Decisions, Uncertainty, and the Brain

Decisions, Uncertainty, and the Brain

The Science of Neuroeconomics

Paul W. Glimcher

A Bradford Book

The MIT Press
Cambridge, Massachusetts
London, England

This book was set in Sabon on 3B2 by Asco Typesetters, Hong Kong and was printed and bound in the United States of America.

Library of Congress Cataloging-in-Publication Data

Glimcher, Paul W.
 Decisions, uncertainty, and the brain : the science of neuroeconomics / Paul W. Glimcher.
    p.   cm.
 "A Bradford book."
 Includes bibliographical references and index.
 ISBN 0-262-07244-0 (hc. : alk. paper)
 1. Cognitive neuroscience. 2. Brain—Mathematical models.
3. Microeconomics. 4. Reflexes. 5. Dualism. I. Title.
QP360.5 .G565   2003
153—dc21   2002026328

10 9 8 7 6 5 4 3 2 1

For C.S.S. and D.M.
whom I most miss having missed

Contents

Acknowledgments

I owe a tremendous amount to a number of colleagues and friends who have been instrumental in the development of the ideas presented here. First and foremost I need to acknowledge the critical role played by many of the young scientists who have worked in my laboratory. The ideas in this book are as much theirs as mine. In chronological order those critical young scientists are Ari Handel, Michael Platt, Michael Brown, Vivian Ciaramitaro, Hannah Bayer, Michael Dorris, and Brian Lau.

Next, I need to acknowledge the critical role that Randy Gallistel and his book *The Organization of Action* have played in forcing my generation of scientists to revaluate the importance of reflex-based theories for understanding the brain. Many of the ideas in the first several chapters of this book are a further development of ideas Randy first presented in that terrific book.

I also need to thank my three closest colleagues and friends, who have provided continuous feedback and constant inspiration: Michael Platt, Eero Simoncelli and David Heeger. Michael in particular deserves my deepest thanks. He introduced me to behavioral ecology when he was a post-doc in my lab. Today he is a professor in his own right, a close friend, and probably the leading scientist attempting a fusion of ecological and neuroscientific approaches. Many of the really good ideas in this book are his. Michael, thanks for lending them to me.

To Hannah Bayer I also have to express special gratitude. Hannah was the only person to read this book as it was being written. Her continual feedback was invaluable. She is the best reader I could have had. Thanks also to Matthew Glimcher for assistance with some of the more technical portions of the manuscript.

Finally, a number of colleagues read and commented on an early draft of the manuscript. Their comments were invaluable. They were Randy Gallistel, Martin Davis, Paul Zak, Michael Platt, Vivian Ciaramitaro, David Heeger, Stu Greenstein, Michael Dorris, Brian Malone, Jeff Erlich, Brian Lau, Mehrdad Jazayeri, Hemai Parthasarathy, Sam Feldman, and Maggie Grantner.

Further Reading

For a working neuroscientist who becomes interested in applying neuro-economic approaches to studies of the brain, this book provides only the most cursory of introductions. In order to really use the insights of economic theory in the study of behavior, brain, and mind, one has to have a thorough grounding in ecological biology and in modern economics. With that in mind, I include here a list of some of my favorite sources for learning about the study of economics in biology. I encourage everyone to explore these books.

Economics

Funderberg, D., and Tirole, J. (1991). *Game Theory*. Cambridge, MA.: MIT Press.

Kreps, David, M. (1990). *A Course in Microeconomic Theory*. Princeton, NJ: Princeton University Press.

Behavioral Ecology

Krebs, J. R., and Davies, N. B. (1997). *Behavioral Ecology*. 4th ed. Oxford: Blackwell Science.

Maynard Smith, J. (1982). *Evolution and the Theory of Games*. Cambridge: Cambridge University Press.

Stephens, D. W., and Krebs, J. R. (1986). *Foraging Theory*. Princeton, NJ: Princeton University Press.

Preface

The philosopher Thomas Kuhn (1962) has argued that science often progresses by fits and starts. At critical times in the history of any discipline, an individual or group of individuals defines a theoretical framework. That framework then serves as a foundation for inquiry.

Many of the greatest brain scientists of the last four centuries have believed that René Descartes played that critical role in defining how we study the connection between the biological brain and the behavior of humans and animals. Pavlov, for instance, argued that for physiologists "Our starting point has been Descartes's idea of the nervous reflex," and other neuroscientists from Marshall Hall in the early 1800s to Charles Sherrington in the 1900s have expressed similar sentiments. Descartes's framework, or paradigm, described how the sensory energies that impinge on an organism give rise to appropriate behavioral responses.

In his book *The Structure of Scientific Revolutions*, Kuhn suggested that paradigms like this succumb to alternative frameworks in a two-stage process. First, he proposed, scientists begin to accumulate data that fit poorly into the existing paradigm. Second, the paradigm begins to be challenged by alternative frameworks that attempt to reconcile all available data into a single alternative conceptual approach. It is a central thesis of this book that about 50 years ago psychologists and biologists interested in brain function began to gather data that fit poorly into the existing Cartesian framework, and that at the present moment in neurobiological history a number of alternative frameworks are being developed and tested.

One of these alternative frameworks has been of particular interest to my research group, and since the early 1990s we have joined a rapidly expanding coterie of social, behavioral, and physiological scientists exploring this alternative paradigm. We and others believe that a mathematically rigorous and conceptually complete description of the neural processes which connect sensation and action is possible, and that such a description will ultimately have its roots in economic theory. In the 1970s, social scientists and economists largely completed the development of what is now called classical microeconomics. This theoretical framework was intended as a tool for describing, at a mathematical level, the computations that would be required if an organism were to use incoming sensory data and a stored representation of the structure of the world to select and execute an optimal course of action. This seemed a powerful tool for describing computations that the brain might perform, and it quickly became very influential, perhaps even foundational, in cognitive science. By the late 1970s, however, evidence began to accumulate that humans often failed to select and execute optimal courses of action in their day-to-day lives, and this called into question the utility of economic approaches as tools for social and cognitive scientists.

More recently, however, biologists have returned to economic theory, using it as a tool for studying the decisions animals make about what to eat or with whom to mate. These biologists have returned to economics on the assumption that in the environment for which an animal has evolved, the decisions the animal makes may more nearly approximate optimal courses of action than do the decisions of humans operating in our modern society. Although this assumption has been controversial, there is no doubt that in many cases economic theory has allowed us to predict and define the behavior of animals with tremendous precision.

Economic theory offers physiologists a second advantage, one that might be even more important than its often debated predictive power. Economic theory allows us to define both the optimal course of action that an animal could select and a mathematical route by which that optimal solution can be derived. Without a doubt, the nervous systems of animals cannot produce perfectly optimal courses of action, but it is equally true that they cannot ever produce courses of action that are better than optimal. Economic theory thus provides us with one critical tool for understanding the nervous system: It places a clear boundary on what is possible and allows us to ask what nervous systems do in that light. If that were all that economics offered physiologists, that might be enough, but it offers another critical advantage. It provides us with a language for describing the computational architecture within which *all* possible solutions can be computed. In this volume I argue, as a member of a group of social, behavioral, and physiological scientists, that economic theory may well provide an alternative to the classical Cartesian paradigm.

Descartes believed that all of behavior could be divided into two categories, the simple and the complex. Simple behaviors were those in which a given sensory event gave rise deterministically to an appropriate motor response. We call these behaviors reflexes after Descartes's use of the verb *réfléchir* in his book *Passions de l'Âme* (1649). The second class of behaviors Descartes identified were those in which the relationship between stimulus and response was unpredictable, or chaotic. These behaviors, Descartes proposed, were the product of a more complicated process he called the soul, but which a modern scientist might label cognition or volition. Since the early twentieth century, physiologists and philosophers have returned again and again to debate this dualist notion. Many have questioned whether there is any real need for Descartes's second (cognitive) mechanism. Could all behavior be explained by reflexlike mechanisms? In fact, many have quite reasonably wondered whether cognitive mechanisms can even be considered scientific notions.

In the subsequent pages I will make two arguments about these issues. First, I will argue (as many others have before me) that if cognitive mechanisms are defined using tools like those developed for economic analysis, then they are in fact quite scientific. Second, I will argue that reflexes are not scientific. To be quite explicit, I will argue that reflexes are a framework for thinking about the connection between sensation and action that is outdated and mechanistically inadequate; that at a physiological level there is no such thing as a reflex. At first that may seem a shocking claim, but I am actually not the first to make it. Many distinguished physiologists working during the twentieth century have also made that claim in one form or another.

In summary, then, like many others I will argue that the Cartesian dualism which has frustrated neurobiologists for at least a hundred years operates from a false premise. But I will argue that the false premise is that the reflex is a useful model for describing anything. Instead, I will argue that the reflex is a primitive model which works well only in overly simple "toy worlds," not in the real world that animals inhabit. A mathematically rich cognitive theory, however, would face no such limitations. It could, by definition, solve the most difficult problems that any environment could present. It would, almost by definition, eliminate the need for dualism by eliminating the need for a reflex theory.

This book, then, has two sets of closely intertwined goals. At a neurobiological level it champions a conceptual approach to understanding the nervous system that is being developed by a growing number of researchers. This conceptual approach begins by arguing that there are two main models of how the nervous system connects sensation and action: the reflex model and the cognitive model. I then challenge, and I hope disprove, the utility of the reflex model for understanding the nervous system. Without the reflex model, I go on to outline what a mathematically complete cognitive model might look like and how one would begin to test that model empirically.

At a philosophical level this book attacks dualism in a slightly unusual way. It begins by arguing that the central error of dualism is the belief in reflex-type mechanisms. Reflex-type mechanisms are attractive for many reasons, but an appropriately developed cognitive theory does not call for them, even in principle. Of course, the existence of a mathematically complete cognitive theory raises important questions about determinism, free will, and the stochastic nature of complex behavior, issues that are dealt with at the end of the book.

I
Historical Approaches

1

René Descartes and the Birth of Neuroscience

Vaucanson's Duck

In 1738 the 29-year-old French watchmaker Jacques de Vaucanson exhibited in the garden of the Tuileries what may be one of the most celebrated robots of all time, a life-size mechanical duck that stood on an elaborate wooden base (figure 1.1). Largely covered with feathers, Vaucanson's automaton was almost indistinguishable from a real duck. When activated, the robotic duck raised its head, looked about, flapped its wings, and even ate from a bowl of grain. The food the duck ate was processed internally, pressed into pellets, and excreted. A feat that must have elicited cries of delight from the children in Vaucanson's audience. The duck performed all of these behaviors so precisely that audiences often refused to believe it was an artificial construct.

The production of this behavior, which would have been unremarkable in a real duck, was accomplished by a clockwork of springs, cams, and levers hidden in the robot. The duck was a machine in which the geometric interaction of carefully shaped pieces of metal, wood, and rubber produced a nearly perfect simulacrum of a predetermined fragment of normal duck behavior.

Vaucanson's duck raised for eighteenth-century audiences ancient questions that still haunt modern neuroscience: Are the mechanical interactions that occur inside each of us sufficient to generate the complex patterns of behavior that we actually produce? What is it that defines us as human beings, the complexity of the behavior that we produce or the specific patterns of interacting matter that appear to generate our behavior? Is there some property that lies beyond our current understand-

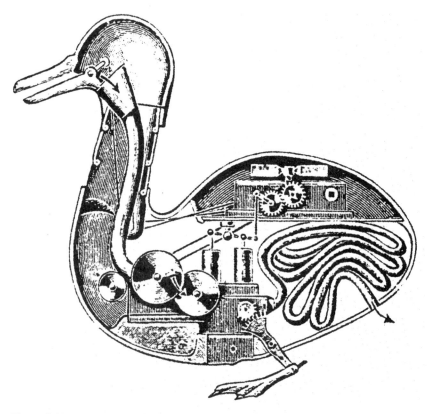

Figure 1.1
Vaucanson's duck (Eco and Zorzoli, *The Picture History of Inventions*. Macmillan, 1963).

ing of both behavior and causal material interactions which is critically responsible for the interaction of behavior, brain and mind?

Vaucanson's duck asks us to decide whether we can hope to understand human or animal brains by understanding the clockwork interplay of matter from which they are constructed. It asks us to decide whether any mechanical device could ever be used to understand how a real organism, like a duck, might actually work. Are physical principles enough, or does the essence of *duckishness* include some property that no machine or model, however complex, can ever capture?

Answering this question has been a central goal of neuroscience, psychology, philosophy, and even mathematics over the course of the last several centuries. Over the course of the period since about 1900, each of these disciplines has made enormous progress toward an answer. Today, one could even argue that there is surprising unanimity among mainstream scholars about how this question *should* be answered. But despite this unanimity, there is no certainty that the common answers to these questions are anything like correct.

Like many contemporary books in neuroscience, this volume is an attempt to develop, at a physiological level, answers to the question of how behavior, brain, and mind are related. To accomplish that goal, the book proceeds in two stages. First, it examines what we, as a scientific culture, believe today. How we came to our current synthetic view from a series of physiological and mathematical insights that have developed since the seventeenth century. The second half of the book provides an alternative to this current synthesis. It presents a viewpoint that has been gaining adherents since the 1990s among economists, psychologists, and neurobiologists who have begun to combine forces in order to explore a radically different model of how behavior, brain, and mind are related. This book is, in some sense, a manifesto for this alternative viewpoint, which is coming to be known as neuroeconomics. But before turning to that new synthesis, we begin by examining how our modern physiological views of behavior, brain, and mind evolved.

René Descartes

It is almost an axiom in scholarly circles that neuroscience, as we conceive of it today, began in the seventeenth century with the work of the French mathematician, philosopher, and physiologist René Descartes (figure 1.2). Descartes was born in 1596 in the town of La Haye, France, now known as Descartes. His family was of the minor nobility, and he was trained in the Jesuit educational system that dominated seventeenth-century ecclesiastic France, taking both a bachelor's and a law degree.

Descartes is probably best known today, three and a half centuries after his death in 1650, for his studies of metaphysics. His efforts to answer the question What is it that we can truly know about the universe? He answered that question with the famous Latinate assertion *Cogito ergo sum*, I think, therefore I am. For Descartes, this assertion seemed axiomatically true, and throughout his metaphysics he argued that any idea as clear and distinct as the *cogito* must also be true.

Figure 1.2
René Descartes (Hulton Archive, BE023664).

In addition to his study of metaphysics, Descartes was a mathematician at a time when proofs were still made geometrically. Arrangements of triangles were used to express theorems about ratios and square roots. Spirals were used to demonstrate the rates at which classes of numerical quantities increased. Descartes produced a number of geometric proofs of this kind. He was a creditable mathematician, inventing analytic algebra and producing a textbook on mathematics, among other accomplishments.

But it was as a physiologist that Descartes's work was most lastingly influential and unique. As we will see, his work as both a metaphysician and as a mathematician had led him to believe that almost any phenomenon in the physical world could be fully described in the simple geometric terms that described interacting physical processes. This led him to suggest mechanical explanations for even the most complex physiological events. It was in developing this line of thought that he was most revolutionary, because no one before Descartes had ever seriously proposed that phenomena as complex as behavior could be viewed as the product of purely physical interactions in physiological systems.

In the 1630s Descartes made this proposal explicit by describing a model of how physical interactions in the material world could give rise to humanlike behaviors. A linkage between behavior and a mechanical system of the type that Vaucanson would use to construct his duck a century later:

I assume their body [the body of an imaginary creature similar in all ways to humans] to be but a statue, an earthen machine formed intentionally by God to be as much as possible like us. Thus not only does He give it externally the shapes and color of all the parts of our bodies; He also places inside it all the pieces required to make it walk, eat, breathe. (Descartes, 1664)

How could such a mechanical device ever hope to produce complex behavior if it could rely only on the geometric interactions of clockwork internal components?

We see clocks, artificial fountains, mills, and similar machines which, though made entirely by man, lack not the power to move of themselves, in various ways. And I think that you will agree that the present machine could have even more sorts of movements than I have imagined and more ingenuity than I have assigned, for our supposition is that it was created by God.

Similarly you may have observed in the grottoes and fountains in the gardens of our kings that the force that makes water leap from its source [hydraulic pressure] is able of itself to move diverse machines and even to make them play instruments or pronounce certain words according to the various arrangements of the tubes through which the water is conducted. (Descartes, 1664)

Given then, that mechanical processes can in fact produce some kinds of behavior, what kinds of mechanical interactions would a model human employ?

And truly one can well compare the nerves of the machine that I am describing to the tubes of the mechanisms of these fountains, its muscles and tendons to divers other engines and springs which serve to move these machines, its animal spirits to the water which drives them, of which the heart is the source and the brain's cavity the water main. Moreover, breathing and other such actions which are ordinary and natural to it, and which depend on the flow of the spirits, are like the movements of a clock or mill which the ordinary flow of water can render continuous. External organs which merely by their presence act on the organs of sense and by this means force them to move in several different ways, depending on how the parts of the brain are arranged, are like strangers who, entering some of the grottoes of these fountains, unwittingly cause the movements that then occur, since they cannot enter without stepping on certain tiles so arranged that, for example, if they approach a Diana bathing they will cause her to hide in the reeds; and if they pass farther to pursue her they will cause a Neptune to advance and menace them with his trident; or if they go in another direction they will make a marine monster come out and spew water into their faces, or other such things according to the whims of the engineers who make them. (Descartes, 1664)

The material world was, Descartes argued, a spectacularly complex clockwork that could be studied, explained, and described by lawful physical principles. The material world could explain, at least in part, even the relationship between behavior and brain.

In the 1630s, when Descartes wrote those words, he was essentially alone in arguing that even aspects of human behavior could be the subject of physical study, but he was not alone in arguing for a scientific and material explanation of the universe. This was the end of a period during which a close-knit group of European scholars were working together to lay the foundation for our modern scientific view of the world. In particular, four Europeans working during this period were developing similar arguments about how we could study and understand the world around us. In England the philosopher and politician Francis Bacon was arguing for a concerted European effort to construct a logical and materialistic explanation for physical phenomena with an experimental method. The English physician William Harvey (who had briefly been Bacon's doctor) was applying this experimental approach to the study of a very specific physiological problem, the puzzle of why the blood is in constant motion. In Italy, the physicist Galileo Galilei was attempting to devise a systematic approach to physical phenomena observed in the heavens and on earth. Finally, in France and Holland, Descartes was attempting to bring all of these threads together in an effort to devise a new approach to the study of behavior, brain, and mind. All four of these men were struggling to give birth to what we think of today as science.

For them this struggle was taking place against the backdrop of medieval Scholasticism, an intellectual system that had dominated European thought for 500 years. In order to understand how much these four men, and Descartes in particular, accomplished for modern neuroscience, it is essential to understand the Scholastic tradition within which they were educated and which they worked so hard to change. The Scholastic tradition in physiology and medicine was a well developed and well codified body of knowledge. It represented the accumulated wisdom of the Greek and Roman cultures as translated and analyzed by generations of scholars. This tradition included clearly presented views on the relationship between behavior, brain, and mind. As educated men, Bacon, Harvey, Galileo, and Descartes would all have been intimately familiar with the writings of the great ancient authors, a familiarity that most scientists lack today. So in order to better understand what Descartes accomplished, we must first turn to the ancient physiologists whose studies defined the biomedical world Descartes inherited.

Understanding the Ancients

For a physician or physiologist working in Europe anytime between 1200 and 1600 there were a number of biomedical texts available: texts on the structure of the body and the brain, texts on the functions of organs, and texts on the treatment of disease. Almost all of these books were attributed to a single individual, the Roman physician Galen.

By the year 1000 Galen was, quite simply, the most influential biologist in the history of man, a position he retained until well into the eighteenth or nineteenth century. For a millennium, no European or Arab scholar could claim even a passing knowledge of physiology without having read Galen's books in detail.

Born in A.D. 129 or 130 in the town of Pergamum, Galen was educated in what was even then considered an ancient and classical medical tradition. A tradition rooted in the much earlier works of Hippocrates and, to a lesser extent, Plato. Galen completed his basic medical training at the age of 19. He had studied the works of the ancient authors and gained some valuable practical experience of medicine in Pergamum, but at that point he moved to Alexandria to pursue further study. In modern terms, he moved to Alexandria to pursue a fellowship in something like internal medicine.

In Galen's time, the second century, Alexandria was the seat of medical and academic scholarship. The famous library and eminent medical school there were without peer anywhere in the world. It contained manuscript copies of essentially every extant book, and one can only imagine the experience of a promising 19-year-old physician from the provinces who suddenly found himself among the entire accumulated medical knowledge of civilization. While in Alexandria, Galen had the opportunity to read medical books that had been written throughout the Roman Empire. He would have read ancient works, too, like the writings of Hippocrates and his colleagues; of famous challengers to the Hippocratic tradition; and of the modern supporters of both views. Galen probably read thousands of biomedical texts, texts that have almost all been lost in the intervening two millennia.

After 5 years at Alexandria, poring over the library's contents and studying with famous and influential physicians, Galen did what any conscientious young doctor would have done: He returned home to Pergamum. There he took up residence and received his first appointment, official surgeon to the Pergamum gladiators, a job that certainly must have provided steady work.

Galen's reputation as a learned physician grew in Pergamum, and at about the same time that Marcus Aurelius was crowned emperor

(A.D. 161), Galen decided to move to Rome, the administrative seat of the world. According to Galen's own reports, while living in Rome he lectured, demonstrated anatomical dissections, and proved himself a much more brilliant and thoughtful physiologist than any living member of the Roman medical establishment. Generally, he seems to have made an academic nuisance of himself. We know that much of this self-aggrandizement must be true; he obviously was well known and respected, because after only a few years in the city, he was appointed physician to the emperor. We also know that he made powerful enemies among the medical elite of Rome. Only 6 years after arriving, he was forced to flee Rome—as he tells the story—under cover of darkness, in order to evade his enemies. In 168 he was back in Pergamum.

But Galen was not to remain in Pergamum for long. A year later Marcus Aurelius recalled him to Rome by imperial order. And in the years that followed, he served as a physician and adviser to Aurelius and to Aurelius's son, Emperor Commodus.

Throughout all of these years, Galen wrote voluminously on subjects ranging from autobiography to practical philosophy, but he focused his efforts on analyzing and codifying the complete body of medical knowledge available to a physician of the emperor. His medical books served, and were meant to serve, as a complete distillation of the physiological knowledge of the world, a final common source for medicine. Of course achieving this level of coverage was not something that could be completed in a single volume. Galen wrote between 130 and 500 books during his life. (The exact number is hotly debated, but was probably much closer to 130 than to 500.) Unfortunately, only about 80 of Galen's books survive today.

Modern readers, perhaps surprisingly, find Galen quite readable. His writing reveals a physician who was arrogant, passionately judgmental, fantastically well read, and obviously brilliant. He rarely hesitates to provide us, his successors by almost 2000 years, with a clear insight into his character and his motivations. In his book *On the Passions*, for example, he admits (somewhat obliquely) to being both too passionate and too judgmental in his nature. In the second century he strikes a modern tone when he blames his mother for these qualities:

Now, personally, I cannot say how I got my nature. It was, however, my great good fortune to have as my father a most good-tempered, just, efficient, and benevolent man. My mother, on the other hand, was so irascible that she would sometimes bite her serving-maids, and she was constantly shouting at my father and quarreling with him, worse than Xantippe with Socrates. (Galen, A)

For physicians and physiologists educated during the Scholastic period that followed, the two most important of Galen's books were probably *On the Usefulness of Parts* (Galen, B) and *On the Natural Faculties* (Galen, C). These are works with which Descartes was intimately familiar. In them Galen lays out a complete medical system, a theory of physiology. It was this system that became the de facto standard for medical belief and practice throughout the Middle Ages and into the Renaissance. Any physician educated in Europe or in the Arab world would have read every word of these two books in medical school, and perhaps dozens of other works by Galen. Being a doctor without knowing exactly what Galen had written about every organ and every disease would have been as unthinkable before 1800 as being a doctor without going to medical school would be today. In this way the medical world of Rome in the second century was projected forward as the unchallenged archive of all physiological knowledge.

The medical world of Galen was, therefore, the medical world of Europe throughout the Middle Ages and during the early Renaissance. And in that world, the fundamental tension that Vaucanson's duck would represent fifteen centuries later had already been the subject of debate for centuries. The Greek philosophers Epicurus and Democritus (whom even Galen would have considered Ancients) had argued that the world was composed entirely of matter and that causal interactions among this matter must, in principle, account for all physical events. Democritus's theory that all matter was composed of tiny, indivisible elements that he called *atoms* pertained as clearly to the human bodies of Galen's gladiators as it did to the stadiums in which they fought. Motion in matter is caused, Democritus and his colleagues proposed, when atoms collide with each other. These tiny mechanical interactions combine to yield all the material events that we observe in the world around us.

Democritus and his intellectual forebears had realized this raised an essential dilemma. If all the events that take place in the universe are the product of tiny particles colliding with each other according to simple physical laws, then the behavior each of us produces must also be the product of these tiny, lawful material collisions. Our own actions must therefore be *predetermined* by simple physical laws. What we will do in the future must be as determinate as the movement of a stone down a steep hill. And thus our own sense that human behavior is unpredictable, even volitional, must be no more than an illusion.

Plato's response to this line of argument, which was at least as well known to Galen as to any of us, was to argue that the world was much more than it seemed, that the true nature of the world existed on a metaphysical plane that our physical senses could not penetrate. We humans are all, Plato argued both to Galen and to us in the metaphor of the cave presented in his book *The Republic*, unable to perceive reality as it truly exists. Instead, the reality we see can be likened to the shadows cast on a wall by *true reality*. What seems to us to be the material world is simply a dim reflection of the true causal world. It is in that inaccessible true causal world that the real relationship between behavior and mind is forged.

Plato's views on this issue were not unchallenged in the ancient world. For Galen the most significant of these challenges came from his own hero, the fourth century B.C. physician and contemporary of Plato, Hippocrates. In Galen's time the writings of Hippocrates were almost 600 years old and had become the foundation of the corpus of Roman medicine. The views of Hippocrates were often challenged during Galen's life, but always taken very seriously. For Galen, the ideas of Hippocrates were almost without exception the final word in medical truth.

Unlike Plato, Hippocrates was a physician, and as a physician he recognized that, at least for some diseases, cause and effect can be deduced, and theoretical frameworks can be developed which explain physical phenomena in terms of simple materialistic causes. Seeking to reconcile the materialistic worldview of a physician with the notion that human behavior was unpredictable, and thus must reflect something more than simple material interactions, Hippocrates suggested a brilliant compromise. Humans were, he proposed, a combination of material and nonmaterial processes. The body itself was, he acknowledged, a physical object governed by the interaction of material components, but all of the body was in turn governed by a nonmaterial process, the soul.

For Galen, as the great interpreter and codifier of Hippocrates, bodies were complex physical machines. The actions of those machines reflected both material interactions and causal forces associated with the non-material human soul. Physical diseases could reflect injury to either of these two processes: the material process of the body or the nonphysical process of the soul. Accordingly, Galen devoted his writing not only to a study of organ physiology but also to the study of human morality, because both of these domains could play critical roles in disease.

How could Galen explain the ability of these two disparate processes, the material body and the nonmaterial soul, to interact and produce behavior? The answer was that sensations gathered by the material body were passed to the nonmaterial soul for analysis. The soul then produced organized behavioral responses by activating the nerves and muscles of the body. For Galen the question of how these two processes interacted reduced to a question of *where*. Where was it that the soul interacted with the body to receive sensation and produce movement? Was the answer to this central question, as Aristotle had argued, that the heart served as the critical link between the material and nonmaterial properties of humans? Or was it, as Hippocrates had argued, the brain and spinal cord that linked behavior and mind?

In seeking an answer to that question, Galen describes what could be loosely called an experiment in his book, *On the Doctrines of Hippocrates and Plato* (Galen, D). You know when you go to a really important festival, Galen asks us, and they have plans to sacrifice a bull by cutting out its heart? You must have noticed that if the priests are really good, they get that heart out and onto the altar so fast that the heart still beats as it sits on the stone. Have you ever noticed what the bull is doing when this happens? You probably noticed that the bull, even when deprived of his heart, is still moving, even running around. Now how could that be the case if the source of all behavior, if the ability of the soul to elicit movement in the physical body, was resident in the heart? Once the link between mind and body had been broken by the removal of the heart, the body should have become immobile.

Now consider, he goes on, the kind of sacrifice in which the priests cut the spinal cord in the neck with a sword. You must have noticed that as the spinal cord is cut, the bull immediately drops to the ground, deprived of all power to move. The only explanation for this, Galen concludes, is that body and mind are linked thorough the organs of the brain and spinal cord. For Galen this largely resolved the question of how behavior and mind are related. They are related thorough the organ of the brain.

Galen goes on in this book, and in others, like his dissection guide *On Anatomical Procedures* (Galen, E), to further develop this theme. The soul must take physical residence in the brain, from whence it can receive sensations that are gathered by the sense organs and use that information to exert its will, via the spinal cord, on the muscles of the body. The soul does this by means of the pneuma. (The Greek word *pneuma* is strictly translated today as "breath," but even as recently as Descartes's time the function of respiration was unknown. For Galen, breath had more to do with a nonmaterial force or spirit that could play a causal role linking mind and body than it did with aerobic metabolism.) For Galen, then, the mind was a nonphysical process resident in the brain that, through the vehicle of the pneuma, actuated behavior. Mind and body are related because the mind receives sensory information from the body and in turn actuates the body's musculature.

Galen's work was monumental. And it would be fairly accurate to say that in the year 200 his books represented the accumulated anatomical and medical knowledge of human history. But with the rise of medieval Scholasticism his works became more than a compilation of existing knowledge. They became the unquestionable authority on all things medical.

The Scholastic period was marked by a turn away from direct observation and toward a study of *The Ancients*. The dominant view of this period was that the Greeks, and to a lesser extent the Romans, had gained an essentially complete knowledge of the universe. The goal of any scholar, therefore, was to attempt to recover that knowledge by a study of these ancient authors. This was as true for knowledge about mathematics or philosophy as it was for knowledge about medicine. Galen became the spokesman for The Ancients on all medical matters, and his writings became the definition of biomedical truth.

This shift toward the study of ancient sources, and the absolute belief in the infallibility of those sources, affected all areas of endeavor, but it had an enormous impact on medicine and physiology. During this period, Galen's work became *The Standard* for understanding physiology and thinking about how the mind and body were related. It was his notion that sensory data were passed to the nonmaterial mind, which then activated the material body that formed the core of neuroscience before Descartes.

The Renaissance

Almost a millennium after Galen, in the early twelfth century, the first hint of the upcoming Renaissance began to show itself in medical and physiological circles. At that time there were four major medical schools in Europe: Salerno and Bologna in Italy, and Paris and Montpellier in France. Manuscripts from those schools indicate that by the twelfth century a new practice entered medical education, the dissection of pigs. This was terribly important because it meant that the study of Galen's anatomical writings was being supplemented by the examination of actual bodies, albeit the bodies of pigs. To the best of our knowledge the first medical school dissection guide was produced around this time, the *Demonstratio Anatomica*, probably written in Salerno.

What is important to consider in thinking about these dissections is that it had been a millennium since the last formal dissections or experiments had been performed, during the Roman period. In the intervening centuries texts, not bodies, had been the source of all anatomical knowledge among medical professionals. But it is equally important to remember that these dissections in the twelfth century were not meant to challenge or test the authority of the Galenic texts; they were meant to serve as teaching tools. Challenging Galen's texts would have been unthinkable in the twelfth century. Were you, a medical student, to discover a discrepancy between the body of your pig and Galen's text, you would never have thought of this as a challenge to Galen's accuracy. Much more likely was the possibility that this reflected an error on your part, or at worst an error in the copying or translation of Galen.

By 1300, these dissections of pigs began to be supplemented by an even more audacious undertaking, the dissection of human cadavers. This probably began at the medical school in Bologna, but by the middle of the century had spread to all four of the great European medical schools. Ultimately, this kind of direct observation could only demonstrate the limitations and errors of Galen's texts, even though a direct challenge to Galen's authority was still hundreds of years off. But when that challenge came, it came suddenly and revolutionized Western medicine in a decade after a millennium of stability.

The critical step in challenging Galen's authority was the work of a Belgian-born physician, Andreas Vesalius (figure 1.3). Vesalius, like any academic physician of his period, had received a proper education in the classics and had an excellent knowledge of both Latin and Greek. Like all medical students, he was obliged to read Galen in incredible detail by his mentors, who included Jacobus Sylvius (for whom the cerebral aqueduct is named). In 1536, an outbreak of war caused Vesalius to return from Paris to his native Louvain, and there he procured his first corpse, which he apparently stole from an execution block along a roadside. Throughout the next year Vesalius conducted one or more anatomies (human dissections), demonstrating to medical observers in Louvain a level of manual skill in dissection that was widely acknowledged to be extraordinary. Over the course of the next 10 years or so, Vesalius continued to teach and dissect, and his teachings began to take on a clearly challenging tone with regard to the established doctrine of Galen's corpus. This series of challenges reached a head in 1543 when Vesalius published his great anatomical monograph, *De Humani Corporis Fabrica*, a book often referred to as the beginning of modern anatomical science.

In the *Fabrica*, Vesalius set out to offer an alternative to the medieval method of study and proposed directly that experimental anatomy was the only appropriate method for understanding the body. In the dedication of the *Fabrica* he wrote:

I am aware that by reason of my age—I am at present 28 years old—my efforts will have little authority, and that, because of my frequent indication of the falsity of Galen's teachings, they [the books of the *Fabrica*] will find little shelter from the attacks of those who were not present at my anatomical dissections or have not themselves studied the subject sedulously; various schemes in defence of

Figure 1.3
Andreas Vesalius (Octavio Digital Publishing's *De Humani Corporis Fabrica*).

Galen will be boldly invented unless these books appear with the auspicious commendation and great patronage of some divine power [Charles V, to whom the *Fabrica* was dedicated].

The preface continues in a similar manner:

that the detestable manner by which usually some conduct the dissection of the human body and others present the account of its parts, like latter day jackdaws aloft in their high chair, with egregious arrogance croaking things that they have never investigated but merely committed to memory from the books of others, or reading what has already been described. The former are so ignorant of languages that they are unable to explain their dissections to the spectators and muddle what ought to be displayed according to the instructions of the physician who, since he has never applied his hand to the dissection of the body, haughtily governs the ship from a manual. Thus everything is wrongly taught in the schools, and days are wasted in ridiculous questions that in such confusion less is presented to the spectators than a butcher in his stall could teach a physician. (Vesalius, 1543; O'Malley, 1964)

Vesalius's work is often cited as *the* defining moment that began modern biology. It was an effort that brought together the spirit of inquiry which characterized the Renaissance with a willingness to challenge authority, an approach that would come to define modern biomedical science. (In fact, the woodcuts for the *Fabrica* were most likely made in the Venetian painter Titian's workshop.)

The work of Vesalius and the other great sixteenth-century anatomists thus provided Descartes and his colleagues with two critical advances over their medieval forebears. First, the growing body of accurate anatomical knowledge that these physicians provided served as a starting point for a more modern and observationally based physiology. It became possible to use very precise anatomical data about the central nervous system to formulate theories about how behavior could be generated by living animals. Second, and perhaps more important, Vesalius made it possible to challenge the ideas of Galen and the ancient wisdom that he represented.

Francis Bacon

In Europe, the challenge to the scientific wisdom of the ancients was conducted simultaneously on several fronts. Perhaps the most theoretical and direct challenge was brought by the English nobleman and philosopher Francis Bacon. In many ways Bacon's challenge must have been an essential starting point for Descartes.

Bacon was, without a doubt, one of the great intellects of the seventeenth century. Over the course of a checkered career he served as a member of Parliament, Solicitor General, Attorney General, Lord Keeper, and Lord Chancellor, but all of this political accomplishment reflected an incredibly cynical nature. He was, by his own admission, a servile flatterer who probably was as comfortable taking bribes as offering them. In fact, after being created first Baron Verulam and later Viscount St. Albans, Bacon was convicted of bribery and sentenced to imprisonment in the Tower of London. He was released from the Tower after a brief imprisonment but was officially excluded from the verge of the court. This was an English sentence that prevented Bacon from placing himself within 12 miles of the official current residence of the sovereign, who was at that time James I. At a scholarly level this must have been an incredible problem for Bacon. James was almost always resident in London, and this would have prevented Bacon from entering any of the great libraries of that city.

Bacon's fame, at least among natural scientists working in the nineteenth and twentieth centuries, stems from his philosophical writings in general and from his most celebrated philosophical work, the *Novum Organum* (New Organ, 1620). The *Novum Organum*, as Bacon saw it, was a book designed to serve as a replacement for Aristotle's treatise on how knowledge could be acquired, a book known as the *Organum* in Latin. (Bacon, to be sure, never underestimated himself.)

Partly as a result of his conviction for bribery, and partly because he was not great at finishing huge undertakings, Bacon never really completed the *Novum Organum*, although he did finish and publish a significant portion of it. In fact, the *Novum Organum* was supposed to be only the first book of his larger work *The Great Instauration*, a six-volume series. Bacon had very high hopes for the *Instauration*, beginning it with the lines "Francis of Verulam [his latin nom de plume at the time] reasoning thus with himself came to this conclusion that the knowledge of his thoughts would be of advantage to present and future generations."

While the *Organum*, like Bacon, was in many ways deeply flawed, it was also very influential and really was one of the first books to expand on the idea that *experimental* science would be important for developing a deeper understanding of the natural world. This is an idea he presented clearly in the preface to *The Great Instauration*. It should be widely admitted, he argued,

That the sciences are in an unhappy state, and have made no great progress; and that a path must be opened to man's understanding entirely different from that known to men before us, and other means of assistance provided, so that the mind can exercise its rightful authority over the nature of things.

It should be said frankly that the wisdom which we imbibed principally from the Greeks seems merely the boyhood of knowledge, with the characteristics of boys, that it is good at chattering, but immature and unable to generate. For it is fruitful of controversies and barren of works.... In the same way also, the sciences as we know them have charming and fair seeming general features, but when it comes to details, down to the parts of generation as it were, where they should yield fruit and works, then arguments and barking disputations arise, and in these they terminate, and are all the issue they can yield.

Furthermore, if these sciences were not altogether defunct, what has been the case throughout the many ages now past could, it seems, hardly have come about, that they have stuck more or less motionless in their tracks and have made no advances worthy of mankind, often to the point where not only what was once asserted remains an assertion still, but where also a question once raised remains a question still, not answered by discussion but fixed and fed thereby.... In the mechanical arts, on the other hand, we see the opposite happening, for they grow and become more perfect by the day, as if partaking of some breath of life; and in the hands of their first authors they often appear crude and somewhat clumsy and shapeless, yet in the course of time they take on new powers and usefulness, to such a degree that men's eager pursuit of them ceases and turns to other things before these arts shall have reached the summit of their perfection. By contrast, philosophy and the intellectual sciences stand like statues, worshipped and celebrated, but not moved forward. In fact they sometimes flourish most under their first authors, only to decline thereafter. For when men ... have once surrendered their minds and have given their allegiance to the opinion of some man, they bring no enlargement to the sciences themselves, but merely act as servile functionaries and attendants to glorify certain authors....

Now what the sciences need is a form of induction that will analyze experience and take it apart, and through due exclusions and rejections necessarily come to a conclusion. And if that common art of logic and reasoning by induction involved so much labor and exercised such great intellects, how much more work is involved in this other method, which is drawn not only from the inner recesses of the mind, but also from the very bowels of Nature? ...

To remedy these things, I have sought most carefully everywhere to find helps for the sense, and supply substitutes where it forsakes us, and correctives where it is at variance [with the truth]. *And I try to bring this about not so much with instruments as by experiments. For the subtlety of experiments is far greater than that of the sense itself, even though assisted by the most delicate of instruments* [my italics]. (I am speaking of those experiments that are skillfully and expertly thought out and framed for the purpose of the inquiry.) I do not therefore attach much importance to the immediate and natural perception of the sense; but I arrange it so that the sense judges only the experiment, the experiment the point in Nature. And for this reason I think that, as regards the sense (from which all knowledge of Nature must be sought, unless we wish to act like madmen), we stand before it as a priest of a religion and skillful interpreter of its oracles; and while others only profess to support and cultivate the sense, I do so in actual fact. These then are the preparations that I make for kindling and bringing to bear the light of Nature. (Bacon, 1620)

Bacon was an experimentalist arguing that ancient Scholastic beliefs should be discarded in favor of new ideas derived from experimental data. Historians often joke that this novel devotion to experiment ultimately cost Bacon his life. In March 1626, at the age of 65, Bacon was driving in his carriage north of London across a field of snow when he began to wonder whether snow would delay the putrefaction of flesh. Seized with a desire to examine this idea experimentally, Bacon purchased a chicken and stuffed it with snow. The story goes that while doing this, Bacon caught bronchitis (from the dead chicken, one wonders?) and died a month later.

William Harvey

The two people who went farthest in describing the new science that Bacon advocated were the famous Italian astronomer/physicist Galileo Galilei and the English physician William Harvey. In most essays on the experimental method, scholars proceed from this point to describe Galileo's science and his philosophy. Without a doubt, Galileo stands as the central figure in the general development of the scientific method because he gave birth to modern physics when he invented the scientific method used in physics today. In addition, Galileo was a prolific writer, and although his work can be hard for a modern scholar to read (fairly boring, actually), he did deal openly with major philosophical questions about the role of experiment and direct observation in the acquisition of knowledge. Finally, the fact that the Church charged Galileo with heresy for defending the intellectual results of his experiments after a long and very public trial, certainly does not hurt his modern reputation. (Although I am sure Galileo did not see any advantage in having to publicly recant his heretical beliefs and spend the end of his life under house arrest.)

From the point of view of physiology, however, Galileo's work was less significant than the work of William Harvey. At the same time that Galileo was advancing physics through observation and experiment, William Harvey was demonstrating that even the bodies of men could be studied and understood as material phenomena, using the new experimental approach that Bacon was championing.

One of the major physiological questions facing medical scientists in the middle of the seventeenth century was to understand the purpose and function of the heart and blood. In Harvey's day it was widely known that arteries pulsed, as did the heart, and that veins did not. Why did the heart and arteries pulse, and why was the pulse so absolutely critical for life? What function, if any, did the veins serve? Capillaries had not yet been discovered, so there appeared to be no connection between the arterial system and the venous system, although both were clearly connected with the heart. Finally, what role did the lungs play in relation to the heart? Great vessels connected the heart and lungs, but to what end? And how was all of this related to the breath, Galen's pneuma, which was also essential for life?

Before Harvey, efforts to answer these questions with anatomical study had proven largely fruitless. One could, for example, observe changes in the size of the heart during each beat, but what did that mean? Many of Harvey's colleagues had suggested that the expansion of the heart (what we would call the filling phase) was driven by an expansion of the blood itself when exposed to some factor that was present inside the heart. Descartes, who was writing at this time and who would later challenge Harvey directly on this point, argued that the heart played a central role in heating the blood. He argued that this heated blood then traveled through the arteries to heat the body. It was, however, William Harvey who realized that in order to solve this mystery, one would have to follow the advice of Francis Bacon and develop a set of experiments to test a series of hypotheses.

The passages that follow are taken from Harvey's masterwork, *Exercitatio Anatomica de Motu Cordis et Sanguinis in Animalibus* (An Anatomical Disquisition on the Motion of the Heart and Blood in Animals, 1628). In this book, which is actually quite short, Harvey describes a series of experiments, which he calls "demonstrations," by which he tests the hypothesis that the left side of the heart pumps blood into the arteries. That the blood flows through a theoretical construct we now call a capillary (which would be discovered decades later by Malpighi) to the veins. That the blood then flows slowly through the veins, which have valves to prevent backflow, to the right side of the heart. That the right side of the heart pumps blood to the lungs where it goes through a second set of capillaries (and is presumably exposed to some factor in the breath or air) and then enters the left side of the heart to repeat the process. The extract below details the experiment by which Harvey attempts to prove that the blood flows in only one direction through the veins. Of course this is critical to his overall argument and, just as important, it flies in the face of most accepted knowledge about the venous system (figure 1.4).

But that this truth may be made the more apparent, let an arm be tied up above the elbow as if for phlebotomy (A, A, fig. 1). At intervals in the course of the veins, especially in labouring people and those whose veins are large, certain knots or elevations (B, C, D, E, F) will be perceived, and this is not only at the places where the branch is received (E, F), but also where none enters (C, D): these knots or risings are all formed by valves, which thus show themselves externally. And now if you press the blood from the space above one of the valves, from H to O, (fig. 2) and keep the point of a finger upon the vein inferiorly, you will see no influx of blood from above; the portion of the vein between the point of the finger and the valve O will be obliterated; yet will the vessel continue sufficiently distended above that valve (O, G). The blood being thus pressed out, and the vein being emptied, if you now apply a finger of the other hand upon the distended part of the vein above the valve O, (fig 3.) and press downwards, you will find that you cannot force the blood through or beyond the valve; but the greater effort you use, you will only see the portion of the vein that is between the finger and the valve become more distended, that portion of the vein which is below the valve remaining all the while empty (H, O fig. 3).

It would therefore appear that the function of the valves in the veins is the same as that of the three sigmoid valves [in the heart] which we find at the commencement of the aorta and pulmonary artery, viz., to prevent all reflux of blood that is passing over them.

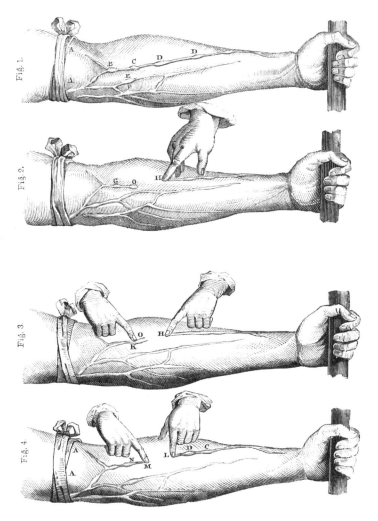

Figure 1.4
William Harvey's figures 1–4 (Octavio Digital Publishing's *Exercitatio Anatomica de Motu Cordis*). Note: Image above is from a later edition than the one reproduced in the Octavio edition. The image in the Octavio edition is much nicer.

That the blood in the veins therefore proceeds from the inferior or more remote to superior parts, and towards the heart, moving in these vessels and in this
and not in the contrary direction, appears most obvious.

But this other circumstance has to be noted: The arm being bound, and the
veins made turgid, and the valves prominent, as before, apply the thumb or finger
over a vein in the situation of one of the valves in such a way as to compress it,
and prevent any blood from passing upwards from the hand; then, with a finger
of the other hand, streak the blood in the vein upwards till it has passed the next
valve above, (N, fig. 4) the vessel now remains empty; but the finger at L being
removed for an instant, the vein is immediately filled from below; apply the finger
again, and having in the same manner streaked the blood upwards, again remove
the finger below, and again the vessel becomes distended as before; and this repeat, say a thousand times, in a short space of time. And now compute the
quantity of blood which you have thus pressed up beyond the valve, and then
multiplying the assumed quantity by one thousand, you will find that so much
blood has passed through a certain portion of the vessel; and I do now believe
that you will find yourself convinced of the circulation of the blood and its rapid
motion. (Harvey, 1628)

Most of the *De Motu* is devoted to a series of similar experiments that,
together, are intended to prove Harvey's hypothesis that the heart cir-
culates the blood through the vascular system. As a set of sequential
experiments the book is overwhelmingly convincing; it is hard to imagine
doubting the conclusions it presents. (Although Descartes seems to have
been very pig-headed about this.) But as a philosophical work, many
modern students find the book a bit disappointing. At each experiment,
Harvey draws his conclusions but he never seems to draw attention to
the fact that he is inventing a new way to do science. He never organizes
the experiments clearly enough around the hypotheses they test, nor does
he draw attention to the process of hypothesis testing around which the
book is organized. He never draws any attention to the fact that he is
changing more than cardiac physiology: that he is changing all of biology.

This may in part reflect Harvey's essentially conservative nature; he
was, after all, a quintessential establishment figure. In London, Harvey
served as physician to James I (the same king from whose court Bacon
was excluded) and was a close friend to King Charles I after James's
death. The execution of Charles at the end of the English Civil War came
as a huge personal blow to the aging Harvey, and the radical government around Cromwell always distrusted Harvey because of his association with the monarchy.

Despite these setbacks, and Harvey's conservative nature, his work had an enormous impact on physiology and Harvey was quickly venerated as the leading biologist of his century. Busts of Harvey were placed in the Royal College of Physicians and elsewhere with inscriptions alluding to his divine nature and certain immortality. In short, Harvey came to define biological experimental science as we know it today.

There is, however, no escaping the fact that while Harvey was doing science, he was not writing like a modern physiological scientist. This may in some measure have precluded his approach to our problem of how mechanistic approaches to bodily functions could be reconciled with our perception that human behavior is fundamentally unpredictable.

Descartes's Synthesis

How can we reconcile Vaucanson's duck with our own sense of free will and the inescapable observation that so much of human behavior seems chaotic and unpredictable? The behavior of Vaucanson's duck is fully determined by its construction. Cams and levers interact; the mechanical laws of cause and effect dictate not just how the duck will behave in the next second, but how all of its behavior will be structured. If humans are just very complicated versions of Vaucanson's duck, as Democritus and his colleagues suggested, then all of our actions are predetermined, human unpredictability and free will are illusions, and in a moral sense no person can be held causally responsible for his or her actions. But what is the alternative? That nonmaterial events, events which lie outside the province of descriptive or experimental science, account for human behavior. That the tools of science that Galileo, Bacon, and Harvey were developing could *not* be applied to studies of how the mechanical hardware inside of humans and animals *makes* us behave. How, in short, can we hope to develop a truly scientific approach to behavior, brain, and mind, which seems to require a mechanistic approach, when free will and moral responsibility seem to require a nonscientific approach? Even Harvey had shied away from this problem.

Descartes, really quite brilliantly, thought of a solution to this dilemma by proposing a two-tiered system that would become the standard solution to the puzzle of behavior, brain, and mind for at least three centuries:

"These men will be composed, as we are, of a soul and a body; and I must first describe for you the body; then, also separately, the soul; and finally I must show you how these two natures would have to be joined and united to constitute men." With those words Descartes began his masterwork on the problem of how the neurobiological basis of behavior could be made the subject of scientific study, *L'Homme* (The Treatise on Man).

Descartes proposed that all observable human behavior could be divided into two categories, the simple and the complex. Simple behaviors were those in which a given sensation always, deterministically, produced the same behavioral response. Touching a man's foot with fire always causes him to withdraw the foot. This tight mechanistic linkage between sensation and action, Descartes argued, showed two things. First, that the behavior was entirely, or almost entirely, unaffected by free will. Second, that it had exactly the mechanistic properties which the emerging scientific method could engage. Complex behaviors, in contrast, were those in which the linkage between sensation and action was unpredictable and subject to the vagaries of volition. These behaviors, Descartes proposed, more nearly followed the Galenic model. They were produced when sensory data were transmitted from the nervous system to the nonmaterial soul, the soul made a decision about what course of action to undertake, and this volitional command was then passed to the machinery of the body for execution.

Descartes laid out this basic framework in a number of works, but he developed it most completely in *L'Homme* which was completed in 1637. *L'Homme* was written during the 1630s as the second section of a much larger work called *The World*. *The World* was to have been composed of two or three major portions: *The Treatise on Light*, *The Treatise on Man*, and perhaps his work *On the Soul*. Current evidence indicates that *Light* and *Man* were both completed in 1637; *Soul* may have been drafted at the same time and destroyed by Descartes. In any case, no copy of *On the Soul* exists today.

The 1630s were, however, not a very good decade for the emerging scientific method. In 1630 Galileo had published his masterwork, *Dialogo Sopra i Due Massimi Sistemi del Mondo, Tolemaico e Copernicano*, A Dialogue Concerning the Two Chief World Systems, Ptolemaic and

Copernican (Galilei, 1630). In that book Galileo had presented his voluminous evidence that the Earth, and the other planets, revolved around the sun. Six years earlier Galileo had traveled to Rome to discuss his Copernican views with Pope Urban VIII, who had been a friend and patron when he was still Cardinal Barberini. This was important because the Copernican system was controversial for two reasons. First, the Copernican system was a direct contradiction of the Scholastic Aristotelian tradition, a tradition in which the Earth lay immobile at the center of the universe and the bodies in the heavenly sphere circled around it. This was the wisdom of the Ancients. Second, the wisdom of the Ancients on this point was supported by Holy Scripture. The Bible distinctly describes the sun as *traveling across the heavens* from dawn to dusk in a number of places. In defense of both Aristotelian Scholasticism and Holy Scripture, the Vatican had ruled that the sun must circle the Earth.

In fairness, Urban found himself in a tough spot when he confronted his old friend Galileo, who was insisting that the Earth must circle the sun. The Counter-Reformation was in full swing as the cardinals and the pope tried desperately to defend themselves and the Church against the rapidly growing Protestant disciplines of northern Europe. Johannes Kepler, a German Protestant, had produced an elegant geometric system for describing the motions of the heavenly bodies that contradicted both the wisdom of The Ancients and Holy Scripture. Finally here was Urban's arrogant old friend Galileo presenting very compelling empirical evidence supporting Kepler's geometric presentation of the Copernican system as an accurate description of the true universe. After six audiences Urban and Galileo worked out an essential compromise. Galileo would have to accept that the Earth was the center of the universe; he could, however, as a purely hypothetical exercise, continue to work out his mathematical and empirical analyses of the Keplerian system. But it was to be understood that this was an intellectual endeavor only, not an effort to prove that Copernicus was right.

The product of this discussion, the *Dialogo*, presents the transcript of a fictional discussion, involving three friends, about the two world systems. Although the book does contain a preface stating that the work is purely hypothetical, nobody who has read the book can be in any doubt about what Galileo is attempting to prove. Galileo quite effectively demolishes the Ptolemaic system. Then, after demolishing this system, which he had promised Pope Urban VIII he would defend, the *Dialogo* gives the last word to the character charged with defending the Ptolomaic system, a character who has been unceremoniously named Simplicio. After having been humiliated and ridiculed throughout the book, Simplicio is permitted to say, as the book closes, "Well, it may look Copernican in every respect, but God can do whatever he wants and it ain't really Copernican at all." Suffice it to say that Urban was less than delighted with this, and Galileo, though in poor health, was immediately ordered to Rome to face the Inquisition. In a plea bargain, Galileo confessed to having overstated his case and to having inadvertently produced the appearance of heresy. The book was of course banned, and Galileo was placed under house arrest for the remainder of his life.

When news of this scientific debacle reached Descartes, a subject of His Most Catholic Majesty King Louis XIII (although Descartes was then resident in Holland), he made the only rational decision that he could, and decided to suppress *The World* rather than risk the Inquisition. As a result *L'Homme* was not published in complete form until 1664, 14 years after Descartes's death. Descartes probably made the right decision. In 1667 the Church placed all of Descartes's works on the Index of Forbidden Books.

Even though *L'Homme* did not reach the press until the 1660s, the effect of this book and of a closely related book, *Les Passions de l'Ame* (The Passions of the Soul, 1649) was enormous. In these books Descartes argued that the essentially dual nature of human behavior permitted a wide range of physiological investigations into the relationship between behavior, brain, and mind. Like Epicurus, Descartes argued that the brain was an organ which existed within the material world. Many classes of behaviors were the deterministic product of this organ acting alone. The scientific method could always be used to explain these simple deterministic behaviors. But like Galen, Descartes argued that human behavior was also the product of the nonmaterial soul. That it was the complex, unpredictable, nondeterministic behaviors which were the product of this nonphysical organ. In studying these behaviors one had to be content, as Galen had been, with identifying the brain locus at which the soul exerted its effects on the brain and the body. Descartes even carried this Galenic notion inside the brain, arguing that the site of this interface was the pineal gland.

Descartes's dualism was thus *the* critical conceptual advance that permitted physiological studies of behavior to begin. Based upon the Cartesian dualist formula, simple deterministic behaviors would become the province of purely physiological study: Whenever a stimulus always produced a fixed behavioral response in a man or animal, then the deterministic material approach of science could be used to understand how the clockwork of the brain generated that behavior. But the dualist approach also recognized that unpredictable and nondeterministic behaviors did exist, and that the clockwork scientific explanations available to seventeenth-century scientists could not hope to mechanistically explain those behaviors. Complex and unpredictable behaviors would remain the province of philosophers, inaccessible to physiological study because these behaviors were the product of processes that resided outside the physical world within which physiologists could construct experiments.

Vaucanson's mechanical duck challenged his eighteenth-century audiences to decide whether a real duck was more than an assemblage of mechanical components that produced ducklike behavior. For the philosophers in Vaucanson's audience, who lived in a post–Cartesian world, the answer to that question was both yes and no. For many simple behaviors, the mechanical duck and a real duck were very much the same at a philosophical level. Both were causal deterministic machines that yielded predictable behavior. But for these post–Cartesians some portion of a real duck was also much more. The apparent ability of the real duck to behave unpredictably was evidence that a nonmaterial process, which lay outside the province of science, was also, at least occasionally, at work.

2

Inventing the Reflex

Enlightenment Views of Determinism in the Physical and Biological World

In the middle of the seventeenth century two new ideas became the foundation for modern science. Bacon championed the first when he argued that a deeper understanding of the physical world could be accomplished only if scholars were willing to challenge the ideas of the Ancients. As he put it: "It should be said frankly that the wisdom which we imbibed principally from the Greeks seems merely the boyhood of knowledge, with the characteristics of boys, that it is good at chattering, but immature and unable to generate." Recognizing the limitations of existing knowledge, however, was only the first step toward developing what we think of today as science. The second, and equally critical, step was a new approach to obtaining a deeper understanding of the physical world. That new approach, which we often call the *scientific method*, was a method both for describing the physical world and for testing the accuracy of our descriptions. A method rooted in the most sophisticated and logically rigorous system of thought available in the seventeenth century: analytic geometry.

Determinism in Geometrical Mathematics and Geometrical Physics
The goal of the scientific method is to develop descriptions, or models, of the physical world that are predictive. Models that can tell us how the physical world will behave in the future. One of the first scientific models of this type grew from the application of geometrical proof to the study of planetary motion. In the early seventeenth century, Kepler had shown

that Nicolaus Copernicus's model of the solar system could be fully described using a few simple mathematical tools. Kepler demonstrated that the orbital path of each planet could be described as a simple ellipse. The square of the time that a planet took to complete a circuit of its elliptical orbit was equal to the cube of the distance from the sun to that planet. The fraction of a single orbital period that it took each planet to cover any given segment of an orbit was equal to that fraction of the total area of the orbital ellipse covered as a sector during that portion of the orbit. This simple geometric system did a very effective job of describing the paths that the planets had taken in the past, but it also did something more; it predicted where the planets would be in the future. Kepler was able to show that his predictions were accurate to within 2 minutes of arc.

Vaucanson's mechanical duck was not very different from Kepler's solar system. The duck executed a preprogrammed series of movements. Ellipsoidal cams drove rods and levers in a geometric sequence. Like the solar system, the geometrically programmed actions of the duck were fixed and deterministic. This similarity was no accident. Kepler's model epitomized a revolution in the way Europeans thought about the physical world. And by the eighteenth century that revolution had influenced every aspect of European society. As I put it in the last chapter: "For many simple behaviors, the mechanical duck and a real duck were very much the same at a philosophical level. Both were causal deterministic machines that yielded predictable behavior." This, in large measure, reflected the growing use of rigorous mathematical syntax to define and test theories about the physical world. This philosophical reliance on determinate mathematics, however, also implied a significant bias in the way that scientists thought about the world. Believing that the future state of the world could be predicted with analytic geometry not only implied that the world was deterministic, it also rested on the assumption that the world *must be* deterministic.

Two men, in particular, were at the forefront of this growing European movement to use determinate mathematics as a tool for analyzing and describing the physical world. These men were Wilhelm Leibniz and Isaac Newton. Leibniz first presented this view publicly in his work on counting and logic *De Arte Combinatoria* (The Art of Combination,

1666), which was published just two years after Descartes's *L'Homme*. In the *Combinatoria*, Leibniz suggested explicitly that all thoughts and ideas which referred to events in the physical world *must*, in principle, be reducible to simple logical expressions derivable from the laws of mathematics. Since the laws of mathematics, he argued, precisely describe the way material objects interact in physical reality, all novel statements made within the grammatical constraints of mathematical syntax would therefore be accurate predictions of the behavior of the physical world. Even the development of completely new ideas could, he believed, be reduced to a fixed logical process in which the syntax of proof would so closely echo the reality of the physical world that new ideas about the physical world would flow deterministically from preexisting mathematical constructions.

Leibniz's proposal was a landmark because it hinted that a set of deterministic logical rules could be applied to solve *any* problem that could be stated. Indeed, Liebniz went so far as to suggest that any proposition that could be stated in a human language could, in principle, be reduced to a statement in a *universal characteristic* language. If this universal characteristic were constrained by an appropriate mathematical grammar, then the universal characteristic would simply not permit the generation of false or contradictory statements. Leibniz's goal was to build, from mathematical first principles, a logical system of language. Although he initially suggested that the final construction of the characteristic ought to take a few smart men only about five years, the project was never completed.

While Leibniz may initially have been alone in his belief that a universal characteristic was actually possible, the idea that more sophisticated determinate mathematical constructs would allow scientists to describe more complex phenomena was widely accepted throughout Europe during the Enlightenment. Both Leibniz and Newton implicitly applied this approach in their development of *the calculus*. The calculus, particularly in Newton's hands, was *the* tool for achieving Kepler's and Galileo's goal of a fully developed mathematical system that described deterministic clockworks like the solar system with a simple set of immutable laws. In a very real way, Newton's *laws of motion*, which were based upon the calculus, were the ultimate vindication of Descartes's approach.

These predictive mathematical rules appeared to verify that the solar system was indeed a determinate clockwork in constant motion, exactly as Descartes, Bacon, and Galileo had hoped.

Determinism and Behavior

How could the most complicated motion of all be reduced to a deterministic natural law? How could the motion of humans and animals be described with the same mathematical precision that had been achieved in studies of the solar system? In the last chapter I argued that the invention of dualism by Descartes was a critical first step toward answering this question. Descartes argued that at least some classes of human behavior, those which are simple and deterministic, could be explained by deterministic scientific laws. Descartes's dualist theory, however, went much further than this first step. His theoretical work also attempted to provide for physiologists the same level of insight that Kepler had provided for astronomers: a nearly complete scientific model of how simple behaviors might be produced by the determinate physical nervous system. (See figure 2.1.)

To understand, next, how external objects that strike the sense organs can incite [the machine] to move its members in a thousand different ways: think that

[a] the filaments (I have already often told you that these come from the innermost part of the brain and compose the marrow of the nerves) are so arranged in every organ of sense that they can very easily be moved by the objects of that sense and that

[b] when they are moved, with however little force, they simultaneously pull the parts of the brain from which they come, and by this means open the entrances to certain pores in the internal surface of the brain; [and that]

[c] the animal spirits in its cavities begin immediately to make their way through these pores into the nerves, and so into the muscles that give rise to movements in this machine quite similar to [the movements] to which we [men] are naturally incited when our senses are similarly impinged upon.

Thus, if fire A is near foot B, the particles of this fire (which move very quickly, as you know) have force enough to displace the area of skin that they touch; and thus pulling the little thread cc, which you see to be attached there, they simultaneously open the entrance to the pore [or conduit] where this thread terminates [in the brain]: just as, pulling on one end of a cord, one simultaneously rings a bell which hangs at the opposite end.

Now the entrance of the pore or small conduit de, being thus opened, the animal spirits from cavity F [the ventricle] enter and are carried through it—part

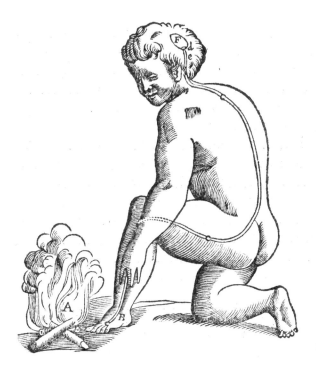

Figure 2.1
Descartes's Reflex Man (Author's personal collection).

into the muscles that serve to withdraw this foot from the fire, part into those
that serve to turn the eyes and head to look at it, and part in those that serve to
advance the hands and bend the body to protect it. (Descartes, 1664)

In this passage from his *Treatise on Man*, Descartes provides us with
his second critical contribution to neural science, a theory of how the
brain actually produces deterministic patterns of behavior. As he puts it
in the concluding paragraph of *L'Homme*:

I desire you to consider, I say, that these functions [the ones produced by this
model of the sensorimotor process] imitate those of a real man as perfectly as
possible and that they follow naturally in this machine entirely from the disposition of the organs—no more nor less than do the movements of a clock or other
automaton, from the arrangements of its counterweights and wheels.
  Wherefore it is not necessary, on their account, to conceive of any vegetative or
sensitive soul or any other principle of movement and life [to account for non-
volitional behaviors or the behaviors of animals] than its blood and its spirits,
agitated by the heat of the fire which burns continually in its heart and which is

of no other nature than all those fires that occur in inanimate bodies. (Descartes, 1664)

Descartes was applying the same mechanistic logic that served Kepler, Galileo, and even Harvey to understand the motion of humans and animals. His model of how sensory signals lead to the generation of movement comes down to us today in a very specific form. As he put it in *Les Passions*:

Article 36. Furthermore, if that [animal which appears suddenly] is very unusual and very frightful ... in some men this so predisposes the brain that the spirits *reflected* from the image thus formed [of the fearful beast] on the gland [the pineal] turn to flow in part into the nerves serving to turn the back and move the legs for running away.... (Descartes, 1649)

From this passage, at least in part, Descartes's model of how sensory signals lead mechanistically to movement derives its modern name, *the reflex*.

The Cartesian model of the reflex clearly has a geometric character. The many woodcut illustrations for *L'Homme*, which Descartes designed before his death, show lines that carry signals from the outside world into the brain. Points of intersection and reflection are labeled with letters, just as in a Euclidean proof. For Descartes, the reflex is a piece of analytic geometry. But the reflex model is also quite different from the truly mathematical models of physicists like Kepler, which could be rigorously analyzed and tested. Descartes appeals in concept to the reflex as a model of how "these functions imitate those of a real man as perfectly as possible," but he provides us with no empirical proof that the model does indeed imitate the motions of a real man with any precision. This stands in stark contrast to Kepler's model of the solar system, which can be both rigorously analyzed and shown to be quantitatively accurate. Perhaps surprisingly, it was not until several centuries later that the physiologists studying behavior would adopt Kepler's empirical approach and begin to test the assertion that Descartes's system could indeed imitate the functions of a real man with any precision.

Nondeterministic Behavior

Descartes proposed his reflex as a model for only one class of human behavior, those behaviors in which the linkage between sensation and action was completely deterministic. But he also argued that there was another class of behavior which could not be described as the product of predictable, deterministic processes.[1] Complex behaviors existed, he asserted, that reflect a nondeterministic process which lies outside the domain of scientific inquiry. Descartes, however, provided no empirical evidence that these nondeterministic behaviors do in fact exist. An omission that raises a critical question which has haunted philosophers since Descartes: Is there good evidence that humans really can produce nondeterministic behaviors? Behaviors that cannot be described as the product of a determinate mathematical process? Are there truly responses that humans can generate which are not fully determined by "the disposition of the organs—no more nor less than do the movements of a clock or other automaton, from the arrangements of its counterweights and wheels"? Or was the emerging Newtonian revolution something that could be applied to the study of all classes of human behavior?

This was, and continues to be, a central question. Preserving the existence of a nondeterministic free will is, after all, a principal reason for proposing the two-track system of dualism. But what if one were to rely only on scientific principles for thinking about the connections between sensation and action in man? Would this necessarily lead us to conclude, first, that all behavior is truly deterministic and, second, that all behavior must be underlain by something like Descartes's reflective mechanism?

In 1748 the Scottish philosopher David Hume, building on the work of Newton and Descartes, addressed this issue directly in his *An Enquiry Concerning Human Understanding*:

when irregular events follow from any particular cause; the philosopher and physician are not surprised at the matter, nor are they ever tempted to deny, in general, the necessity and uniformity of those principles, by which the animal economy is conducted. They know, that a human body is a mighty complicated machine: That many secret powers lurk in it, which are altogether beyond our comprehension: That to us it must often appear very uncertain in its operations:

1. In fact there is significant scholarly debate about whether or not Descartes actually believed in the existence of nondeterministic, or volitional, behavior. It may be that this attribution of unpredictable behavior to an action of the soul was a bow to the authority of the Church. In his writings he specifically indicates that animals lack any form of volition; that they, at least, should be viewed as fully determinate mechanisms.

And that therefore the irregular events, which outwardly discover themselves, can be no proof, that the laws of nature are not observed with the greatest regularity in its internal operations and government.... The philosopher, if he be consistent must apply the same reasoning to the actions and volitions of intelligent agents.

Hume was suggesting that all human and animal action could be reduced to a complex series of deterministic interactions. Like Descartes, he argued that deterministic behavior should be explicable by the same kind of natural law that Newton had applied to the inanimate world, but unlike Descartes, his approach was to suggest that the operations and government of the human mind could be described exclusively with the deterministic mathematical tools of the scientific revolution.

The Birth of Analytic Mathematics: The End of Geometric World Models

The development of the calculus had an enormous impact on European science. It allowed mathematicians and physicists to analyze and describe continuous processes, like the instantaneous properties of objects in motion. It also provided fundamental tools, like differentiation and integration, that would come to be as important to mathematics as addition and subtraction. Perhaps just as important as these innovations was the influence of the calculus on the way that mathematicians *thought* about problems. As we will see, one long-term effect of Newton, Leibniz, and the calculus was to shift mathematical reasoning away from the constraints of analytic geometry and toward a more formal grammatical syntax while retaining the fundamentally determinate approach of classical mathematics.

Before Newton and Leibniz invented the calculus, mathematics had been concerned primarily with the study of discrete phenomena and with simple systems of equations. Kepler produced his main insights about the solar system using simple geometry of a kind that would have been basically familiar to the ancient Greek mathematicians. Newton's laws of motion, and the calculus from which they derive, however, provided a very different set of tools. They made it possible to describe and analyze continuous phenomena, like the trajectory of a moving body. Using a differential equation, it became possible to set up and solve equations that answered questions like, When does a moving body reach maximum velocity? without resort to any geometric representations. This was a critical step in thinking about the world as a deterministic place because it meant that a whole range of previously unpredictable events (in the mathematical sense) could now be analyzed with tremendous precision and with a mathematical syntax that had been stripped of geometrical allegory. The implications of this approach were nowhere more clear than in the work of the two great mathematicians of the late 1700s and early 1800s, Joseph-Louis Lagrange and Pierre-Simon Laplace.

Lagrange was a mathematical titan revered by scientists and philosophers throughout Europe. Born in Italy, he moved to Paris in the mid-eighteenth century because that city was rapidly emerging as the intellectual center of the Continent. It was Lagrange who almost singlehandedly emancipated mathematics from geometry through the vehicle of the calculus.

The first major problem that Lagrange tackled as a young mathematician was to use Newton's law of gravitation and an extension of the calculus to explain the rotation of the moon. This was an exceptionally difficult problem, and one that Galileo had been unable to solve, because it involved the interaction of three gravitational bodies: the sun, the Earth and the moon. Kepler's solution to celestial problems was to apply simple ellipses as models of planetary motion. Planets circled the sun. But as Newton's law of gravitation made clear, the orbit of any celestial body must be influenced not just by the sun but also by every other body in the system. The simplest example of this, Lagrange reasoned, was a three-body problem in which sun, Earth, and moon interact gravitationally. Armed with the calculus, Lagrange was able to derive a set of equations that not only accurately described this system but also allowed one to predict the position and orientation of the moon at any future time. Lagrange's mathematics was beginning to do exactly what deterministic material scientists were hoping for; these functions were beginning to make it possible to predict the future for increasingly complex clockwork systems.

Lagrange's mathematical brilliance placed him squarely in the center of the European world during a turbulent time. He found himself in Paris during the French Revolution, and watched noble-born friends like the great chemist Antoine Lavoisier go to the guillotine. While he tried unsuccessfully to argue for the lives of his friends, he very slowly matured a volume that was to be a turning point for mathematics. Slowly, because in middle age Lagrange was rocked by depression and despair (it was only through the relentless efforts of a beautiful young Parisian, who first courted and then married him), Lagrange's masterwork, the *Mécanique Analytique*, was completed in 1788.

The *Mécanique Analytique* was a compilation of the mathematical advances accomplished in the hundred years since Newton's death. It represented the logical extension of the Newtonian approach to the study of complete classical mechanical systems and it introduced a number of critical advances. One of its most interesting features is that although it is five volumes in length, the book contains not a single geometric figure. This is a point that Lagrange notes in his introduction. This book, he suggests, provides equations that quantitatively describe the geometry of three-dimensional spaces in time without requiring resort to the figures which had limited the scope of mathematics during the dominance of analytic geometry. It was explicitly Lagrange's goal to liberate the syntax of post–Newtonian mathematics from geometry. It is a tribute to his brilliance that he largely succeeded.

However, at the end of the eighteenth century, amid the heat of the French Revolution, it was Lagrange's brilliant young colleague Pierre-Simon Laplace who came to personify the analytic and deterministic approach Lagrange had begun to develop (figure 2.2). Born to a poor family in the provinces, he used his brilliant mind and his unfailing ability to flatter and cultivate those in power to become the preeminent intellectual force on the Continent during the Napoleonic period.

Early in his career Laplace came to Paris and distinguished himself as a mathematician and as a teacher at the French military academy (where, among others, he had the young Napoleon Bonaparte as a student). As the revolution erupted, Laplace's humble birth, which he had previously sought to conceal, served him well and he rose to become Lagrange's peer. As the revolution ended, he announced his undying admiration for Napoleon and continued his rise during the emperor's reign. With the defeat of Napoleon, Laplace, in a final move, was able to announce his

Figure 2.2
Pierre-Simon Laplace (Hulton Archive, IH05166).

deep and ongoing commitment to the Bourbon monarchy, an act for which he was created Marquis de Laplace.

Like Lagrange and other mathematicians of his time, Laplace was concerned with refining models of the solar system through the extension and refinement of the calculus. But in his masterwork, the *Mécanique Céleste*, Laplace took mathematical analysis far beyond even what Lagrange had attempted (Laplace, 1789–1827). Laplace believed that the ultimate accomplishment in celestial mechanics would be to develop a set of equations which allowed one to model the gravitational interactions of every body in the solar system. He believed that the Newtonian system could be extended beyond the complex three-body problem that Lagrange had tackled, that a complete mathematical model of the solar system was possible. Such a model would allow one not only to predict the locations of any body at any time in the future with unparalleled precision, but also would allow Laplace to answer what he considered the ultimate question: Is the solar system a stable process or is it doomed to eventual destruction? If Laplace was able to capture the motions and interactions of the sun and its planets and moons, he ought to be able not only to determine the precise position of any body at any time in the future, but also to determine whether, and when, the solar system would change or decay from its current state. And it is absolutely fair to say that he accomplished this. His calculations indicated that the orbits of the planets were in a kind of equilibrium, stable in their current configuration for eternity. While this may not be exactly true today (Laplace was unaware of things like tidal forces), its impact was very important in establishing the notion that the universe was a very deterministic place, just as Newton and Hume had suggested.

Laplace, and essentially all European mathematicians and scientists, believed that the *Mécanique Céleste* had succeeded in reducing the cosmos to an orderly, fully understood system. The behavior of all of the planets and moons at any time in the infinite future could be known. At the time this was widely believed to represent the culmination of astronomical science. The goal that remained, Laplace argued in his *Système du Monde* (Laplace, 1796), was to bring terrestrial science to this same level of determinate perfection.

Beyond Clockworks: Analytic Models of the Determinate Brain

After Laplace, the mathematical foundations of our deterministic worldview continued to develop. Understanding the terrestrial sphere seemed to become more and more possible as mathematics, chemistry, and physics continued to grow. At every stage, more and more evidence accumulated that physical law was an adequate tool for describing *all* physical systems, even biological systems, a conclusion that strengthened one of Descartes's original claims.

Perhaps the most startling biological revelation made in this regard during the eighteenth century came from the work of the Italian physiologist Luigi Galvani. In 1791 Galvani published his *De Viribus Elec-*

tricitatis in Motu Musculari Commentarius (Commentary on the Effect of Electricity on Muscle Motion). This was a landmark work that went far toward integrating the emerging physics of electricity with the motive force in muscle contraction. In it, Galvani demonstrated that electrical stimulation of either nerves or muscles led to muscle contraction, a finding that led him to suggest that it was a form of electricity which was responsible for the movement of animals. As he put it in one of his manuscript notes:

Accordingly, on an early evening in September 1786, we placed some frogs horizontally on a parapet, prepared in the usual manner by piercing and suspending their spinal cords with iron hooks. The hooks touched an iron plate; behold! a variety of not infrequent spontaneous movements in the frog. If, when they were quiescent, the hook was pressed with the finger against the iron surface, the frogs became excited almost as often as this type of pressure was applied. (translated in R. M. Green, 1953)

In time, Galvani perfected this technique of electrical stimulation by developing what he called "bimetallic arcs" (a primitive two-metal battery) to use in place of the iron hooks. Although Galvani became embroiled in an enormous controversy with Alessandro Volta over the existence of this "animal electricity," his experiments can only have strengthened the growing conviction among physiologists that at least some of the clockwork gears which made up a moving animal were beginning to be understood:

it would perhaps not be an inept hypothesis and conjecture, nor altogether deviating from the truth, which should compare a muscle fiber to a small Leyden jar, or other similar electric body, charged with two opposite kinds of electricity; but should liken the nerve to the conductor, and therefore compare the whole muscle with the assemblage of Leyden jars. (Galvani, 1791, part four)

With these ideas in the physiological forefront, it seems only logical that physiologists would begin to believe that Descartes's concept of the reflex was becoming testable in a scientific sense. As a result, a number of experimenters began to examine the relationship between different classes of behavior and the different components of the nervous system. While many scientists undertook these tests, including Johannes Müller the dean of German physiology, one man in particular seems to have defined the modern version of the Cartesian paradigm with his work. That man was the British physiologist Marshall Hall.

Hall was a scientist just at the moment in European history when the practice of science, particularly in Britain, was about to become the province of trained professionals rather than the domain of wealthy amateurs. Hall was born into a reasonably well-to-do manufacturing family in Nottingham, clearly a member of the middle class. Like many members of that social group, his family was Methodist, setting them outside the ranks of the Anglican elite. Since he was a Methodist, Oxford and Cambridge universities were essentially closed to Hall, driving him further from the privileged elite that ruled British science. Hall was forced to pursue his medical studies at the University of Edinburgh in Scotland.

Edinburgh was, however, a cosmopolitan and innovative place at that time. Because it was the finest nonecclesiastical institution in the United Kingdom, it attracted the best non–Anglican minds from throughout the English-speaking world. Catholics from Ireland, Protestants from America, and Jews and Dissenters from England traveled to Edinburgh, which became the center of extra–Cambridge medicine. Nearly all of the leading American physicians from that period came to Edinburgh for their educations before founding institutions in post–Revolutionary metropolises like Philadelphia.

It is important to remember that Hall was trained as a physician at a time when the distinction between physicians and surgeons was enormous. Physicians were the elite practitioners of medicine who diagnosed and prescribed, rather than treating illness directly. Surgeons were viewed as manual, although educated, laborers, and so by obtaining for himself the rank of physician, Hall was able to enter the world of gentlemen, despite his mediocre pedigree.

After leaving Edinburgh, Hall returned briefly to his hometown of Nottingham, then relocated to London as quickly as decency permitted (and perhaps a bit more quickly than that). In London, he established a medical practice and began to devote himself to writing papers for the *Philosophical Transactions of the Royal Society*, at least in part to further secure a place among the upper classes of the capital.

The Royal Society of London (fig. 2.3) was, at that time, the epicenter of British science. It was founded in 1662 as the Royal Society of London for the Promotion of Natural Knowledge by the Adherents and Disciples

Figure 2.3
The Royal Society (Hulton Archive, HN7180).

of Francis Bacon. At its evening meetings the intellectuals of Britain verbally presented their papers, almost in a salon atmosphere, to the aristocracy of the British Empire. Thereafter these papers were published in the Society's *Philosophical Transactions,* one of the oldest scientific periodicals of Europe. At the time that Hall moved to London, the Royal Society could already count among its past presidents Robert Hooke (one of the inventors of the microscope) and Sir Isaac Newton. In addition to presenting and publishing papers in the *Philosophical Transactions,* the fellows of the Royal Society met regularly to, for example, elect new members from among the ranks of "scientifically minded gentlemen" whose contributions to science merited their receipt of the coveted initials F.R.S. (Fellow of the Royal Society). It was into this community that Hall hoped to project himself when he moved to London and began to submit papers for presentation at the Royal Society.

The Royal Society at this time was in a critical stage of transition. It, and British science in general, were still the province of the upper classes, but more and more often educated members of the middle class were forcing their way into this intellectual enclave. One side effect of this dramatic change was that it tended to polarize the Royal Society into two groups, Anglican insiders of high birth and outsiders of essentially all other categories.

Hall's early work centered on what were then called "the diseases of women," and his publications on obstetrical and gynecologic material were competent if a bit self-aggrandizing. Among other things he published one manuscript that argued against the then common practice of bloodletting. It was on the basis of this work and on his rising position in the London medical establishment that Hall was, finally, elected a fellow of the Royal Society in 1832.

It was in 1833, however, that Marshall Hall, M.D., F.R.S., presented his landmark paper, "On the Reflex Function of the Medulla Oblongata and Medulla Spinalis." Other writers before Hall had performed similar experiments, and others had even used the word "reflex" to describe some of these properties, but Hall's paper so clearly lays out our modern concept of both Cartesian dualism and the reflex as a model for how the nervous system produces fully deterministic behaviors, that I believe his presentation at the Royal Society served as one of the half-dozen most critical points in the history of neural science.

In the middle of this landmark presentation Hall epitomizes both his discovery and his theoretical interpretation of it with the following experiment:

The spinal marrow of a frog was divided [or transected] between the [levels of the] anterior and posterior extremities. *It was immediately observed that the head and the anterior extremities alone were moved spontaneously and with design* [my italics], the respiration being performed as before. But the posterior extremities were not paralyzed: they were drawn upwards, and remained perfectly motionless, indeed unless stimulated: by the application of any stimulus, they were moved with energy, but once only, and in a manner perfectly peculiar

[stereotyped]. The stimulus was not felt by the animal, because the head and anterior extremities remained motionless at the time it was applied. *Nothing could
be more obvious, and indeed striking, than the difference between the phenomena of the functions of sensation and volition observed in the anterior part of
the animal and those of reflex function in the posterior: in the former there
were spontaneous movements with obvious design: in the latter the mere effect
of stimulus* [my italics]. (Hall, 1833)

In these passages Hall quite clearly defines a physiological version of
Descartes's dualism that would come to characterize studies of the nervous system for the next century. The spinal cord is the seat of the Cartesian clockwork, the deterministic organism. The brain, in particular the
brain above the medulla, is the seat of volition, or will. Hall, however,
does not stop there; like Descartes, he goes on to offer a quite specific
model of how the clockwork deterministic nervous system operates:

I have been compelled, therefore, to adopt a new designation for them [this class
of phenomena], and I shall now give the reasons for my choice of that which is
given in the title of this paper.
 This property [of reflex action] is characterized by being *excited* in its action,
and *reflex* in its course: In every instance in which it is exerted, an impression
being made upon the extremities of certain nerves is conveyed to the medulla
oblongata or the medulla spinalis, and is reflected along other nerves to parts
adjacent to, or remote from, that which has received the impression.
 It is by this reflex character that the function to which I have alluded is to be
distinguished from every other.... In this kind of muscular motion, the motive
influence does not originate in any central part of the nervous system, but at a
distance from that centre: it is neither spontaneous in its action, nor direct in its
course; it is on the contrary, *excited* by the application of appropriate stimuli,
which are not, however, applied immediately to the muscular or nervo-muscular
[*sic*] fibre, but to certain membranous parts [sense organs], whence the impression is carried to the medulla, *reflected*, and reconducted to the part impressed, or
conducted to a part remote from it where the muscular contraction is effected.
                                    . . .
 In the case of the reflex function alone, the muscles are excited by a stimulus
acting mediately and indirectly in a curved and reflex course, along the superficial
subcutaneous or submucous nerves proceeding to the medulla, and muscular
nerves proceeding from the medulla. (Hall, 1833)

In fairness, Hall's model for how the reflex is accomplished is still
quite primitive, and nothing like the very specific cellular model that
Sherrington would develop a half-century later. He argues that sensory
and motor nerves are connected in the spinal cord by a hazy process he
calls reflection. But the critical step in Hall's presentation is that he has

single-handedly brought the Cartesian paradigm into the modern scientific period. Descartes's hypothesis has been stated quite clearly. The "animal economy" consists of two main classes of movement: volitional movement and reflex movement. Volitional movements show spontaneity and reveal willful design. Reflex movements are simple and deterministic; they "reflect" "the mere effect of stimulus." Volition can be localized to the brain, above the level of the medulla. Reflexes can be localized to the spinal cord. While understanding the mechanism of volition clearly lay outside Hall's empirical domain, he argues that the mechanism of the reflex can be modeled as some type of sensorimotor reflection.

No doubt Hall was inspired in drawing these conclusions not only by Descartes but also by the neuroanatomical studies of Sir Charles Bell and François Magendie. In 1822 Magendie, who was the intellectual center of French neurophysiology, performed a critical experiment (Magendie, 1822a, 1822b). He sectioned a few of the spinal nerves entering the dorsal columns of the spinal cord and found that his animal subjects had lost all sensation in tissue innervated by these nerves. Startlingly, he noted that these portions of the body still possessed muscle tone and that under some conditions the animals could be induced to move these muscles. In contrast, when the nerves entering the spinal cord ventrally were cut, the animal lost all ability to move but retained sensation. From these observations Magendie drew the conclusion that sensory information entered the spinal cord exclusively through this dorsal route and that motor signals left the spinal cord exclusively along a ventral trajectory.

Hall would have been very aware of this work because it had provoked a firestorm of controversy in London. Sir Charles Bell, the most senior British neuroanatomist of the period and a central figure at the Royal Society, had privately published a similar report in 1811. In the 1820s he very publicly attacked Magendie, claiming priority in the discovery of independent sensory and motor roots for the spinal cord. In fact, Bell's report was a good deal less rigorous than Magnendie's and dealt only with the sensory roots, but Bell was adamant about establishing priority for what he considered (perhaps in retrospect) the most important discovery of his career. Pierre Flourens (who hated Magendie) even made the claim that Bell once said, "My discovery will place me by the side of Harvey."

Bell's delusions of grandeur aside, Marshall Hall must have been profoundly struck by this observation that sensory signals entered the spinal cord dorsally and motor signals left the cord ventrally. His comment that "In the case of the reflex function alone, the muscles are excited by a stimulus acting mediately and indirectly in a curved and reflex course, along the superficial subcutaneous or submucous nerves proceeding to the medulla [of the spinal cord], and muscular nerves proceeding from the medulla" must have been motivated by this observation.

Vaucanson's Duck in a Deterministic, but Analytic, World

Hall's paper and his later researches were well received on the Continent, but a combination of Hall's obstreperous character and his middle-class origins limited the impact of his work in Britain at the time. In fact, Hall often had trouble getting his later manuscripts accepted for publication in the *Philosophical Transactions*. A number of his papers were rejected as too purely derivative of the 1833 paper or of containing claims that were incompletely substantiated. Hall took rejections of this sort quite personally, and almost always responded to a rejection by campaigning vigorously for a second hearing or by seeking the personal intervention by a high-ranking member. Interestingly, one of the older men to whom he turned was the mathematician and inventor Charles Babbage.

Babbage was a mathematician who held the Lucasian Chair in mathematics at Cambridge, the same chair that Newton had held just a few decades previously. With the death of Humphry Davy in 1829, the presidency of the Royal Society passed for a brief time to an unremarkable gentleman, Davies Gilbert. Gilbert was, essentially, a caretaker president, but one who became the specific target of Babbage's efforts to reform the Royal Society. In 1830 Babbage published *Reflections on the Decline of Science and Some of Its Causes*, a polemical manuscript which argued that science in Great Britain was in terrible decline and that at the core of this decline was an absolute failure of the Royal Society to promote British science. This book led, ultimately, to the end of Gilbert's term as president and to a new election. Babbage and his coterie of scientists and reformers promoted Babbage's close friend, the astronomer John Herschel, for the post of president. Unfortunately, Herschel found himself running against His Royal Highness the Duke of Sussex, King George IV's third son. After a contentious election the Duke of Sussex was ultimately victorious, and it was largely through a combination of his good offices and public pressure that Babbage was not expelled from the Royal Society.

Babbage was a mathematician who had made his name in two ways. First, he had published a few papers on analytic functions, the mainstay of mathematical research at that time. Second, and perhaps much more important, Babbage made his name by bringing to Britain many of the mathematical advances made on the Continent since Newton's death. Having then made his name, Babbage devoted much of his energy to defending the Royal Society from what he perceived as mediocrity, an effort that included Herschel's ill-fated run for the Society's presidency. It was in his capacity as an outsider's insider that the younger and much less important Marshall Hall often turned to Babbage for support. We might well imagine that Babbage was, at best, an uncertain ally for the young physician. In *The Decline of Science* Babbage had written:

The honor of belonging to the Royal Society is much sought after by medical men, as contributing to the success of their professional efforts [their medical practices], and two consequences result from it. In the first place the pages of the *Transactions of the Royal Society* occasionally contain medical papers of very moderate merit; and, in the second, the preponderance of the medical interest introduces into the Society some of the jealousies of that profession. (Babbage, 1830)

All this suggests that Babbage, as was probably typical of mathematicians in his time, did not think of physiology as a *real* science. He did not see physiology as a science that could be attacked using the tools mathematicians were then developing. Defending the excellence of British science did not include the promotion of medical physiologists like Hall. But Babbage did think very deeply about how these new mathematical tools could be used and about what kinds of problems they could solve in other areas.

Babbage's main scientific contribution lay in this direction with his design of the first general-purpose mechanical computer, the Babbage analytic engine. In some ways, the idea of the analytic engine represents a critical step in the way that Western scientists were beginning to think about mathematics, models, and determinism. On the Continent, Lagrange and Laplace had demonstrated that the universe was one vast clockwork which could be better described with differential equations than with geometric objects. If this is so, then an analytic engine, which could represent equations stripped of figural geometric notation, could in a very real sense serve as a model of the real universe. It would serve as a computational model of the universe in the same way that Vaucanson's duck had served as a geometric model of a real duck. When Lagrange demonstrated that mechanical systems could be modeled without the use of physical geometric representations, he made it possible for Babbage to begin to model the clockwork of a deterministic world in a new way, with an analytic engine.

Unfortunately, Babbage's analytic engine was never built, and over a hundred years would pass before technology would catch up with Babbage's dream. But this notion is critical. The clockwork automata of the mathematicians that continued to influence physiologists were beginning to come of age.

3

Charles Sherrington and the Propositional Logic of Reflexes

Testing the Limits of Determinate Analytic Mathematics

To post–Newtonian mathematicians like Laplace it must have seemed that determinate mathematics would eventually become a tool that could describe *any* event or process in the physical universe. Mathematics would someday be bounded only by the limits of thought. But at a philosophical level it is important to remember that this need not necessarily be true. The logical system of human thought in which determinate mathematics is grounded could be self-limited. Physical processes might exist that cannot, in principle, be resolved or described with any of the tools determinate mathematics could ever provide.

Certainly in Babbage's time there was no way to know in advance whether, or how, a given mathematical problem could or would be solved. Mathematical proofs were a kind of art that relied on the intuition and creativity of mathematicians. Leibniz, in particular, had been frustrated both by this artful quality of Enlightenment mathematics and by the absence of any clear proof that determinate mathematics would some day become a complete system for describing the entire physical world. In his writing he voiced this frustration, proposing that someday all ideas would be reduced to a simple set of logical symbols and that a set of logical operators could be applied to these symbols in order to create and test, in a mechanical way, all possible new ideas.

Unfortunately, Leibniz made very little headway toward developing his universal characteristic. As a result the idea of the universal characteristic was more of an open challenge than a complete logical system. Leibniz had argued that a fully developed and internally self-consistent

Figure 3.1
George Boole (Hulton Archive, IH000935).

logical system could be created, and that this system would reduce mathematics to a mechanical and inductive process. But for a century and a half there was no clear evidence that Leibniz's challenge would, or could, be answered.

In the mid-1800s the self-taught English mathematician George Boole (figure 3.1) began to answer Leibniz's challenge when he published two books that now serve as two of the foundations of modern logic. In 1847 he published *Mathematical Analysis of Logic*, and in 1854 *An Investigation of the Laws of Thought*. In these books Boole argued that classical logic had become too entangled in the limitations of human language and, partly as a result, had failed to achieve Leibniz's central goal of permitting the testing of new ideas in any domain.

As Boole put it in *The Laws of Thought*:

The design of the following treatise is to investigate the fundamental laws of those operations of the mind by which reasoning is performed; to give expression to them in the language of a Calculus, and upon this foundation to establish the science of Logic and construct its method; to make the method itself the basis of a general method for the application of the mathematical doctrine of probabilities; and finally to collect from the various elements of truth brought to view in the course of these inquiries some probable intimations concerning the nature and constitution of the human mind. . . .

To accomplish these goals, Boole began by proposing a new syntax for logical reasoning, the language of a logical calculus. Ever since the time of the ancient Greeks, logical statements had taken the form of syllogisms. For example, in a more modern context:

I have seen a portrait of John Wilkes Booth; John Wilkes Booth assassinated Abraham Lincoln; thus I have seen a portrait of an assassin of Abraham Lincoln. (Church, 1944)

Boole argued that instead, logicians should adopt the language of mathematical algebra for making logical statements. Logical statements should be symbolic and mathematical rather than linguistic. Taking, for example, the form

$$xy = 0.$$

Boole felt that this new approach might ultimately allow the creation of a complete and self-contained logical system on which all of mathematics could be based. He thus began *The Laws of Thought* by providing ten basic postulates, or axioms. These postulates range from definitions of identity among algebraic objects to definitions of a set of legal operations that can be made among algebraic objects. The ten basic postulates are not things that Boole proves, but rather assertions that serve as a starting point. Having provided these basic postulates, Boole goes on to accomplish much of what Leibniz had imagined. He shows that if one begins with a few elementary operations, like *A and B, A or B, A not B*, these basic elements can be combined in many different ways to produce logical sentences, and the logical sentences produced in this way can be used to derive many thousands of common mathematical theorems. Much of determinate mathematics, Boole shows, can be derived from a few simple axioms and a handful of logical operators.

In *The Laws of Thought* Boole had succeeded in producing a symbolic logical system. He showed that something like the universal characteristic was, in a general sense, possible. Boole could not, however, make the claim that his logical system was all-inclusive; he was not able to show that his logic was a fully complete system for expressing all mathematically possible concepts. Boole could not rule out the possibility that there were proofs and theorems which could not be described within his system. In this regard he started, but did not complete, Leibniz's process of reducing determinate mathematics to a single overarching logical system that was coextensive with all of reality.

One of the people who came closest to that goal was a successor of Boole's in the late nineteenth century, the German mathematician Gottlob Frege. Frege explicitly set for himself the goal of showing that logic and all of mathematics were, in principle, coextensive. He set out, in a very formal way, to develop exactly the logical system that Leibniz had proposed, a system we now think of as propositional logic. Frege's basic idea was most fully developed in his 1893–1903 *Grundgesetze der Arithmetik* (The Basic Laws of Arithmetic). Frege's goal was to reduce all logical thought to a system of operations that would have its roots in mathematics. This would mean that, in principle, mathematical tools could be used to examine, test, and solve any problem that could be stated in those terms. Were Frege to succeed, this would be a major philosophical landmark, perhaps the ultimate mathematical achievement in a Cartesian world. And the two-volume *Grundgesetze* appeared to be just such an accomplishment. Although not widely read at the time, the *Grundgesetze* seemed to contain a complete description of a universal characteristic language.

Following very close inspection of the *Grundgesetze*, however, the English philosopher and mathematician Bertrand Russell noted a harrowing inconsistency in Frege's program. Using Frege's own system of logical grammar, Russell was able to construct a self-referential sentence that seemed to be self-contradictory. Something that had the flavor of the sentence "I am now lying." If you are lying, and this sentence is therefore a lie, does that mean you are telling the truth? And if you are telling the truth, then how can you be lying? Russell was able to show that statements of this kind were inescapably possible in the logical system of the *Grundgesetze*. He brought this to Frege's attention just as the second volume of the *Grundgesetze* was going to press. Frege responded by including an additional proof that he hoped would make self-contradictory statements impossible within the framework of predicate logic, but Frege's proof is widely considered inadequate, a fact of which he must have been aware.

Frege's inability to build a system of logic that was free from internal contradiction raised a critical question: Was it impossible to construct a logical-mechanical system that would always be internally consistent? Were there classes of problems, such as those which involve recursive statements like "I am now lying," that can never be presented in a consistent, resolvable, and noncontradictory manner by any logical system? If this were true, then even simpler systems based upon determinate mathematics, like Boole's, would be profoundly limited in what they could model or describe.

At the beginning of the twentieth century, two groups of mathematicians began to address this absolutely critical problem: Russell and his colleague Alfred North Whitehead in Britain, and David Hilbert and his students in Göttingen, Germany. Both groups realized how much was at stake, and both were absolutely convinced that the Cartesian–Newtonian paradigm of formal systems rooted in determinate mathematics could be shown to be a complete model of all logically possible realities, if only mathematicians could overcome the limitations Russell had found in Frege's approach.

Russell and Whitehead tackled this problem by attempting to refine Frege's basic approach, incorporating advanced concepts from set theory into the framework of the "universal logical language." Their masterpiece, the *Principia Mathematica* (Whitehead and Russell, 1910–1913), represents the fruit of this research effort, which was very much in the tradition of Frege's work. In the *Principia* Russell and Whitehead defined a formal mathematics, and appeared to show that it could be extended to resolve all questions that, in principle, could ever be asked in mathematical form.

Hilbert's approach, though less philosophical, was to have more far-reaching implications. He hoped to develop direct mathematical proofs to show that there were virtually no limits to the kinds of problems that determinate mathematics could solve. The Hilbert program was, in a nutshell, to develop proofs for three ideas in number theory. First, he wanted to prove that mathematics (and in particular number theory) was *complete*; any true mathematical statement could necessarily be proven within the domain of mathematics from a fixed set of axioms. Second, that mathematics was *consistent*, if one could prove that $2 + 2 = 4$, then one should never be able to prove a contradictory statement like $2 + 2 = 5$. Finally, he wanted to prove that all mathematical problems were *decidable*; any mathematical proposition could be tested as true or false by a definite method. In the early 1900s Hilbert's students seemed well on their way to proving each of these three critical assertions.

At the end of the nineteenth century, determinate mathematics had reached this critical stage. Mathematicians and philosophers had converged on the idea that complete logical systems of thought were possible. Anything that was true could be proven by using the tools of a mathematical system which rested on a small number of axioms. If one started with a few basic axioms and a few basic mathematical operators, then any idea or operation could be synthesized from these basic elements.

Charles Scott Sherrington: The Confluence of Logic and Physiology

Working at the same time that Marshall Hall was codifying the reflex as a model for determinate behavior, George Boole had laid the foundations for predicate logic. Boole had argued that even if one permits only a dozen or so different kinds of primitive operations in a system of logic, it is still possible to reconstruct much of determinate mathematics. Simple operations like *and, or, not* were, Boole showed, building blocks from which much more complicated logical structures could be built.

At the end of the nineteenth century, the growing certainty that determinate mathematics could be used to describe and model any physical system influenced the way that many philosophers and scientists thought about Boole's accomplishment. By 1900, Frege, Russell, and Hilbert were arguing that an appropriately designed calculus of predicate logic could be used to reconstruct all of determinate mathematics, and thus could be used to describe any physical system. If this were true, it would imply that determinate models of the nervous system rooted in predicate logic must be the necessary and sufficient tool for understanding how sensory signals gave rise to deterministic motor responses. Ultimately, this suggested that the goal of a neurophysiologist was to break down the signals conducted by the nervous system into a small number of primitive operations and rules from which *any* arbitrarily complex behavior could be produced.

As these philosophical and mathematical advances were beginning to influence the intellectual mainstream, literally dozens of scientists in Germany, France, and England were beginning to investigate the neurobiological hardware that gave rise to Marshall Hall's determinate reflexes. One man, however, was clearly the premier thinker in this group. His research program, which spanned more than half a century, seems to have captured both the scientific rigor and near certainty of success that characterized the ongoing mathematical studies of logic. That man was the English physiologist Charles Scott Sherrington (figure 3.2). As Sherrington wrote in the preface to the second edition of his masterwork, *The Integrative Action of the Nervous System*, it was the combination of Descartes's model and a logical-analytic process that would form the core of a theory of the biological basis of deterministic behaviors:

A "reflex" can be diagrammatized as an animal reacting to a "field" containing it. Animal and field are of one category, . . . they are machines which interact—a point taken by Descartes. His wheelwork animals geared into the turning universe. Cat, dog, horse, etc. in his view had no thoughts, no ideas; they were trigger puppets which events in the circumambient universe touched off into doing what they do. . . . Experiment today [puts] within reach of the observer a puppet animal which conforms largely with Descartes' assumptions[: the decerebrate[1] preparation. Indeed, after a decerebration is complete,] the animal is found to be a Cartesian puppet: it can execute certain acts but is devoid of mind. (Sherrington, 1947)

Sherrington was, unsurprisingly, a member of the English scientific elite. Educated at Cambridge and a professor at Oxford, he was elected a fellow of the Royal Society in 1883 (at the age of thirty-six) and served as its president from 1920 to 1925. It was Sherrington who formulated our modern notion of the reflex as a model for how the periphery and spinal cord connect sensation and action, using a syntax of axioms and

1. In Sherrington's case the decerebrate animals were usually cats. The animals would be deeply anesthetized, and then the connection between the brain and spinal cord would be surgically severed.

Figure 3.2
Charles Scott Sherrington (Hulton Archive, HE8929).

primitive operators that was not very different from the syntax of logical calculus Boole had described:

The concept of the reflex therefore embraces at least three separate structures,—an *effector* organ, e.g., gland cells or muscle cells; a conducting nervous path or *conductor* leading to that organ; and an initiating organ or *receptor* whence the reaction starts. The conductor consists, in the reactions which we have to study, of at least two nerve-cells,—one connected with the receptor, and the other with the effector. For our purposes the receptor is best included as part of the nervous system and so it is convenient to speak of the whole chain of structures—receptor, conductor, and effector—as a *reflex-arc*. All that part of the chain which leads up to but does not include the effector and the nerve-cell attached to this latter, is conventionally distinguished as the *afferent-arc*.

The reflex-arc is the unit mechanism of the nervous system when the system is regarded in its integrative function. *The unit reaction in nervous integration is the reflex*, [Sherrington's italics] because every reflex is an integrative reaction and no nervous action short of a reflex is a complete act of integration. The nervous synthesis of an individual from what without it were a mere aggregation of

commensal organs resolves itself into coordination by reflex action. But though
the unit reaction in the integration is a reflex, not every reflex is a unit reaction,
since some reflexes are compounded of simpler reflexes.

. . .

The reflex-arc consists, therefore, of at least three neurones. It is convenient to
have a term distinguishing the ultimate neurons FC [final common] from the rest
of the arc. For reasons to be given later it may be spoken of as a final common
path. The rest of the arc leading up to the final common path is conveniently
termed the afferent arc. (Sherrington, 1906)

The concept of the reflex that Sherrington and his colleagues evolved
was a model of how the nervous system connected sensory events and
motor responses. Perhaps because it was a system that appeared to be
consistent, complete, and fully determinate, it quickly came to dominate
studies of the nervous system.

Sherrington's System: The Logic of the Nervous System

Sherrington's reflex arc is familiar to every medical student or anyone
who has taken an advanced undergraduate course in brain sciences. The
basic concept is often illustrated by the stretch response (figure 3.3). The
function of the stretch response is to keep a muscle at the same length
despite increases in the load it carries, increases that would have the
effect of stretching the muscle.

Consider yourself standing with your arms by your sides. Now raise
your right forearm by bending your elbow at 90°. Rotate your palm so
that it faces upward. In this configuration the biceps muscle in your upper arm supports the forearm against the pull of gravity. Now, abruptly
drop a weight into your palm. Initially the forearm drops a few centimeters as the biceps muscle is stretched by the weight, but after a very
short delay the biceps produces an increase in contractile force, raising
the forearm back to its initial position.

How is this accomplished? We know that the increase in contractile
force is caused by an increase in the activity of the motor neurons, Sherrington's final common path. We also know that within the body of
the biceps muscle there are stretch receptors which increase their firing rate when the muscle is elongated, Sherrington's receptor. We also
know that neurons with long axons connect the stretch receptor to the
spinal cord, Sherrington's conductor. Together, then, the receptor and

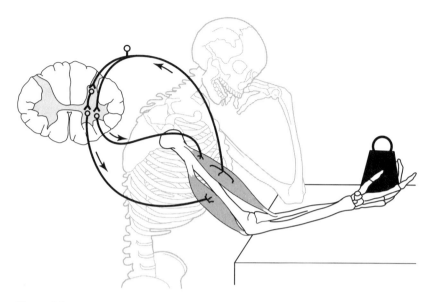

Figure 3.3
The stretch reflex.

the conductor that carries the stretch signal into the spinal cord compose the afferent-arc as Sherrington described it. How, then, do we connect these neurons to produce a stretch reflex? The answer is that if we directly connect the afferent-arc to the final common path, the stretch reflex which we have built performs exactly like the stretch response we observe in our own behavior. Adding weight stretches the muscle, increases the firing rate of the receptor, increases the activity of the conductor. This conductor passes into the spinal cord via the dorsal nerve roots, where it makes contact with the motor neuron. It increases the activity of the motor neuron, leading to an increase in the force produced by the muscle. Of course it is the simplicity of this model that is its beauty. Every element of this reflex circuit is necessary for the production of this behavior. It is the simplest circuit that could produce the stretch response.

A simple reflex circuit thus contains just a few logical components and operations from which any simple excitatory reflex of this type can be built up. We need to posit the existence of a receptor, a conductor (which together form the afferent-arc), a final common path, and the operation of excitatory conduction. With these simple tools we can explain a fairly complex behavior.

Sherrington noticed, however, that there are classes of behaviors which cannot, in principle, be constructed from these three or four primitive logical components. When the biceps contracts during the stretch response, the triceps muscle, which acts to pull the forearm down in this configuration, simultaneously relaxes. That seems a more difficult response to explain, because now activation of the stretch receptor somehow has to inactivate the motor neurons of the triceps.

To resolve this paradox, Sherrington made a brilliant proposal, perhaps based in part on the work of the Russian physiologist I. M. Sechenov (Sechenov, 1863). What if we posit the existence of an additional logical component, neurons in the spinal cord that are inhibitory? Neurons that, when excited, act to inhibit the neurons with which they communicate. If that were the case, then the biceps stretch receptor and the afferent-arc might connect not only to the final common path for the biceps but also to an inhibitory neuron which was in turn connected to the motor neurons of the triceps. With this addition, the model circuit could now simultaneously excite the biceps and inhibit the triceps. Like the excitatory reflex, it would contain the minimum number of components (assuming that receptors or conductors could not be inhibitory) required to produce this response.

The question that this explanation raises, of course, is whether behaviors much more complicated than a stretch reflex can be built up by the coordination of many reflexes, and how many basic tools, like excitatory and inhibitory neurons, does one require to build an adequately complex system of reflexes?

Sherrington was deeply interested in this problem, and he built models of progressively more complex reflex circuits to answer that question. One reflex model that communicates this particularly well is the scratch response of the dog, a response Sherrington studied extensively. Imagine taking a dog that, like Marshall Hall's frog, has had its spinal cord severed at the level of the neck. Support the dog in a sling and with a blunt probe attached to a battery, stimulate a point on the dog's back. The dog's hind leg moves up to scratch at this electric flea.

What Sherrington noticed about this behavior, and what Marshall Hall had missed, is that the dog invariably scratches at the flea about four times per second, at 4 Hz. Now add a second flea adjacent to the first. Again the dog scratches, and again at a rate of 4 Hz, regardless of the fact that the intensity of stimulation has doubled. Now reduce the intensity of the original flea and apply it alone. It may take longer for the hind leg to begin scratching, but again it scratches at 4 Hz. How can this insensitivity of the response frequency to stimulus strength be explained by a reflex model? Sherrington argued that if one assumed that within the reflex arc there was a fatigable element that could activate the muscle for only a brief time before needing to rest for about 0.25 second, then the observed 4 Hz behavior would be exactly what a scratch reflex circuit would produce. Thus, by adding a fatigable (or refractory) element to his tool kit of reflex operators, Sherrington made it possible for the nervous system to generate highly periodic, or cyclic, behaviors from sensory stimuli that had no intrinsic periodic structure.

In the experiments he uses to develop this idea in *The Integrative Action*, Sherrington presents spectacular data to show that the refractory element cannot be in either the afferent limb or the final common path, and thus, by exclusion, he argues that it must lie at the synapse (a word he invented) which connects the afferent-arc to the motor neuron. By this brilliant bit of deduction Sherrington strengthens his preexisting claim that it must be the synapse at which integration (by which he means computation) occurs, and not within neurons. This focus on the synapse was important, because it endowed the reflex model with the ability to perform mathematical computations at a discrete logical point in the reflex circuit.

What about two reflexes that are mutually exclusive? That is to say, what about two reflexes which might both be elicitable at the same time but which should never co-occur? How do reflexes compete for access to the final common path? This is also an issue that Sherrington was deeply concerned with, and he discussed it at length in a number of papers and in *The Integrative Action*:

When two receptors are stimulated simultaneously, each of the receptors tending to evoke reflex action that for its end-effect employs the same final common path but employs it in a different way from the other, one reflex appears without the other. The result is *this* reflex or *that* reflex but not the two together.... The flexor-reflex when it occurs seems therefore to exclude the extensor-reflex and *vice versa*. If there resulted a compromise between the two reflexes, so that each reflex had a share in the resultant, the compound would be an action which was neither the appropriate flexion nor the appropriate extension.

...

Thus there dominates now this group, now that group in turn. It may happen that one stimulus ceases coincidently as another begins, but as a rule one stimulus *overlaps* another in regard to time. Thus each reflex breaks in upon a condition of relative equilibrium, which latter is itself a reflex.... These reflexes may in regard to one another be termed antagonistic; and the reflex or group of reflexes which succeeds in inhibiting its opponents may be termed "prepotent" for the time being. (Sherrington, 1906)

By permitting reflexes to perform the logical operation of inhibiting (or reinforcing) each other, Sherrington's model became capable of an even higher level of computation. The ability of reflexes to interact in this manner opened an even broader behavioral arena.

One final question that Sherrington addressed with his reflex model was to explain how complex sequences of responses could be described as the product of a set of reflex-operators. Consider, for example, walking forward in a straight line. Walking begins when one leg swings up and forward. The foot is then planted and the limb assumes a load-bearing stance. Only during the load-bearing stance can the opposite leg begin its swing up and forward. To build behaviors of this type, Sherrington argued, reflexes would have to be chained together. The core of this idea is that the reflex responsible for swinging the left leg forward has two actions. First, it must strongly inhibit the swing reflex in the right leg. Second, as it finishes, it must strongly reinforce activation of the stance reflex in the left leg, which must in turn be strongly reinforced by the swing reflex of the right leg. Working together, these simple reflexes can be configured to construct a chain of responses that result in forward progression.

Sherrington's accomplishment here cannot be overstated. In the 1630s Descartes suggested that there was some way to build a deterministic nervous system by connecting sensory and motor elements. Physiologists like Marshall Hall strengthened the general conviction that this was in fact possible, but it was Sherrington who offered something like a calculus of the reflex. Sherrington described a series of elemental operations (what Boole might have called physiological postulates) from which, he hypothesized, all deterministic behavior could be generated. While it is important to note that Sherrington did not provide us with a proof that his system must in principle be capable of producing all deterministic behaviors, it seems clear that he was trying to accomplish something very like what Boole and Frege were attempting to do in the mathematical domain.

Sherrington's students and colleagues recognized that this work served as a logical foundation upon which all of neural science could be built. After his death Sherrington was often referred to as the Newton of the twentieth century.

Dualism

It is important to point out, however, that Sherrington retained Descartes's original dualistic approach to behavior as a whole. At the end of *The Integrative Action* he puts it this way:

Pure reflexes are admirably adapted to certain ends. They are reactions which have long proved advantageous in the phylum, of which the existent individual is a representative embodiment. Perfected during the course of ages, they have during that course obtained a stability, a certainty, and an ease of performance beside which the stability and facility of the most ingrained habit acquired during an individual life is presumably small. But theirs is of itself a machine-like fatality. Their character in this stands revealed when the neural arcs which execute them are separated, e.g. by transection of the spinal cord from the higher centers of the nervous system. They can be checked, it is true, as we have seen, by collision with other reflexes as ancestral and as fatally operative as themselves (Lectures V and VI). To these ancient invariable reflexes, consciousness, in the ordinary meaning of the term, is not adjunct. The subject as active agent does not direct them and cannot introspect them.

Yet it is clear, in higher animals especially so, that reflexes are under control. Their intrinsic fatality lies under control by higher centres unless their nervous arcs are sundered from ties existing with those higher centers. In other words, the reactions of reflex-arcs are controllable by mechanisms to whose activity consciousness is adjunct. By these higher centres, this or that reflex can be checked or released, or modified in its reaction with such variety and seeming independence of external stimuli that the existence of spontaneous internal processes expressed as "will" is the naive inference drawn. *Its spring of action is not now our question* [my italics]; its seat in the nervous system seems to correspond with that of processes of a perceptual level. It is urgently necessary for physiology to know how this control—volitional control—is operative on reflexes, that is, how it

intrudes and makes its influence felt upon the running of the reflex machinery....
No exposition of the integrative action of the nervous system is complete, even in
outline, if this control is left without consideration. (Sherrington, 1906)

Sherrington himself believed that there were classes of behavior that
lay outside the province of determinate reflex models. But the Sherringtonian paradigm, in this very nearly complete form, led others to question that belief. Hume and Laplace had suspected that all events in the
physical world, including all human behavior, might be the product of
deterministic processes. As Hume had said, "A human body is a mighty
complicated machine.... That to us it must often appear very uncertain
in its operations: And that therefore the irregular events, which outwardly discover themselves, can be no proof, that the laws of nature are
not observed with the greatest regularity in its internal operations and
government."

What if it could be shown that the postulates of the Sherringtonian
reflex system were in principle adequate for the generation of *any* possible behavior? To put it in Hilbert's terms, what if one could show that
the reflexological system was complete? What strong reason would we
have to believe that a second volitional system would have to coexist
with the reflexological system? This raises a critical question for neurobiology: Is the reflexological system as Sherrington stated it, or in some
modified form, complete? That is, of course, a question that is still very
much in debate, but among the first people to argue that the answer to
this question must be *yes* was the Russian reflex physiologist Ivan Pavlov
(figure 3.4):

The physiologist must thus take his own path, where a trail has already been
blazed for him. Three hundred years ago Descartes evolved the idea of the reflex.
Starting from the assumption that animals behaved simply as machines, he regarded every activity of the organism as a *necessary* reaction to some external
stimulus, the connection of the stimulus and the response being made through
some definite nervous path: and this connection, he stated, was the fundamental
purpose of the nervous structures in the animal body. This was the basis on
which the study of the nervous system was firmly established. In the eighteenth,
nineteenth, and twentieth centuries the conception of the reflex was used to the
full by physiologists. Working at first only on the lower parts of the central nervous system [e.g., the spinal cord], they came gradually to study more highly
developed parts, until quite recently Magnus [a student of Sherrington's],
continuing the classic investigations of Sherrington on the spinal reflexes, has

Figure 3.4
Ivan Petrovitch Pavlov (Hulton Archive, IH014740).

succeeded in demonstrating the reflex nature of all the elementary motor activities of the animal organism. Descartes' conception of the reflex was constantly and fruitfully applied in these studies, but its application has stopped short of the cerebral cortex.

It may be hoped that some of the more complex activities of the body, which are made up by a grouping together of the elementary locomotor activities, and which enter into the states referred to in psychological phraseology as "playfulness," "fear," "anger," and so forth will soon be demonstrated as reflex activities of the sub-cortical parts of the brain. A bold attempt to apply the idea of the reflex to the activities of the [cerebral] hemispheres was made by the Russian physiologist I. M. Sechenov, on the basis of the knowledge available in his day of the physiology of the central nervous system. In a pamphlet entitled "Reflexes of the Brain," published in Russia in 1863, he attempted to represent the activities of the cerebral hemispheres as reflex—that is to say, as *determined* [Pavlov's italics].

Thoughts he regarded as reflexes in which the effector path was inhibited, while great outbursts of passion he regarded as exaggerated reflexes with a wide irradiation of excitation.... All this, however, was mere conjecture.

...

I shall now turn to the description of our [Pavlov's laboratory's] material, first giving as a preliminary an account of the general conception of the reflex, of specific physiological reflexes, and of the so called "instincts." Our starting point has been Descartes' idea of the nervous reflex. This is a genuine scientific conception, since it implies necessity. It may be summed up as follows: An external or internal stimulus falls on some one or other nervous receptor and gives rise to a nervous impulse; this nervous impulse is transmitted along nerve fibres to the central nervous system, and here on account of existing nervous connections, it gives rise to a fresh impulse which passes along outgoing nerve fibres to the active organ, where it excites a special activity of the cellular structures. Thus a stimulus appears to be connected of necessity with a definite response, as cause with effect. It seems obvious that the whole activity of the organism should conform to [such] definite laws.

. . .

Now although *the signalling stimuli* [the stimuli that trigger reflexes developed by the organism over the course of its life] do play a part in these comparatively simple reflexes we have given as examples, yet this is not the most important point [of Pavlov's extension of the concept of the reflex]. The essential feature of the highest activity of the central nervous system, with which we are concerned and which in the higher animals most probably belongs entirely to the [cerebral] hemispheres, consists not in the fact that innumerable signalling stimuli do initiate reflex reactions in the animal, but in the fact that under different conditions these same stimuli may initiate quite different reflex reactions; and conversely the same reaction may be initiated by different stimuli.

In the above-mentioned example of the salivary reflex [of the dog], the signal at one time is one particular vessel [or bowl], at another time another [bowl]; under certain conditions one man, under different conditions another—strictly depending upon which vessel had been used in feeding and which man had brought the vessel and given food to the dog. This evidently makes the machine-like responsive activities of the organism still more precise, and adds to it qualities of yet higher perfection. So infinitely complex, so continuously in flux, are the conditions in the world around, that the complex animal system which is itself in living flux, and that system only, has a chance to establish dynamic equilibrium with the environment. Thus we see that the fundamental and most general function of the hemispheres is that of reacting to signals presented by innumerable stimuli of interchangeable signification. (Pavlov, 1927)

It is Pavlov's claim, made in a less mechanistic way by Hume and in a more formal mathematical way by Laplace, that Descartes was wrong in proposing a dualistic system. Descartes's "truly scientific" and "determined" reflex system *can* be enough to account for all of the many classes of behavior that we observe. Pavlov's claim is thus twofold: All behavior is deterministic, and the calculus of reflexes is an adequate system for describing all possible deterministic behavior.

Unlike the more rigorous mathematicians, however, Pavlov simply states this as an assertion. Although his argument does loosely borrow the structure of a mathematical system, it does not in any formal sense offer a proof that the calculus of reflexes *must* be an adequate system for describing all possible behaviors in the way that the *Principia Mathematica* argues that it is a formal system which can be used to demonstrate the truth of any assertion, including Pavlov's.

Pavlov's conjecture is critical because it allows an effort to resolve the paradox of Cartesian dualism. As I wrote in the first chapter of this book: "Descartes's dualism was thus *the* critical conceptual advance that permitted physiological studies of behavior to begin. Based upon the Cartesian dualist formula, simple deterministic behaviors could become the province of purely physiological study. But... complex and unpredictable behaviors would remain the province of philosophers, inaccessible to physiological study because these behaviors were the product of processes that resided outside the physical world in which physiologists could construct experiments."

Pavlov was arguing that a dualistic approach was unnecessary for two reasons. First, he argued that all behavior was in fact deterministic. Second, he argued that any possible deterministic behavior could be produced with an adequately sophisticated reflex-based system.

The Gödel Theorem: Finding the Limits of Determinate Mathematics

In 1931 a crushing blow was delivered to David Hilbert's program to develop a complete and consistent logical calculus that could encapsulate mathematics in the style pioneered by Russell and Whitehead. In a famous paper published in the journal *Monatshefte für Mathematik und Physik*, the Czech mathematician Kurt Gödel was able to show that forms of the statement "I am now lying" were inescapably possible in any formal arithmetic system. By making this observation, Gödel had actually derived an answer to the first of Hilbert's three propositions: Mathematics was, by construction, incomplete. There were true statements that could not be proven.

But Gödel went further, demonstrating that if all assertions could be imbedded in recursive statements in such a way as to make them inconsistent, Hilbert's second proposition as well his could be disproved. What he noted, in essence, was that his proof that some statements were unprovable could itself be expressed as a formal proof. From this observation it followed, Gödel showed, that the consistency of the logical system itself could not therefore be proved. Gödel had, in 1931, provided a death blow to Hilbert's hope that formal mathematical systems could be proven to be both complete and consistent. It was true that by excluding some classes of statements, a logical system could be made consistent within a limited domain, but no logical mathematical system could be both complete and consistent.

Alan Turing and Computability

Hilbert had proposed that mathematics was complete, consistent, and decidable. Gödel had shown that Hilbert had been wrong: Mathematics could not be complete and consistent. In 1936 a young English mathematician, Alan Turing, attacked the third of Hilbert's propositions, the issue of decidability: Was there a deterministic method or mechanical process that could, with absolute certainty, decide whether or not *any* mathematical statement was provable from a given set of axioms?

Hilbert had believed that there was, that some mechanical process must exist which could determine whether or not some proposed mathematical statement is a logical consequence of a given set of axioms. Turing attacked this problem in a unique way (Turing, 1936). He began by defining a method as a "mechanical process" if it were a mathematical technique that a machine could perform. Hilbert's decidability proposition then reduced to the question, Could a machine be designed that could determine whether a given logical inference is correct?

In order to answer that question, Turing began by trying to design a machine that would answer this question for as many types of mathematical statements as possible. To be specific, what he did was to design, on paper, a general-purpose machine that could compute the value of any real number which could be defined by a definite mathematical rule. Such a *Universal Turing Machine* could, for instance, compute the value of π, specified by the Taylor expansion series, to any arbitrary number of decimal places. Computations of this type Turing referred to as "computable numbers." He went on, however, to show that there were many specific problems that such a machine could not solve. Recursive problems in which one machine received the output of another machine as an input were particularly difficult. Such logical situations often constituted logical problems that could not be resolved by Turing's machine. Just as Russell's original self-referential statement had broken Frege's system, Turing's observation had identified concepts that were in principle non-computable. So Turing had, in this odd way, falsified Hilbert's third proposition: There was no mechanical process that could determine whether any statement made within a mathematical system was, in principle, provable.

Turing had, however, also done something of tremendous practical importance. He had shown that one of his machines, a Universal Turing Machine, could all by itself compute the values of any *computable function*, and he argued convincingly that this class of function encompasses all that *can* be computed by classical means. This insight made modern computer science possible because it specified both the capabilities and the limits of mechanical deterministic computers.

At one level this was a final defeat for the Hilbert program and the approach pioneered by the *Principia Mathematica*. The repercussions of these findings are still being worked out by mathematicians and logicians. It now seems inarguable that systems of mathematical proof are limited, inherently capable of inconsistency, and there is no way to tell mechanically whether any mathematical statement will be provable. But while these conclusions had a huge impact in mathematics, they also had implications for physiology.

Pavlov and others like him had made two important proposals. First, they had suggested that all behavior was deterministic. Second, they had argued that reflex theory (which was effectively a logical calculus) could be a complete descriptor for all possible deterministic behaviors. If both of these proposals were true, then a reflex-based analysis of the nervous system might someday be able to explain all of behavior. After the 1930s and 1940s the second of these proposals had been shown to be false within the domain of mathematics. No logical calculus could ever be complete, and this raised the possibility that there might be behaviors which could not be produced by simple, axiomatically based systems like reflexology.

This observation meant one of two things: Either reflex-based approaches could not be used to describe all classes of behavior that animals can produce or the behaviors that animals can actually produce are limited to those which a determinate axiomatic system like reflexology could describe. While either of these could be true, Gödel and Turing had cast a new and significant doubt on the power and flexibility of Sherrington's reflexological program.

By the 1950s, insights like these had made it clear that in order to understand the relationship between determinate mathematics, logic, and neural computation, three central questions would have to be answered by modern physiologists: (1) How large is the set of deterministic behaviors actually produced by living organisms? (2) What fraction of those deterministic behaviors can be modeled within the traditional framework of reflex-based approaches? (3) Are there behaviors that are either nondeterministic, and thus outside the domain that reflexlike systems can explain, or deterministic but "noncomputable"?

4
Finding the Limits of the Sherringtonian Paradigm

In the last chapter I wanted to make it clear that there are significant uncertainties faced by any programmatic approach which uses determinate mathematical models to explain how behavior, brain, and mind are related. All classical approaches to the problem of behavior, brain, and mind—approaches like Sherrington's—have been rooted in this determinate approach. This is not to say that these approaches are failures, or even that these approaches are necessarily wrong. Indeed, it is beyond question that these approaches have been both useful and successful at an empirical level, but a century after their inception it seems reasonable to begin to question their validity.

Sherrington's reflex-based program was the first of the classical approaches to develop a workable grammar for relating brain and behavior. Its existence motivated generations of scientists because it showed that physiologists could successfully relate the structure of the brain to the production of behavior. It is no accident that Sherrington is so often compared to Newton; both men laid the foundations for radically materialist views of the world. Newton showed that the physical world could be studied and understood using simple determinate laws. Sherrington showed that the biology of behavior could also be approached in this manner. He and his students changed the study of brain from a haphazard effort to derive a few general principles into a programmatic effort to explain all aspects of the relationship between brain and behavior. By the second half of Sherrington's life there was a growing certainty among neurophysiologists that the Sherringtonian paradigm would succeed, and would succeed quickly.

As with many scientific revolutionaries, Sherrington's accomplishment may have been more philosophical than empirical. He accomplished the philosophical goal of convincing all of us that behavior can be dissected using the tools of physiology. That concept is what made modern neuroscience possible. But Sherrington also achieved an empirical goal: he convinced the bulk of the scientific establishment that reflex theory was the right empirical tool for achieving this philosophical end.

That these two aspects of Sherrington's work remain intertwined is unsurprising. Neither goal could have been accomplished alone, but half a century after his death there has been very little effort by scientists and historians to disentangle these two contributions. Ever since the Gödel theorem was published, scientists have had to accept the notion that Sherrington's empirical approach may not be complete. This should, at the very least, lead us to reexamine the Sherringtonian reflex as a scientific tool.

Reflexes: Empirical Fact, Philosophical Paradigm, or Both?

Despite the dominance of reflex theory in the scientific mainstream, ever since the early 1900s a number of scientists have challenged this approach in a number of ways. None of those specific challenges, however, have succeeded in supplanting the reflexological paradigm, which remains our central framework for neuroscience. Nothing could make this clearer than the allocation of textbook space used today to describe physiological processes that are believed to be produced by reflex-arc mechanisms. Take as an example the third edition of the dominant textbook in neuroscience today, *Principles of Neural Science* (Kandel, Schwartz, and Jessel, 1991). *Principles* contains hundreds of references to the word "reflex." The book devotes an entire chapter to describing the stretch reflex, which, it is argued, defends muscle length against changes in load exactly as Sherrington might have proposed. In *Principles* the stretch reflex is not even described as a model of a physiological circuit that achieves a stretch response; instead, the behavior itself is described as a stretch reflex.

The reflex is, first and foremost, a theory of how patterns of input delivered to primary sensory neurons can be channeled and modulated to produce patterns of muscle activation that yield simple, deterministic motor actions. Simple circuits can be described using the rules (or postulates) of reflex theory that should, in principle, be able to produce these simple deterministic motor actions. These hypothetical circuits, among other things, predict the existence of synapses that connect some sensory neurons to some motor neurons in the spinal cord. And it is inarguably true that many of those direct synaptic connections have been observed. But does this prove that the reflex-arc is the only, or even *the correct*, model of these sensorimotor processes? Surely other models may also predict the existence of these synapses.

It may seem that I am going into obsessive detail by making the point that reflexes are a theory and not a fact. After all, nearly everyone believes that there are reflexes. Indeed, many people will no doubt respond to my line of argument by saying that I am simply mistaken in asserting that the reflex is a theoretical construct. While reflexes may have been a theory in Sherrington's time, these people argue that today reflexes are a proven, observable fact. We call the stretch *response* the stretch *reflex* because, they continue, it has been proven beyond a reasonable doubt that the stretch response and the stretch reflex are physiologically equivalent. Many people make this argument, but is this really true? Do we really have enough evidence to conclude that the stretch response is produced by a stretch reflex circuit like the one Sherrington might have described?

In this chapter I will review several arguments suggesting that even a behavior as simple as the stretch response cannot be accounted for by the stretch reflex hypothesis. Over the last hundred years many intelligent and respected physiologists have suggested that the reflex is not an adequate model for explaining *any* determinate behavior. Many of these physiologists have argued that there simply are no such things as reflexes in the real world.

In this chapter I will present these historical arguments in two stages. First, I will describe a series of classical explanations and experiments which suggest that reflexes alone cannot produce all of the different behaviors we see animals produce in the real world. Second, I will review experiments and theoretical studies suggesting that behavior is not organized around reflexes, as Sherrington suggested, but rather that behavior is organized hierarchically around clear systemwide *goals*.

The Reflex Model Is Not Adequate to Account for All Determinate Behavior. Additional Mechanisms Are Required

Since the beginning of the twentieth century a number of prominent physiologists have argued that there are simple, deterministic behaviors which cannot be modeled using the basic postulates of reflex theory outlined by Sherrington and his colleagues. Each of these physiologists has made this argument in a slightly different way, but the arguments share a common theme. Reflexes are, by definition, mechanisms that use sensory signals (or sensory energies, as Sherrington put it) to activate a set of motor neurons. Sherrington and his colleagues were very clear that this was an essential feature of their theory: "From the point of view of its office as the integrator of the animal mechanism, the whole function of the nervous system can be summed up in one word, *conduction*" (Sherrington, 1906). The operative concept in reflexes is that the role of the nervous system is not to originate activity of any kind but instead to conduct sensory stimuli into motor neurons. In reflex theory the role of the nervous system is passive; it initiates nothing on its own.

Sherrington's Cat

If this were true, how could one explain the fact that humans and animals often appear to generate spontaneous behaviors, becoming active in the apparent absence of any sensory stimulation? To make this point clear, imagine what we might think of as Sherrington's cat. One afternoon while Sherrington's pet cat, René, is sound asleep, we kidnap René and take him to a bunker placed deep underground. In the bunker we have prepared a kitty sensory deprivation tank. This is a completely soundproofed and light-tight container filled with a very dense saline solution on which the cat can safely float even if asleep. Before bringing the cat to the bunker we have adjusted the temperature of both the saline solution and the air so that it is identical to René's body temperature. The chamber air has been filtered and is completely odorless. Finally, before the cat goes to sleep, we apply a strong anesthetic to his tongue, so that taste stimuli produce no neural activity. Being careful not to wake Sherrington's cat, we place him in the chamber, close it, and seal the lid.

The point of this endeavor is to eliminate, as completely as possible, all sensory stimuli from René's environment. Sherrington proposed that the whole function of the nervous system is conduction, and we have placed his cat in an environment in which there is nothing to conduct. Under these conditions pure reflex theory makes the following prediction: The cat will sit unmoving, indefinitely, until we provide some kind of sensory stimulus.

To test this hypothesis we perform the following experiment: At a totally unpredictable time, hours after the chamber was sealed, we suddenly open the lid. In the instant before light and sound from the bunker impinge on René's nervous system we ask: Is the cat in motion? Is there any evidence that the cat has, in the hours since we left him, moved from the original position in which he was placed?

We all (Sherrington included) share a common conviction about what we would observe if this experiment were performed. We all expect that as the lid of the chamber is opened, there is at least some chance that we will find René swimming angrily around in the silent chamber. How can that be if reflex theory is *the* correct model for neural function?

Sherrington himself offered a resolution for this paradox (although the cat in the tank might not have been the framework within which he would have presented his speculations). Sherrington argued that under these conditions the cat's body is itself a source of sensory signals to the cat's brain.

Sherrington and other physiologists of his day divided sensory signals into two main categories exteroceptive and interoceptive. Exteroceptive signals were those sensory energies which originated in the external environment. Interoceptive signals were those sensory energies which arose in the internal environment. The grumbling of the cat's stomach as it emptied would be an interoceptive signal. So Sherrington's first answer to the puzzle of the cat in the sensory deprivation tank would be to say that the internal environment is never completely silenced. The internal environment remains a source of sensory input that can trigger reflex responses. Sherrington's cat is swimming around when we open the chamber because he got hungry.

It might seem at first blush that Sherrington could have offered a second explanation: The cat is swimming around because, as an act of volition, it decides to swim around. The cat is swimming around because of the action of a neural system that, by definition, lies outside Sherrington's model. My own guess is that Sherrington would not actually have said that. In *Integrative Action* he argued: "The reactions of reflex-arcs are controllable by mechanisms to whose activity consciousness is adjunct. By these higher centres, this or that reflex can be checked or released, or modified in its reaction with such variety and *seeming independence* [my italics] of external stimuli that the existence of spontaneous internal processes expressed as 'will' is the naive inference drawn" (Sherrington, 1906). I think that the conclusion Sherrington wants us to draw is that the cat *would* be inert if we could eliminate *all* sensory input. But it would have to be absolutely all sensory input.

Even this resolution of the paradox of Sherrington's cat seems disappointing to many (but not all) physiologists and philosophers. To make it clear why this seems disappointing, consider a variant of the Sherrington's cat story. Before the cat goes to sleep on the day of the experiment, we take him to surgery. There, in a long but certainly conceivable operation, we cut all of the cat's interoceptive sensory nerves, effectively silencing the internal environment. When the cat awakes from anesthesia in the surgical suite, we find that he is a bit clumsy but largely normal. He still eats, walks, and meows. Now we wait for the cat to fall asleep and place him in the sensory deprivation tank. What happens?

While we do not actually know the answer to this question, it is a thought experiment that has tortured many physiologists. Many of us believe that even under these conditions, René must be capable of some movement. But if Sherrington's cat could move under these conditions, what would this imply? It would mean that the nervous system of the cat was capable of more than just conduction; it would mean that his nervous system was capable of generating activity internally and autonomously, a prediction that lies outside the classical reflex theory of Sherrington and his students.

T. Graham Brown and Internal Rhythms

Among the first people to wrestle with this issue was Sherrington's student, friend, and colleague T. Graham Brown. Graham Brown was particularly struck by the observation that under some conditions cats which had their exteroceptive sensory nerves severed could still be induced to walk. This observation seemed to Brown to capture, in microcosm, the puzzle presented in the parable of Sherrington's cat. Could reflexes alone, he wondered, really be expected to account for an observed phenomenon like this "spinal step"?

> The difficulty in explaining this phenomena [*sic*] has been emphasized by Sherrington. He points out that in the intact animal (cat, dog), severance of all the sensory nerve trunks directly distributed to all four feet up to and above the wrists and ankles scarcely impairs the act of progression.... He therefore concludes that the intrinsic stimuli for reflex stepping of the limb are not referable to any part of the skin of the limb.
>
> In continuation of his work on proprioceptive reflexes [reflexes driven by interoceptive stimuli], Sherrington finds in the sensory end organs of the muscles themselves the seat of the intrinsic stimuli for reflex stepping [an interoceptive signal]. He considers that the mode of process in reflex walking is as follows: The spinal step [stepping by animals in which the spinal cord has been cut] is a rhythmic reflex which may be excited by continuous stimuli applied either to the cross section of the divided spinal cord [to continuous electrical stimulation at the site of the spinal cord injury produced by the cut] or to various peripheral points outside the limb itself. The generating stimulus is continuous, but the movement of the limb is determined by the alternate action of two antagonistic reflexes. The primary stimulus sets one of these [two reflexes] in action. This act generates in that limb a proprioceptive [interoceptive] reflex antagonistic to itself. The proprioceptive reflex interrupts the primary reflex, and in this interruption abolishes the stimulus which engendered itself. The primary reflex is then reconstituted and again calls forth the interrupting reflex, and so on. (Graham Brown, 1911)

Graham Brown realized that this hypothesis made a clear prediction: If the spinal cord of a cat could be deprived of *all* sensory input, both exteroceptive and interoceptive, then spinal stepping should be impossible. Just as in the parable of Sherrington's cat, Brown set out to test this hypothesis by designing a sensory deprivation experiment. He began with the observation that under some conditions, an anesthetized cat will briefly produce regular, coordinated stepping motions with its hind limbs. Could this phenomena be elicited in a cat spinal cord that lacked sensory input of any kind?

Brown began by anesthetizing a cat and performing the following surgery. I should warn you that what follows is a pretty brutal description of Brown's surgery. The severity of the surgery was something he was very aware of (and disturbed by), and in all of his papers he adds something like the following statement: "To prevent any possibility of mistake it must be clearly stated that in all of these experiments and for the whole of them the animals (cats) were completely unconscious and remained so until they were destroyed at their [the experiments'] termination" (Graham Brown, 1914).

At the start of the surgery, the spinal cord about half way down the back of the animal was exposed and a lasso of thread was passed around the cord at that point. Next, Brown began to systematically cut all of the sensory and motor nerves throughout the cat's body that communicated with the spinal cord at or below the level of the lasso. In some cases this involved cutting the nerves as they entered and left the lower spinal cord; in others it involved cutting nerves in the legs themselves. The only nerves that he left intact were those motor nerves which activated the two principal muscles of walking in only one of the cat's hind limbs. Next he secured the legs of the cat to metal rods so that actual movement of the legs was impossible, minimizing the possibility that motion of the legs would activate some proprioceptive nerves that he had accidentally failed to cut. Finally, he cut the tendons of the two muscles he hoped to monitor and attached the now free ends of the muscles to tiny mechanical levers that would permit him to monitor the contractile states of the two muscles.

When all of this preparation was complete, Brown finally began to adjust the anesthetic in an effort to elicit rhythmic contractions of the two leg muscles in a manner similar to the pattern of activity produced during normal stepping. Once he observed that pattern, he quickly tightened the lasso, cutting through the spinal cord and removing any input that the spinal cord might receive from the brain. The critical question could then be asked: Can the cat spinal cord continue to step, generating a behavioral output, under these conditions, in which no sensory input of any kind enters the nervous system?

For better or worse, Brown got a slightly equivocal answer. He found that if his complicated surgical procedure took more than about 25 minutes to perform, he never observed stepping of any kind, even if the spinal cord was left intact. But if he completed the surgery within 20 minutes (an absolutely heroic task), adjustments to the anesthesia machine often produced stepping. In those cases, Brown immediately severed the spinal cord by tightening his lasso. Under these conditions

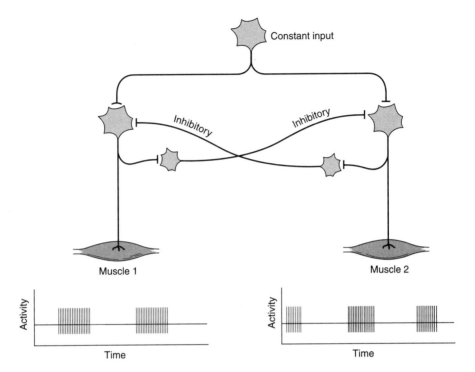

Figure 4.1
Graham Brown's half-center oscillator.

Brown found that the stepping behavior did persist, in the absence of all sensory signals, but only for 20–75 seconds.

To Brown, this seemed a critical observation. For over a minute a spinal cord completely deprived of any sensory input could still produce a coordinated output, and this, he believed, fundamentally challenged Sherrington's notion that the reflex was the only mechanism for the generation of deterministic behavior. (See figure 4.1.)

In other words, the view is here advanced that the functional unit in the nervous system is not the activity of the reflex arc as is usually assumed, but that it is the activity of a unit which we may term the "half-centre"—or, perhaps, the centre composed of linked antagonistic "half-centres." (Graham Brown, 1914)

Over the course of several years Brown continued to develop this idea of the half-center, a self-activating neural structure that could organize and produce behavior in the absence of sensory input. Graham Brown performed a number of elegant experiments to strengthen his argument that reflexes alone could not account for all of the behaviors produced by a cat spinal cord. He even went so far as to develop an elegant model of how oscillatory signals could be produced and maintained in the spinal cord, a now widely accepted theory that describes a self-activating neural oscillator. At the time that these results were published, however, the implications of Brown's work seem not to have captured the imaginations of English physiologists. Sherrington was, by that time, the Dean of Brain Sciences throughout the English-speaking world. He was revered in this way because his reflex theory provided such a powerful theoretical framework within which to view all brain function. Sherrington's ideas were widely regarded as truth, and his central idea was the notion of the reflex.

In fairness, though, Sherrington himself seems to have acknowledged that Brown's experiments did imply that there were some autonomously active processes within the spinal cord. And Sherrington was, in this case as in every other, terribly gracious. Brown's first major publication on this issue appeared in the 1911 volume of the *Proceedings of the Royal Society*. At this time Brown was not a fellow of the Royal Society, and in order to publish in the *Proceedings*, one needed either to be a fellow or to have the paper sponsored for publication by a fellow. It was Sherrington who sponsored Brown's paper.

In 1932 Sherrington and a group of his students published what became essentially the handbook for thinking about reflex theory: *Reflex Activity of the Spinal Cord* (Creed et al., 1932). Toward the end of that book the authors present a cogent synopsis of studies of what they call "rhythmic reflexes," and at one point go so far as to say:

The nervous mechanism answerable for the essential rhythmicity of the scratch reflex and stepping seems a central spinal one, not requiring *rhythmic* impulsion from outside. For spinal stepping Graham Brown has particularly insisted on this.... The phasing of these alternating reflexes can be affected by the proprioceptive and other stimuli which they generate—as well as of course by many other extrinsic stimuli—but their phasing is not *caused* by peripheral stimuli. The self-generated proprioceptive stimuli of the muscles which take part in progression can regulate the act but are not essential to its rhythm.

Despite discussions like these, the broader implications of Graham Brown's work seems not to have been recognized by the English physiological community. Instead, his observations continued to appear as footnotes, or exceptions, presented at the end of textbook discussions of reflex theory.

Erik Von Holtz: Adding to Reflex Theory

Outside the English-speaking neurobiological world, however, a number of German scientists were deeply taken with Graham Brown's work. They began to argue that if autonomously active, deterministic elements were added to classical reflex theory as additional logical operators, then a more complete and accurate description of the neurobiological basis of behavior would become possible. C. Randy Gallistel, in his 1980 book *The Organization of Action*, provides an excellent overview of this evolving trend, and it is his conclusion that the critical first step toward adding self-activating neural elements to the conceptual base of reflexology was made by the German physiologist Erik von Holtz.

Like Brown, Von Holtz believed that rhythmic behaviors were evidence that the nervous system did more than simply conduct, that the nervous system could generate its own activity. As he put it:

If one operates on a tench [a small European freshwater fish], severing all the dorsal [sensory] nerve roots on both sides while leaving the ventral [motor] roots intact (such that no further stimuli can be taken up from the trunk, since the centripetal pathways have been destroyed), the fish is still able to swim around.... Graham Brown performed the same experiment of severing the dorsal roots in mammals with the same result.... The nervous system is not, in fact, like a lazy donkey which must be struck (or, to make the comparison more exact, must bite itself in the tail) every time before it can take a step. Instead it is rather like a temperamental horse which needs the reins just as much as the whip. (Von Holtz, 1937)

Over the course of a long and influential career Von Holtz attempted to develop a theory that would in scope closely parallel Sherrington's reflex theory. He proposed a number of basic integrative postulates that might explain how internally generated rhythms could be interconnected in different ways to yield the richly complex patterns of rhythmic behavior that he had observed.

Von Holtz's proposal was, however, met with considerable skepticism, and the mainstream of physiological investigations continued to rest on a firmly Sherringtonian belief that reflexes alone were the basic mechanism around which the nervous system was organized. Frustrated by this, Von Holtz and his student Horst Mittelstaedt mounted a second attack on reflex theory by proposing the existence of another mechanism that lay outside classical reflex theory: *the reafference principle.*

Ever since the physiology of the central nervous system (CNS) came into existence, one question has remained in focus: What regular relationship exists between the impulses which arrive in the CNS, following evocation by stimuli, and those which are then transmitted (directly or indirectly) to the periphery, that is between *afference* [input signals] and *efference* [output signals]. The CNS is portrayed as the image of an automat [an automatic ticketing machine] which produces, in a "reflex" manner, a given travel voucher in exchange for a specific coin. With simple protective reflexes—such as sneezing and retraction following a pain stimulus—this interpretation is an appropriate one, and it has similarly been used to explain more complex responses, for example equilibration and orienting movements. Rhythmic locomotion can also be understood on this basis, if it is assumed that every individual movement reflexly sets in motion its antagonistic partner and that every extremity provokes movement in its temporal successor (reflex-chain theory). Finally, the higher, experimentally modified behavior patterns are fitted into the picture as "conditioned" reflexes.

The *classical reflex theory* by and large dominates the field although many facts have been recognized which do not concord with it. We know that the respiratory center continues to operate even without rhythmic stimulus impulses [this was a favorite example of Graham Brown's], that the central locomotor rhythms of some invertebrates persist without afference, and that in fish and amphibians an almost negligible residue of afferent nerves suffices for continued movement of *all* parts in a coordinated fashion. In addition, analysis of relative coordination in arthropods, fish, mammals and men has demonstrated the existence of central organizational forces—coupling and superposition phenomena [two elements of Von Holtz's theory of rhythmic behaviors]—whose interaction leads to rules which are formally quite similar to those discovered for the subconscious organization of sensory perception in Gestalt psychology.

These new results resist any description using reflex terminology, and it is therefore comprehensible that, whilst they have a certain influence upon comparative behavioral research and upon human psychology, they have not been assimilated in studies of the actual physiology of the CNS. Even quite recent textbooks are still entirely constructed on the classical reflex concept.[1] The fact that the intact CNS is an actively operative structure in which organized processes are continuously taking place without stimulus impulses, and that even

1. This applies, for example, to the comprehensive work of Fulton [a student of Sherrington's], *Physiology of the Nervous System* (1943), which leads the reader from the simple spinal reflexes up to the operation of the entire nervous system (the conditioned reflex) without attributing any part to spontaneous endogenous activity or to autonomous organizational forces in the CNS. [their footnote]

resting and sleeping represent no more than special forms of central nervous activity, strikes many physiologists as being an unscientific concept. It is believed that the only possible "cause" of any central process must be "the stimulus."[2]

This attitude is, after all, understandable, for nobody will readily give up a simple theory—particularly when it is regarded as a "fact" because of its long history—before a better one is available. The new theory must incorporate both the old *and* the new results and permit predictions both above and beyond the area which one has so far been able to understand. New experiments have led us to an interpretation which we think lives up to this expectation, within demonstrable limits.... The characteristic feature of this new conceptual framework is ... [that] rather than asking about the relationship between a given afference and the evoked efference (i.e., about the reflex), we set out *in the opposite direction* from the efference, asking: What happens in the CNS with the afference (referred to as the "reafference") which is evoked through the effectors and receptors by the efference? (Von Holtz and Mittelstaedt, 1950)

In the remainder of their article Von Holtz and Mittelstaedt present evidence from a series of experiments to suggest that signals which control the motor output of the nervous system are often fed back directly into the nervous system, thus permitting an output headed for the final common path to serve also as an input to some other system. Sherrington and the classical reflex theorists had recognized that feedback from action would have to be a central feature of a coordinated nervous system, but they had argued that the nervous system could monitor the activity of motor neurons only via the afferent arc of the sensory system. As Graham Brown had put it: "Sherrington finds in the sensory end organs of the muscles [the afferent arc of the stretch reflex] ... the seat of the intrinsic stimuli for [the next] reflex." In this conceptualization, feedback from the actions of the muscles enters the nervous system *only* inasmuch as it activates the sensory organs of the body. This is absolutely essential to the Sherringtonian paradigm because Sherrington had argued that "the whole function of the nervous system can be summed up in one word, *conduction*." If activity could pass from the afferent arc into the final common path, and then from the final common path back into the nervous system directly, without passing to the periphery, then

2. This misunderstanding probably has psychological motives as well. It is much more satisfying in view of the naive requirement for causal explanation to be able to relate a visible motor activity of the body to a visible alteration in the environment, than to invoke invisible energy turnover within the CNS. The latter is apparently felt to be semi-psychological. [their footnote]

activity could echo through the nervous system indefinitely. Activity in the central nervous system could become self-sustaining.

To make this distinction clearer, let us return to Sherrington's cat René. Imagine that just before René goes to sleep, he stretches his legs. We then immediately place him in the sensory deprivation tank. As long as he is absolutely stationary and deprived of sensory input, the classical reflex model predicts that he can produce no behavior. But what if, as Von Holtz and Mittelstaedt had proposed, the activity that gave rise to the leg movements of the cat just before he went to sleep could continue to propagate in the nervous system? Under those conditions the cat might spontaneously move at any time, simply because the old activity associated with moving the legs could persist within the nervous system.

In order to develop this idea of reafference, the idea that old efferent (output) signals could become afferent (input) signals in their own right, Von Holtz and Mittelstaedt examined a number of visual behaviors in animals ranging from insects to humans. For the sake of brevity, let me present just one of their examples, a human visual-motor behavior.

Von Holtz and Mittelstaedt noted what seems a trivial phenomenon. When a human rapidly shifts his line of sight to the right, he rotates his eyeball to the right while the world that sheds light on the retina remains stationary. When this happens, from the point of view of someone inside the eyeball who is unaware of its rotation, the world appears to slide across the retina to the left. But when we do shift our eyes to the right, even though our retinas have the "point of view of someone inside the eyeball," we have a strong sense that the world is stationary. It never seems during eye movements that it is the world, rather than our eye, which is in motion.

Now consider another example. Imagine that you are sitting in a movie theater and the image on the screen is shifted abruptly to the left. From the point of view of someone inside the eyeball, this is identical to the situation in which the eye moves to the right. In both situations the image falling on the retina shifts to the left but the experience that we have in these two conditions is completely different. In one we feel as if we are looking around in a stationary world, and in the other we feel as if we are observing a view of the world that is shifting to the left.

These two situations differ in only one fundamental way. In the first example we actually produce a motor command to move our eyes. An efferent signal goes to the final common path. In the second, we do not. So in some way, Von Holtz reasoned, it must be the motor command itself which is responsible for the difference we experience under these two conditions.

Reflex theory offers a clear explanation of how this difference might arise. Stretch receptors in the muscles of the eyes, muscular sense organs, would act through reflex circuits to produce this experiential difference. When the eyes move, these sensory organs become active, and this activity produces, via a reflex, the sense that the world is stationary. If the world slides to the left and the sense organs are silent, then a reflexive sense that the world is in motion is produced. If, however, this explanation is the correct explanation, then reflex theory makes an additional prediction. What would happen if we were to paralyze the muscles of the eye? Paralysis of the eye muscles would effectively disconnect the linkage between the motor command (which would have no effect on the eyeball after paralysis) and the sensory organ embedded in the muscles of the eye. If under these conditions we tried to move our eyes, nothing would happen. The eye and its muscles would not move, the visual world would not move across the retina, and we would have no sensation or experience of any kind.

The theory of reafference, however, makes a different prediction under these conditions. The reafference hypothesis proposes that the command to move the eyes is fed back into the nervous system, and it is this internal feedback that allows us to judge whether it was our eye or the world that was moving. Paralyzing the eye muscles would immobilize the eyes but would not eliminate this internal feedback signal. Imagine that under these conditions we tried to move our eyes 20° to the right. Our internal feedback (the reafference) would report that the eyes have in fact moved 20° to the right. The visual world, however, would be in exactly the same position on the retina as it had been before the movement was attempted. Under normal conditions this could be true only if the visual world had, at the exact same time as our rightward eye movement, also shifted to the right. Reafference thus predicts that if we try to move our eyes to the right while the eye muscles are paralyzed, then we should have the strong sensation that the world has moved abruptly to the right. Under these conditions the subjective experience of shifting one's line of sight should be very like the experience we have when the image is shifted on the movie screen, *even though the image has not in fact moved.*

Surprisingly enough, this experiment has been performed a number of times since the 1930s (the original experiment can be found in Kornmuller, 1932) and always in the same way and with the same result. (See figure 4.2.) The subject (a volunteer, to be sure!) is placed in a comfortable chair facing a large projection screen or other complex visual environment. Next, a tourniquet is applied to one of the subject's arms to limit blood flow to one hand. Then the subject receives an intravenous dose of curare, a drug that completely paralyzes all muscles while leaving the subject awake and alert. One side effect of paralyzing all muscles is that you cannot breathe under these conditions (or open your eyes), so

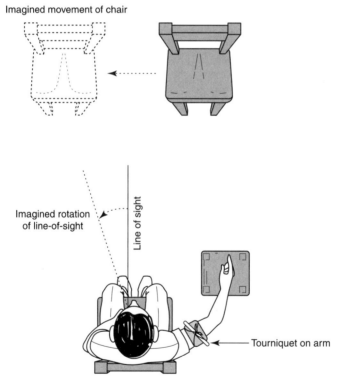

Figure 4.2
Kornmuller's experiment.

the next step is to begin artificial respiration. (Yes, this really is a true story.) Once all of this has been accomplished, we ask the subject, "Are you ok?" He answers by tapping on the chair with the hand of the arm that has the tourniquet, the tourniquet having prevented curare from reaching the muscles of that hand. One tap for yes and two taps for no. At this point we are (finally) ready for the experiment. We pull up the lids of the subject's eyes while he stares straight ahead and once again ask if he feels ok. "Tap." Now we say to the subject, "Look abruptly to the left 20°." We watch his eyes and see that they do not move at all. Now we can ask the question this experiment was designed to answer: Did the world just move abruptly to the left? "Tap."

When our subject recovers from the curare we can, of course, ask him to tell us what it was like. All of the people who have ever undergone this procedure respond the same way: "Whenever I moved my eyes, I had the most profound sense that the world was jumping around, as if it was actively chasing me." Under these conditions we know that the sense organs in the eye muscles must report that no movement has occurred, but the brain clearly believes that a movement *has* occurred. The only way that the brain could have come to this conclusion would be if the motor command itself was used as an afferent signal by the circuit that controls our sense of whether or not the world had moved.

It is important for me to reiterate that this is only one of the many examples that Von Holtz and Mittelstaedt developed. I picked it because is so heroic (or insane), but all of the experiments they describe point in the same direction. Under at least some conditions, output signals produced by the nervous system can become input signals through a kind of internal feedback. This is a possibility that lies outside the basic postulates of reflex theory.

It is hoped that this article will contribute to the gradual disappearance of attempts to describe the functions of the highest developed organ of the body with a few primitive expressions. The sooner we recognize the fact that the *complex higher functional Gestalts* [perceptual experiences] which leave the reflex physiologist dumbfounded in fact send roots *down to the simplest basal functions of the CNS*, the sooner we shall see that the previously terminologically insurmountable barrier between the lower levels of neurophysiology and higher behavioral theory simply dissolves away. (Von Holtz and Mittelstaedt, 1950)

Scientists like T. Graham Brown, Erik von Holtz, and Horst Mittel-staedt were presenting a compelling criticism of classical reflex theory during the first half of the twentieth century. Sherrington had argued that reflexes were *the* organizing unit of the nervous system. He argued that all of the behavior which animals produce can be accounted for by this very simple mechanism. In much the way that the mathematician George Boole had argued that many proofs could be built from a few simple postulates, Sherrington and his students had argued that many deterministic behaviors could be built from a few classes of reflex phenomena. But Sherrington and his students had actually gone farther than this; they had suggested that *all* deterministic behaviors which animals exhibit could be produced with a single set of deterministic reflex-based operators. In a sense they had tried to make an argument more similar to Frege's than to Boole's. Recall that Frege had tried to demonstrate that his logical system could be used to prove anything that was true in much the same way that the classical reflex theorists had argued that a small set of simple operators could be used to model any deterministic behavior. That was, in a sense, Sherrington's deepest and most philosophical claim, and Von Holtz had no explicit problem with this idea. Where Von Holtz parted company with Sherrington was over what operators were necessary for this program. Von Holtz and Mittelstaedt were arguing that one would require reflexes, oscillators, and reafference to accomplish Sherrington's deeper goal, not simply reflexes, as Sherrington had proposed.

In the 1950s Von Holtz made little headway with this argument. Sherrington's students, and the reflex theory they championed, dominated physiological circles. At that time, as Von Holtz repeatedly pointed out, nearly all textbooks on the physiology of the nervous system were essentially manuals for applying reflex theory to the many classes of simple behaviors that Sherrington and his students had studied. In the English-speaking community there was a nearly absolute hegemony of the reflex.

In the 1960s, however, as physiologists began to directly measure the activity of small groups of nerve cells that had been removed from the brain (and the afferent-arcs it included), it became clear that there were in fact groups of neurons which were self-activating. In time, and through a tremendous amount of hard work, half-center oscillators almost exactly like those proposed by Graham Brown were demonstrated in vertebrate and invertebrate nervous systems. Physiological studies of the eye movement systems of behaving animals were also completed, and it became clear that reafferent signals, often called corollary discharges, could be demonstrated. It also became clear that the circuitry for generating deterministic behavior must include more than reflexes; it must also include the oscillators and reafference that Von Holtz and others had proposed.

Neurobiology textbooks today make this sea change abundantly clear. A typical textbook might devote a chapter or two to explaining *how reflexes work* and another to *extrareflexive mechanisms* like reafference and half-center oscillators. Two things, however, have not been changed by this trend: reflexes are still presented as the central tool for understanding the generation of deterministic behaviors, and it is still widely believed that a small set of simple, deterministic operators can be used to model any of the many deterministic behaviors that animals can produce.

Reflexes Are Not, as Sherrington Argued, the Organizational Element for Behavior. Behavior May Be Structured Hierarchically

Working from yet another starting point, a second group of anti-reflexive neurobiologists have argued that while the reflex seems a good model for many simple behaviors, if you examine those behaviors in detail you find that they are organized around well-defined goals rather than being a loose conglomeration of local and independent reflexes. To many physiologists this has suggested that reflexes must be embedded in a goal-directed hierarchy, not simply chained together at a local level, as Sherrington and his students had proposed. Some of these neurobiologists have even gone so far as to suggest that reflexes simply may not exist.

Paul Weiss

Among the first people to make this point explicitly was the Viennese physiologist Paul Weiss. In the 1920s, 1930s, and 1940s Weiss was an important and influential physiologist famous both for his studies of coordinated movement in amphibians and for his studies of the development of the vertebrate nervous system during gestation and infancy. He presented yet another alternative to the reflex model of behavioral coordination that was also not widely influential. Weiss was, in fact, widely disliked by his colleagues, who found him dogmatic about both his own theories and the importance of his work. Despite these personal limitations, Weiss was one of the first physiologists to identify a key structural limitation of the reflex idea: the inability of reflexes to flexibly organize behavior on a organismwide scale.

Reflexes, by definition, tie specific sensory organs to specific muscles. That is the central idea of a reflex, and it is a logical thing to do if activation of a particular sensory organ predicts (from the animal's point of view) that activation of a particular muscle will produce a beneficial movement. The critical notion here is that a specific sensory stimulus is used by the nervous system to elicit a specific and appropriate movement. That has been the core claim of the reflex approach since the time of Descartes. It is important to remember, however, that reflexes *do not* connect sensory stimuli with movements per se; they connect sensory receptors with muscles. It was Weiss who pointed out that there are conditions under which activation of a single muscle can produce widely different movements, depending on the biomechanical state of the body. If the goal of a reflex is to produce a particular movement, but the design of a reflex can activate only a particular muscle, then how can reflexes compensate for the fact that in real biomechanically complex organisms, activation of the same muscle will not always produce the same movement?

To make this clear, consider an example Weiss developed in some detail in a paper published in 1941.[3] Examine the simplest reflex of all, the stretch response. When a muscle that spans the elbow joint and supports the forearm (the biceps) is stretched by an external force that pulls the forearm down, that muscle contracts almost immediately after it

3. A large portion of this paper is reprinted in C. Randy Gallistel's 1980 book *The Organization of Action*, complete with an exhaustive and insightful commentary by Gallistel. I will present Weiss's argument in much less detail than Gallistel has, and I urge the interested reader to examine *The Organization of Action*.

is stretched. At the same time, the muscle that works antagonistically against the biceps and normally acts to pull the forearm down (the triceps) relaxes. This pattern of responding has the effect of defending the angle at which the elbow joint is being held against the external force that attempted to pull the forearm down. This response, mentioned in chapter 3, is one of the simplest reflex-like behaviors that can be described.

Reflex theory predicts that this stretch response is produced by two pathways. First, the physical stimulus of stretching of the biceps activates sensory receptors, the stretch receptors of the biceps muscle. These impulses then directly activate the motor neurons of the biceps and pass indirectly, as inhibitory impulses, into the motor neurons of the triceps. The two subcomponents of a reflex model for this behavioral response are thus the biceps-stretch-receptor to biceps-motor-neuron excitatory pathway and the biceps-stretch-receptor to triceps-motor-neuron inhibitory pathway.

Just as Sherrington would have explained it, the model of this reflex connects specific sensory stretch receptors to specific muscles. But what is the proposed function of this stretch response? What is the evolutionary advantage that we suspect this circuit provides to the animal? Presumably, the function of the stretch reflex is to defend the angle of the elbow joint against an external force that attempts to pull the forearm downward.

Consider, as Weiss did, generalizing the stretch reflex model to the behavioral goal of defending joint angle in a two-dimensional ball-and-socket joint like the human shoulder, as shown in figure 4.3A. In this simplified shoulder joint, four muscles control the position of the limb: an upper muscle, a lower muscle, a left muscle, and a right muscle (only three of which can be seen in the figure). With the limb sticking straight out of the ball-and-socket joint, imagine depressing the limb. Depressing the limb under these conditions would have the effect of stretching the upper muscle, which we will refer to as muscle 1. The two-dimensional angle of the joint would be successfully defended by a model in which stretch receptors in muscle 1 excite motor neurons that activate muscle 1 and inhibit motor neurons that activate the lower muscle, muscle 2. Muscles 1 and 2 thus form an antagonistic reflex pair whose biomechanical

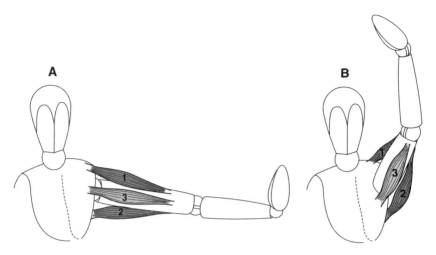

Figure 4.3
Weiss's shoulder joint.

antagonism is reflected, in the stretch reflex model, by the excitatory and inhibitory connections of the stretch receptors.

Next, consider the stretch reflex model for generating the stretch response when the limb begins at a different starting position: not sticking straight out but instead deviated all the way up and to the left, as shown in panel B of figure 4.3. Under these conditions, in order to activate the stretch receptors of muscle 1, we really should push the limb forward and a bit down, not simply down, as before. This is because repositioning the limb up and to the left has temporarily changed the angle at which muscle 1 pulls on the arm. This implies that the linkage between a stimulus (activation of the stretch receptors) and an event in the outside world is less fixed than we might have expected. Depending upon where the limb is positioned, activity in the stretch receptors of muscle 1 could mean many different things. When the limb is sticking straight out, activation of these stretch receptors might indicate that the limb is being pushed down. When the limb is in an eccentric position, it might mean that the limb is being pushed mostly forward and slightly down. What stretch receptor activation means turns out to be a very dynamic function of the current position of the arm.

On close inspection, the same property can be shown to characterize the effects of muscle contraction. When the arm is sticking straight out, activation of muscle 1 pulls the arm straight up. When the arm is deviated all the way to the right, activation of muscle 1 pulls the limb principally backward and only slightly up. What becomes clear from this example is that the linkage between events in the outside world and receptors, and the linkage between patterns of muscle contraction and directions of movement, is not as fixed as one might at first suspect. This seemed to Weiss to place a limit on the utility of reflex theory.

To make this clearer, we return to the stretch reflex. Consider stretching the upper muscle of the shoulder when the arm is deviated all the way up and forward as shown in figure 4.3. It seems obvious that under these conditions the best way to defend the overall angle of the shoulder joint (which is, after all, the function of the stretch reflex) would be for a stretching of the upper muscle to result in an excitation of the upper muscle and an inhibition of muscle 3, not an inhibition of muscle 2. This pattern of activation would defend the two-dimensional position of the limb because under these biomechanical conditions, it is muscle 3 that performs as the principal biomechanical antagonist to muscle 1. The reflex models used to achieve the stretch response when the limb was sticking straight out cannot achieve this coupling. When the limb was sticking straight out, the muscles 1 and 3 operated independently of one another, not as antagonists, and as a result the reflexes active under those conditions were assumed to reflect that independence. But when the limb is deviated up and forward, the biomechanical interactions of the muscles are different and an entirely new set of reflexes is required, reflexes that reflect the biomechanical antagonisms between the muscles under these new conditions. Under these conditions the stretch response would require a reflex that makes an inhibitory connection between the stretch receptors of the muscle 1 and the motor neurons of the muscle 3.[4]

4. The example that I just presented is a highly simplified form of Weiss's argument. To make this argument in an absolutely rigorous fashion, the limb needs to be pulled not along a straight line down and to the right, but along a slight arc that would keep the left muscle at a constant length at all times. Even this crude example, however, conveys the notion that simple fixed reflexes cannot capture the biomechanical complexity that a two-dimensional joint requires in the stretch response.

Weiss pointed out that a four-muscle, two-dimensional joint would require a very large number of reflex mechanisms specialized for each of the many positions of the limb in order to implement a multiposition stretch response. To make matters even more worse, the human shoulder is much more complex than the joint discussed here. The existence of even greater biomechanical complexity hints at just how hard it would actually be to build a complete reflex model for a behavior as simple as the stretch response in a real joint.

What struck Weiss about the reflex idea in this context was how poorly it seemed to be designed to accomplish real-world goals, like keeping the limb in a fixed position. Descartes had been attracted to the idea of the reflex because a minimum of two components, a sensory element and a motor element, were required to produce any action. The two components were the minimum nervous system necessary to produce any given behavior. It was this necessity that made the reflex so attractive to later theorists. As Pavlov said, "Starting from the assumption that animals behaved simply as machines, he [Descartes] regarded every activity of the organism as a necessary reaction to some external stimulus, the connection of the stimulus and the response being made through some definite nervous path: and this connection, he stated, was the fundamental purpose of the nervous structures in the animal body." What Weiss was arguing was that Pavlov and Descartes were wrong. The connection of a stimulus with a muscular response was not the fundamental purpose of the nervous structures; rather, the connection of an event in the outside world and a movement goal was the fundamental purpose of the nervous system. The nervous system had evolved, Weiss argued, so that animals could produce the right movement in response to an external event. Because reflexes by design link receptors to muscles, rather than linking events to movements, they can never capture the goal-directedness that Weiss thought would have to be a central feature of the vertebrate nervous system.

External stimuli must, Weiss argued, be connected to goals, and it was the job of the nervous system to achieve that connection. He felt that connecting receptors directly to muscles would be too disorganized and too complex, given the biomechanical subtlety of real animals.

How could the nervous system be organized if not around reflexes, as Sherrington had proposed? In answer to this question Weiss made a startling proposal. All movements, he suggested, must be the product of a hierarchically organized global system that controls behavior. Little or nothing, he proposed, is organized by the nervous system at the local level of coordination that reflexes were postulated to employ.

Consider an animal with a hierarchically organized nervous system. At the highest level, the nervous system selects global goals, like *go toward that food*. These commands, Weiss proposed, are passed to a lower level in a hypothetical neural hierarchy, say to neural structures that control all four limbs of the animal. This intermediate neural structure passes to each leg, at an appropriate time, a command either to support the weight of the animal or to swing the leg forward. Within an even lower level of hierarchical control that regulates a single leg, commands again filter through a hierarchy, ultimately leading to the activation of specific muscles at specific times.

Unlike the Sherringtonian model of a walking animal, or even the Graham Brown model with coupled half-centered oscillators, Weiss's nervous system structures behavior around goals at a global level. Recall that in Sherrington's model "The sensory end organs of the muscles themselves are the seat of the intrinsic stimuli for reflex stepping ... the movement of the limb is determined by the alternate action of two antagonistic reflexes. The primary stimulus sets one of these in action. This act generates in that limb a proprioceptive reflex antagonistic to itself. The proprioceptive reflex interrupts the primary reflex, and in this interruption abolishes the stimulus which engendered itself. The primary reflex is then reconstituted and again calls forth the interrupting reflex, and so on." The absolutely critical idea here is that in Sherrington's view walking, like all behavior described in reflexological terms, is brought about by the interaction of very local reflexes. Weiss argued instead that walking must reflect the activity of higher centers that execute specific plans.

Thinking about this, Weiss realized that his globally organized hierarchical proposal and the standard local reflexological models made very different predictions under a set of circumstances that he could construct. Imagine a young salamander. When you place food in front of him where he can see it, he walks forward toward the food. If you place a photograph of a predator in front of him, he walks (quickly) backward. Now perform the following experiment. Anesthetize the salamander and

Figure 4.4
Weiss's salamander.

then surgically remove the right and left front legs and reattach them on the opposite sides. Now wait a few weeks or months. Unlike a mammal, the salamander's legs will heal, the nerves will regrow, and soon the salamander will be able to move both legs fairly normally with the left front leg attached to the right front shoulder and vice versa. (See figure 4.4.)

What is interesting about this operation is that it has the effect of reversing the biomechanics of the limbs. The pattern of muscle contraction that moved the right limb forward (with regard to the shoulder) before the surgery now acts to pull the animal backward, as shown in figure 4.4. If we examine all the different patterns of limb motion that the animal can produce after the surgery, we see that the limbs are still capable of both forward and backward movement. Of course, the movements of the front legs that used to propel the animal forward now propel him backward, and vice versa.

Based upon this postsurgical observation, Weiss built the following logical framework. The fact that the forelimbs can move either forward or backward postoperatively means that the "reflexes" for walking forward and backward must be intact postoperatively in the spinal structures that control all four limbs. Of course, for the animal to actually progress forward after the operation, it would have to use the forward-walking reflexes in its hind limbs and the backward-walking reflexes in its forelimbs. If, as the reflexologists proposed, all behavior was organized locally at the level of individual reflexes, then it should be easy for the salamander to progress forward, or at the very worst to learn how to progress forward after the surgery. If we were to put food in front of the salamander after the surgery, we would either expect him to walk toward the food immediately, or at least to be able to learn to walk toward the food.

Weiss argued that if behavior were, in contrast, controlled hierarchically, then the salamander would never be able to learn to walk again. He would always run in place, whether you showed him food toward which he tried to advance or a predator from which he hoped to escape. Like the Push-me-Pull-you of Dr. Dolittle fame, the salamander's forelimbs and hindlimbs would struggle against each other, moving the salamander nowhere.

To test this hypothesis, Weiss performed the surgery I described. Then each day, he spent time with these animals, trying to teach them to progress forward toward food, duplicating the procedures Pavlov had developed for conditioning reflexes in dogs. Weiss found that even after a year of training, the salamanders had made no progress whatsoever in learning to walk either forward or backward. From this result Weiss concluded that reflexes could not be purely responsible for generating this behavior. Instead, he concluded, walking must represent the action of a globally hierarchical nervous system.

Many people have observed that there are, in fact, other possible explanations for Weiss's result. His experiment certainly does not *prove* that the salamander nervous system must be organized hierarchically. Maybe salamanders simply cannot modify their local reflexes based upon experience. Maybe Weiss was a bad salamander trainer. But even if Weiss's experiment is not conclusive, it does raise an important point. It is possible that some aspects of behavior are organized hierarchically around goals rather than locally around afferent-arc-to-muscle reflexes. I think that in practice most neurobiologists working today would agree with Weiss that some kind of neural hierarchy must exist. There must be some hierarchical structure in the vertebrate nervous system, and at least to some extent this hierarchical structure must be organized around the behavioral goals of the organism, not around the contractions of muscles. However, despite this widespread acknowledgment of the need for hierarchical organization, reflexes are still presented as *the* central tool for understanding the generation of deterministic behaviors. It is still believed that a small set of simple deterministic operators which serve to link sensory and motor events can be used to model any of the many deterministic behaviors that animals can produce.

At this point, any professional neurobiologist reading this argument will no doubt be thinking: All of these experiments do point up limitations to reflex theory, but they are limitations that every neurobiologist accepts. No professional neurobiologist working today *really* uses models that are constrained by reflex theory. Our models incorporate many extrareflexive mechanisms like oscillators, reafference, and hierarchical organization.

In the next chapter, I will argue that while we all do pay lip service to this idea, in practice very few of us use these extrareflexive ideas in thinking about how the nervous system produces determinate behaviors. In fact, I want to suggest that even our most sophisticated models are a good deal more firmly rooted in reflexological approaches than most of us are willing to admit. But before we move on to that argument, we turn to one more challenge to the reflexological paradigm.

Nickolai Bernstein

In the 1920s and 1930s Weiss was not alone in drawing the conclusion that the nervous system must be organized hierarchically, and in a very nonreflex manner. The other prominent scientist to draw this conclusion during the 1920s and 1930s was a Russian cyberneticist, Nickolai Bernstein. During this period Bernstein wrote a number of important papers that, like Weiss's papers, had no real impact in the English-speaking world. In fact, Berstein's papers had little enough impact in Russia during this period. He was, after all, preaching an anti-reflex sermon in the very heart of the Pavlovian world. But more recently, both Russian-speaking and English-speaking physiologists have begun to rediscover Bernstein.

Like Weiss, Bernstein believed that the nervous system must be organized around movement *goals*, not around muscle contractions. He believed that the brain had to be hierarchically organized if it was to use muscles to achieve real behavioral goals. Perhaps the clearest statement of this case was made in a paper published in the *Archives of Biological Science* in 1935. In that essay, Bernstein was concerned with reflexes as models not of spinal cord function but of brain function. At the time this paper was written, it had been known for almost a century that there was a strip of tissue in the human brain, the motor cortex, which was connected fairly directly to the motor neurons of the spinal cord: Sherrington's final common path. A number of scientists had proposed that the neurons in this tissue served as a second control on motor output, an upper final common path, from which reflexes could be constructed within the brain itself. It was Bernstein's goal in this paper to point out that a reflex theory of the motor cortex was untenable on basic logical grounds:

Let us suppose that the cells of the gyrus centralis [the motor cortex] are in reality the effector centre for the muscles [within the brain]. Let us further suppose that the activity of these cells must be (as is inevitable in the given [reflex] hypothesis) sharply different from instant to instant on the multiple repetition of a given movement, [because of] changes in the external force field and proprioceptive signals. If we suppose for clarity that we may represent each excited effector cell in the cortex as lighting up like an electric bulb at the moment when its impulse is transmitted to the periphery, then under such an arrangement the effecting of every muscle will be visible to us on the surface of cortex as a zig-zag discharge. The absence of a one-to-one correspondence [between muscle activations and the direction of movement] and all the considerations which have been described as consequences of equation 3c [which explains that muscle excitation depends on both muscle position and muscle velocity] will be obvious in this case because on every repetition of a given movement the zig-zag discharge will be visibly different. Now suppose that this repetitive movement is an automatized act, the realization of a habit of movement, in other words a conditioned motor reflex. From the discussion above it follows as an inescapable deduction that the conditioned reflex of movement operates each time through a new zig-zag—through new cells; in other words, we arrive at the conclusion that the hypothesis of cellular localization of muscles [the idea that activation of a given motor neuron, or in this case cortical neuron, leads to the activation of a given muscle] necessarily leads to a denial of cellular localization of conditioned reflexes. One of these two chess pieces must here be taken, and it is here a very pertinent question which of the two the old-fashioned localizationalist would rather sacrifice. (Bernstein, 1935)

Like Weiss, Bernstein was arguing that in the real world, goals and patterns of muscle contractions were only loosely related. If the whole point of the nervous system was to achieve behavioral goals, it simply could not be organized around local reflexes. The belief that reflexes alone could achieve organized behavior was, he suggested, an artifact of the kinds of experiments physiologists had conducted for the preceding hundred years:

The classical physiology of the last hundred years is characterized by two sharply defined features. The first of these is the study of the operation of the organism under quiescent inactive conditions. Such conditions were artificially secured whenever possible by decortication, by anesthetization of the animal, or by fixing it in a stand under conditions of maximal isolation from the external world. This analytical approach to the study of the quiescent conditions derived from the attempt to study every organ and every elementary process in isolation, attempting to exclude side effects or mutual interactions. In general terms this approach corresponded to the predominance of mechanistic atomism in the natural science of that era. The absolutism of that point of view led to the conviction that the whole is the sum of its parts and no more than this, and that the organism is a collection of cells, that all behavior is a chain of reflexes, and that a sufficient acquaintance with the individual bricks would be enough for the comprehension of the edifice constructed from them. (Bernstein, 1961)

Bernstein further reasoned that in order to understand the nervous system, it would be absolutely necessary to understand the problems that the nervous system had evolved to solve. If one could fully describe the problem-of-coordination that the brain had been designed by evolution to solve, then one could begin to see how the nervous system would have to be structured. To accomplish this goal, Bernstein attempted to develop an entirely new approach to the study of coordinated behavior. First, he said, one must define the problem of coordination faced by the animal. The problem of coordination must be stated as a mathematical formula that it was the job of the nervous system to solve, or compute. Like Weiss, Bernstein was recognizing that muscle contractions and movement goals were very different, but unlike Weiss, Bernstein was trying to develop a set of mathematical tools to relate these two properties. Mathematical tools that would describe, in numerical form, the relationship between the muscle contractions and movements. By 1935 he had made this quite explicit, developing the rudiments of a calculus of movement. The quotation below gives a sense of how Bernstein approached this problem. I have not included enough of the passage for you to follow his mathematical derivation, but I include the equations so you can get a sense of how he hoped to solve the problem of coordination.

The degree of tension of a muscle is a function, in the first place, of its innervational (tetanic and tonic) condition E, and in the second place, of its length at a given instant and of the velocity with which this length changes over time. In an intact organism the length of a muscle is in its turn a function of the angle of articulation α; for this reason we may write that the momentum of a muscle with respect to a joint is:

$F = F(E, \alpha, d\alpha/dt)$

On the other hand, we may assert that the angular acceleration of a limb controlled by a given muscle is directly proportional to the momentum of the muscle F and inversely proportional to the moment of inertia of the limb I. In this way

$d^2\alpha/dt^2 = F/I.$

If there are other sources of force than the muscle operating on the limb, the situation is a little more complicated. Let us limit ourselves for simplicity to only one external force, namely gravity. In the simplest case which we have just described, where we are considering the movement of a single limb segment in relation to a second fixed one, the momentum due to gravity G is, like the momentum of the muscle, a function of the angle of articulation

$G = G(\alpha)$

The angular acceleration of the limb segment under the influence of both momenta together is expressed by the equation

$d^2\alpha/dt^2 = F + G/I$

If we introduce into this equation expressions (1) and (1a) for F and G, we obtain a relation of the following form:

$I(d^2\alpha/dt^2) = F(E, \alpha, d\alpha/dt) + G(\alpha)$

This is the fundamental equation for the movement of a single limb in a gravitational field under the influence of a single muscle where the level of innervation is E. (Bernstein, 1935)

Bernstein went on to develop this notion that the pattern of muscle activations necessary to produce a particular movement could be computed by a fully determined mathematical equation. If a given sensory stimulus made the nervous system want to achieve a particular movement, then the job of the nervous system was to compute the pattern of muscle activations that would be necessary, given the current state of the body and of the world around it, to achieve that movement.

For Bernstein, the problem of coordination broke down into two clearly separate subproblems. First, when one received a sensory input, one had to know what movement that sensory input suggested one should produce. He referred to this as the kinematic problem: Given a sensory stimulus, what is the pattern of limb or joint movement through space that I hope to achieve? This was the problem that the reflexologists had all focused on in their work. But Bernstein's mathematical approach recognized the existence of a second, largely ignored problem. Given a kinematic (or movement) goal, what is the pattern of muscle contractions that will, with the limb in its current state, yield that kinematic goal? This computation of requisite muscle contractions he referred to as the dynamic problem.

In Bernstein's view, the nervous system must solve the problem of co-ordination hierarchically. First, the kinematic problem must be solved. The nervous system must link a sensory stimulus with a desired movement. Second, the nervous system must solve the kinematic-to-dynamic problem; it must compute the muscle force patterns required under current limb conditions in order to produce the desired movement. Like Weiss, Bernstein had derived evidence that a larger hierarchical principle must play a central role in the organization of action. His focus on the difference between the kinematics and dynamics of movements made it clear that reflexes, which by definition ignore this distinction at an organizational level, could not be an adequate model for how determinate behaviors were organized. Reflexologists were, as Bernstein saw it, trying to solve a fundamentally kinematic problem (what movement should I make?) by using a tool that operated exclusively at the dynamical level.

Beyond Reflexes

Graham Brown, Von Holtz, Mittelstaedt, Weiss, and Bernstein are only a few of the important physiologists who have explicitly challenged the utility of the sensory-to-motor linkage that is at the heart of reflex theory. Many other researchers have raised similar challenges. All of these scientists have argued that reflexology, with its focus on a sensory-to-motor linkage, has led physiology down a restricted path since the beginning of the twentieth century. All of them have argued that in order to account for determinate behaviors, the nervous system would have to include elements that lay beyond the boundaries of reflexology. Graham Brown, Von Holtz, Mittelstaedt, and their colleagues all argued that the nervous system was not a passive sensory-to-motor connection, as Sherrington proposed. They argued that instead, the vertebrate nervous system must include active elements that generated behavior in the absence of stimuli. Weiss, in turn, argued that behavior must be organized around goals, not muscle activations, and he showed that muscle activations and goals could often be quite different. Bernstein developed this idea in greater detail, showing at a mathematical level that movements (kinematics) and patterns of muscle force (dynamics) were very different, and suggesting that it was around this very difference that the nervous system must be hierarchically organized.

Physiologists now admit that these are important ideas that should influence the ways we model the connection between sensation and action in determinate behaviors. Unfortunately, these ideas have gained surprisingly little traction. Models and experimental approaches have barely been influenced by these insights. Perhaps this is because none of these other approaches seems to offer an adequate replacement for the reflexological paradigm. These ideas seem to point out the limits of the existing paradigm without offering a fully developed alternative. To make that clear, in the next chapter we turn to a brief overview of some of the most influential theories of behavior and brain modeling that have been developed. These are theories that are rooted in the Sherringtonian paradigm. They are brilliant advances but, like the paradigmatic view within which they reside, they face significant limits and offer no clear solutions to the problems that limit the Sherringtonian paradigm itself.

5

Neurobiology Today: Beyond Reflexology?

In the four preceding chapters I have argued that the reflexological approach was, at heart, an effort to develop a logical calculus, a simple set of basic operations that could be combined in different ways to yield a working model for any determinate behavior. In this regard, the logical calculus of reflexology closely paralleled the work of mathematicians and logicians working to develop a *complete* logical predicate calculus.

The physiologists working on the logic of the nervous system, however, had to engage an issue that was absent from the mathematical debate. Descartes's dualist conjecture proposed that all behavior could be broken down into two categories: simple and complex, or determinate and indeterminate. Unfortunately, the logical calculi being developed by both physiologists and mathematicians could explain only determinate phenomena. Reflexologists like Pavlov addressed this limitation by arguing that Descartes had been wrong. Indeterminate behaviors simply did not exist. Others, like Sherrington, accepted the Cartesian dualist conjecture and explicitly proposed the existence of indeterminate processes that lay outside the domain of any reflex-based approach.

Regardless of whether or not indeterminate behaviors exist, classical reflex-based approaches face an additional problem today. Theoretical and empirical studies have shown that there are determinate behaviors which are poorly described by reflex theory. Rhythmic behaviors like stepping, behaviors that involve feedback, and behaviors that seem to require hierarchical control systems are all poorly described by the passive local elements that Sherrington employed. Not only do the passive logical operators of reflexology do a poor job modeling these behaviors, but empirical work indicates that the nervous system actually generates these behaviors using the kinds of active physiological mechanisms that lie outside of classical reflexology.

None of this is controversial among neurobiologists. Any graduate student in physiology, regardless of his or her opinions about indeterminate behavior, would agree that extrareflexological components are employed by the nervous system. Any graduate student would also agree that these extrareflexological mechanisms are more difficult to understand and more difficult to model than simple reflex behaviors, but neither our student nor any of his or her colleagues would challenge the existence of these mechanisms. In fact, many neurobiologists would view the preceding four chapters as an entirely historical exercise with little or no applicability to modern neuroscience. As one of my colleagues recently put it to me: "That's quite interesting, but it's not as if all that reflexology and dualism influences the way neurobiologists think about the brain today."

In this chapter I want to convince you of just the opposite. Although we all know that reflexological approaches are limited in scope, I believe that Sherrington's calculus of reflexology still forms the core of how we think about the relationship between behavior, brain, and mind. If we look at many of the most subtle and advanced physiological experiments and computational models of the brain, we will find that they contain *only* reflex-based components. These are components that Sherrington would, without a doubt, have considered very familiar.

In order to make that argument, I am going to describe two contemporary models of neurobiological function. These are two of the most widely discussed accomplishments in cognitive neuroscience. One uses computer-simulated neural networks to describe how speech might be learned by human infants. The other describes how monkey brains might produce perceptually guided decisions about where to look.

Before I describe these two research programs, I want to make something absolutely clear. First, I am *not* arguing that these are bad models. On the contrary, I picked these examples because I think that they are important models. They are, in my mind, among the best models of sensorimotor function that exist. Second, I am not arguing that the specific behaviors they model would be better described using extrareflexological tools. The tools used to build these models seem to me to be entirely appropriate. What I want you to see is that the models used to explain neurobiological phenomena are models in which reflexological tools do a very good job of explaining largely deterministic behaviors that are well suited to a reflexological explication. What I want to convince you of is not that we are unaware of the limits of reflex calculus, but that we intentionally circumscribe both the behaviors we study and the models we build to allow us to employ these tried-and-true approaches in our studies of the brain.

NetTalk, a Neural Network That Reads Aloud

Classical Networks

Nowhere is the continued reliance on a reflex-based architecture clearer than in the history of neural network models of the brain, an area in which mathematics and neurophysiology achieve their closest fusion. That history begins with Alan Turing's work (Turing, 1936) on the computability theorem and on the design of modern computers. Turing's computability theorem, in turn, strongly influenced two American neural scientists who are now considered the fathers of computer models of the brain: Warren McCulloch and Walter Pitts. McCulloch and Pitts (1943) realized that Turing had demonstrated a critical feature of *any* logical calculus with his computability theorem. Any machine, *or brain*, that could perform a specific set of simple deterministic calculations could, in principle, solve any *computable* problem. Although such a device could not hope to engage noncomputable problems, it could be shown to be complete within the limited domain of computable problems.

For the Sherringtonian program, this meant that reflexology could be complete within the computable domain if the logical operators Sherrington employed could be shown to be formally equivalent to the specific set of deterministic operators Turing had identified as critical within the computable domain. McCulloch and Pitts hoped to accomplish this goal by proving that neurons could perform each of the requisite deterministic calculations. This would allow one to conclude that a neuron-based machine like the brain was at least as powerful as a Universal Turing Machine.

To that end, they systematically showed that simple mathematical models of single neurons could be hooked together to compute essentially all of the elementary operations of Boolean propositional logic. Three model neurons with appropriate connections and physiological properties could, for example, be hooked together to compute the logical operation *and*. This was an important advance because it made the link between mathematical models of computation and models of the brain very explicit. But as McCulloch and Pitts were aware, it placed a limit on what could be accomplished with these models of the brain. If the actual human brain was limited to Turing's set of computable functions, then these models could mimic any real neural function. If, however, brains were capable of other classes of computation, then some neural processes might lie beyond the realm of what could be modeled with these tools.

You will recall that at the turn of the twentieth century, Pavlov had addressed this uncertainty by contending that even the most flexible behavioral process he could imagine, learning, could be described as fully determinate (Pavlov, 1927). He had argued that reflex calculi could be extended to account for all of behavior, even for the ability of animals to learn. Perhaps because Pavlov provided no explicit physiological model of how this might be accomplished, both Sherrington's students and McCulloch and Pitts had avoided the issue of how brains might learn and whether this could be considered a determinate phenomenon within the computable domain. In the late 1950s, however, a new approach to brain modeling was able to engage this issue directly. It was able to provide rigorous mathematical models of how networks of neurons might actually be capable of learning. This enormous breakthrough was largely the work of one man, the Canadian psychologist Donald Hebb (1949).

Hebb had been interested in how it was that groups of neurons might modify themselves, changing some aspect of their own physiology to store new knowledge or to permit new computation within a network. What Hebb proposed was that neurons might be able to dynamically modify the strength of the synapses that interconnect them, based upon a simple rule that each neuron could compute locally. While the precise form of this rule, now known as Hebbian learning, has been tremendously important, the general idea that such a rule might exist has had an even greater impact. The idea that a simple rule for increasing or decreasing the strength of individual synapses could be used to allow a network of neurons to modify the connections it makes between sensory inputs and motor outputs revolutionized the emerging field of artificial intelligence that was growing from the work of McCulloch, Pitts, and their colleagues.

One of the clear leaders in this revolution was Frank Rosenblatt at Cornell University. During the 1950s and 1960s he became fascinated with building networks of model neurons and allowing them to learn how to solve more and more complicated problems with tools like Hebb's learning rule. Critically, because his networks were designed to learn how to solve their own problems using a very physiological architecture, Rosenblatt's approach was distinct from the discrete logical strategy that McCulloch and Pitts had originally proposed. These networks represented, in some sense, an effort to bridge the narrowing gap between the work of McCollough and Pitts, Sherrington, and Pavlov.

In 1943, the doctrine and many of the fundamental theorems of this approach to nerve net theory were first stated in explicit form by McCulloch and Pitts, in their well known paper on "A Logical Calculus of the Ideas Immanent in Nervous Activity." The fundamental thesis of the McCulloch-Pitts theory is that all psychological phenomena can be analyzed and understood in terms of activity in a network of two-state (all-or-nothing) [by which McCulloch, Pitts, and Rosenblatt mean binary] logical devices. The specifications of such a network and its propositional logic would, in the words of the writers, "contribute all that could be achieved" in psychology, "even if the analysis were pushed to ultimate psychic units or 'psychons', for a psychon can be no less than the activity of a single neuron.... The 'all-or-none' law of these activities, and the conformity of their relations to those of the logic of propositions, insure that the relations of psychons are those of the two valued logic of propositions." (Rosenblatt, 1962)

Rosenblatt, however, went on to argue for an approach distinct from the one McCulloch and Pitts had employed. Although their logical architectures may have been formally equivalent to the Sherringtonian architecture, to Rosenblatt they seemed, at an anatomical level, very different from the classic reflexology of Pavlov and Sherrington. (See figure 5.1.)

As a result, Rosenblatt focused his highly influential research program on a class of network models he called perceptrons. Rosenblatt's perceptrons took many forms, but the dominant architecture in his designs, and the one that he and his students spent the most time developing, was

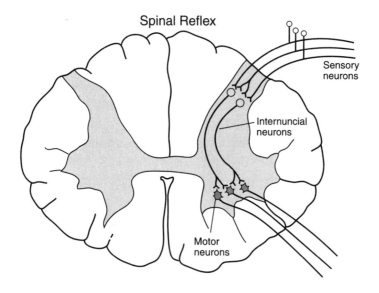

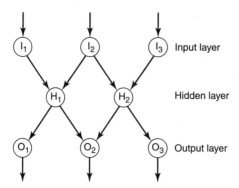

Figure 5.1
Spinal reflexes and three-layer perceptrons.

the architecture with the greatest anatomical similarity to the original Sherringtonian model.

In that class of perceptrons, an array of output neurons was influenced by a second array of internuncial neurons (now usually called hidden neurons) that in turn received their signals from an array of input neurons. In anatomical form these perceptrons were nothing less than a computer simulation of a classic reflex exactly as Sherrington had described it: "The concept of the reflex therefore embraces at least three separate structures,—an effector organ, e.g., gland cells or muscle cells; a conducting nervous path or conductor leading to that organ; and an initiating organ or receptor whence the reaction starts."

Of course perceptrons were not the first formally described neural networks. McCulloch and Pitts had beaten Rosenblatt to that milestone. Perceptrons were not even the first neural networks to learn. The father of artificial intelligence, Marvin Minsky, had beaten Rosenblatt to that accomplishment. But Rosenblatt's perceptrons were among the most physiological networks that had been developed at that time. They employed a three-stage architecture just like Sherrington's, and like Pavlov's dogs they could learn.

Since Rosenblatt's initial work on perceptrons there have been a number a major advances in neural network modeling. The dominant architecture for thinking about neural networks, however, has remained one that would have been quite familiar to both Rosenblatt and Sherrington: a three-layered system of sensory, integrative, and motor neurons linked by variable-strength connections. To explain how models of this type work today, we turn to one of the most widely discussed uses of the Sherringtonian architecture, the NetTalk system of Terry Sejnowski and Charles Rosenberg (Sejnowski and Rosenberg, 1987).

The NetTalk System

Sejnowski and Rosenberg began by asking whether a large, traditionally configured neural network could learn to solve a particularly interesting sensory-to-motor problem, the problem of turning English-language text into speech. In order to make this a tractable problem, they began by defining a relatively simple set of initial goals. First the network would be set the goal of reading a single training text of about 1000 words. These words would be provided as a sequential letter-by-letter input to the network. The task of the network would not be to read the text per se, but instead to select from a prerecorded set of 79 English-language sounds, or phonemes, the series of phonemes that were appropriate for any word in the text. The task of NetTalk was thus to take English letters as an input and select phonemes as an output. (See figure 5.2.)

How did the network receive the letters of the text as an input? Sejnowski and Rosenberg began with a set of 182 sensory neurons that

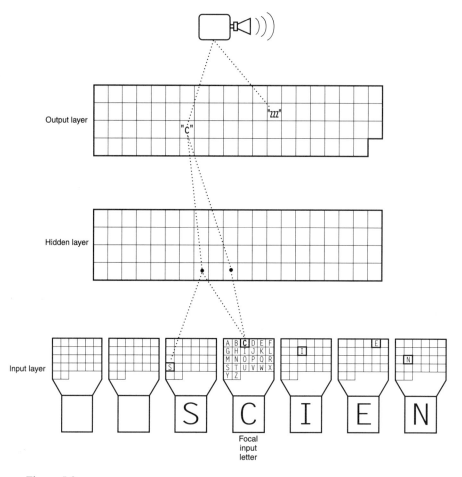

Figure 5.2
The NetTalk network.

served as the inputs to their network. These sensory neurons were then broken into seven groups of 26 neurons each. Within each group, each of the 26 neurons was a specific receptor, in the Sherringtonian sense. Neuron 1 became active only when the letter "A" appeared before it. Neuron 2 was a specific receptor for the letter "B." Each of the seven groups had a specific receptor for each of the 26 letters of the English alphabet. The seven groups of sensory neurons were thus able to provide as input seven sequential letters from the text at a time. The output, or motor, neurons had a roughly similar structure. There were 79 output neurons, one for each of the 79 phonemes that the model could produce. Whenever one of the output neurons became active, the system produced that phoneme. Finally, in order to turn this into a sensorimotor device, the 180 sensory neurons were connected by variable-strength synapses to 80 internuncial, or hidden, neurons, and these hidden neurons were connected by variable-strength synapses to the 79 output neurons.

The next step, which was the major focus of Sejnowski and Rosenberg's experiment, was to have the network learn how to build connections between sensory, hidden, and motor neurons that met the goal of turning text into speech. To do that, Sejnowski and Rosenberg used a very sophisticated neural network learning algorithm called backpropagation. Backpropagation was an enormously important computational advance in neural network circles because it very efficiently implements a class of computation called gradient descent. But for our purposes the mathematical details of backpropagation are unimportant. The important feature of backpropagation is that it allows simulated networks of neurons to learn new sensorimotor patterns of connectivity quickly.

The training phase of the NetTalk experiment went this way: Sejnowski and Rosenberg lined up the seven input groups in a row so that they could look at the first seven sequential letters from the training text. They then advanced the text letter by letter past the seven input groups. Sejnowski and Rosenberg had decided in advance what would be the correct pattern of phonemes for this text. The task faced by their backpropagation algorithm was to compare the phonemes that the network actually produced with the phonemes that it should have produced. Every time the network got closer to getting a phoneme right, the backpropogation algorithm strengthened the synaptic connections within the network responsible for getting closer. Conversely, every time the network got farther from correct, the connections responsible were weakened. The job of the backpropagation algorithm was to work out the sensory neuron-to-interneuron-to-motor neuron connections that solved the text-to-speech problem.

Not surprisingly, when the network began this training process, it did a very poor job. As the letters scrolled by the input array, the network produced an entirely random pattern of phonemes. As the backpropagation algorithm tuned the network, amazing structure began to appear in the output of the machine. Slowly but surely, as it learned, these random sounds turned to a kind of almost intelligible babbling that seemed similar to the way human infants begin to vocalize before they actually speak. As the network continued to learn, this babbling became progressively more structured and English-like until, after 50 runs through the training text, the system was able to perform this particular sensory-to-motor process of converting text to speech with a 95 percent accuracy.

There is absolutely no doubt that this was an amazing accomplishment. NetTalk did learn to turn text into phonemes, and it did this by employing a reflexological strategy. To make this clear, imagine a Sherringtonian reflexologist trying to study the behavior of the NetTalk system at a physiological level. In order to begin with a very simple reflex, our imaginary physiologist might notice that every time the letter "Z" was presented as an input to the central group of 26 sensory neurons, NetTalk always responded by producing the sound "zzz." Now how did it do that? He might begin by looking to see if there was a sensory receptor specialized for detecting the letter "Z" in the input array. Indeed, he would find one sensory neuron in the central group that became highly active only when "Z" appeared. He might also look at the output system to see if there was a final common path for the "zzz" sound. He would find one, a single output neuron that produced the "zzz" sound when active.

Sherringtonian reflex theory would propose that these sensory and motor neurons were linked by one or more interneurons. With this idea in hand, our neurophysiologist might then search through the 80 interneurons of the system for a connection between the input and the output neurons. We have every reason to believe that if he was patient, he would find one: a projection from the "Z" receptor to one or more internuncial neurons that would in turn project to the final common path for the "zzz" sound. Every time a "Z" stimulus would be presented as a sensory input to the fully trained network, a "zzz" motor output would be produced. Reflex theory seems to do a good job of describing how NetTalk works.

Now, examine a more complicated case. Our neurophysiologist might notice that NetTalk is much less predictable when it comes to the letter "C" as an input. Sometimes NetTalk responds to the "C" input by producing a hard "c" sound, as in the word "cat." At other times NetTalk seems to be unaffected by the presence of a "C," remaining silent. This happens when the "C" is preceded by an "S," as in the word "science." Now how can we explain this behavior? Our physiologist would have a simple theory. There is a "C"-to-"c" reflex. We can look for this reflex by studying cases in which the "C" appears at the start of words. He would also reason that there is an inhibitory reflex that operates under some conditions. If an "S" stimulus precedes a "C" stimulus, then an inhibitory reflex is activated that prevents the normal "C"-to-"c" reflex from occurring. If our neurophysiologist studied the NetTalk network carefully enough, he would no doubt be able to find these analogues of the excitatory and inhibitory pathways of classical reflexology as well.

So there seems to be little doubt about two important points. First, reflex theory does a good job of characterizing the NetTalk network. Second, the NetTalk network uses something like the reflex calculus to produce a deterministic sensorimotor linkage in much the way that Sherrington imagined. What does that tell us about the human brain? Does the fact that a reflex machine can solve the text-to-speech problem mean that the human brain does so with this methodology? I think that everyone, Sejnowski and Rosenberg included, would answer no to this question. This is not necessarily how the human brain solves the text-to-speech problem. In fact, we have every reason to believe that the human brain uses elements like self-activation, corollary discharge (or feedback), and a hierarchical organization to accomplish the conversion of text-to-speech that we all perform so easily.

The point that I am trying to make here is not that NetTalk teaches us nothing. NetTalk teaches us quite a lot. What I am trying to convince you of is that NetTalk is, at root, an exploration of reflexological mechanisms and that reflexological mechanisms are, at best, only a tiny subset of the brain mechanisms which underlie behaviors like converting text to speech. Like almost all neural network models that produce complex behaviors, the whole function of NetTalk can be summed up in one word: conduction (to paraphrase Sherrington). And this is a general feature of nearly all neural network models that employ simple sequential connections between inputs and outputs. That kind of direct serial connection, which scientists like Graham Brown and Von Holtz argued was inadequate for modeling many kinds of behavior, still serves as the core approach to neural network modeling.

To develop the notion that we often choose to study only the subset of our behavior that can be well described by a methodology rooted in reflexology, I want to turn to another example. This next example is one of the greatest accomplishments of cognitive neuroscience. It is the product of a 20-year program aimed at understanding how a complex behavior can be described as a linkage between a sensory input and a motor output. This is the work of William Newsome of Stanford University.

Deciding Where to Look

Newsome and his colleagues revolutionized modern sensory neuroscience in the late 1980s and early 1990s when they began to ask a relatively subtle question: What is the neurobiological basis of a subjective sensory experience? As Newsome and some of his closest colleagues put it in 1990:

An enduring problem for sensory neurophysiology is to understand how neural circuits in the cerebral cortex mediate our perception of the visual world. In part, the problem endures because it is difficult; the circuits in visual cortex are formidable both in their number and in their complexity. Of equal importance, however, is that investigation of the visual system has yielded a stream of fascinating insights into the nature of critical information processing. Perhaps foremost among these insights is that individual cortical neurons, in contrast to retinal photoreceptors, respond selectively to perceptually salient features of the visual scene. For example neurons in striate cortex (or VI) [cortical visual area number one] respond selectively to the orientation of local contours, to the direction of motion of a visual stimulus, or to visual contours that fall on disparate locations in the two retinae.

Selective neurons of this nature are often thought to be related to specific aspects of visual perception. For example, orientation-selective neurons could provide the basic information from which we perceive shape and form, direction-selective neurons might play a prominent role in seeing motion, and disparity-selective neurons could mediate the sensation of stereoscopic depth. Although straightforward links between neuronal physiology and visual perception are intuitively appealing, the evidence for such links is generally indirect.

The goal of our research is to explore—in as direct a manner as possible—the relationship between the physiological properties of direction-selective cortical neurons and the perception of visual motion....

Our general strategy is to conduct physiological experiments in rhesus monkeys that are trained to discriminate the direction of motion in a random-dot motion display. In such experiments, we can simultaneously monitor physiological events and perceptual performance. The psychophysical [or behavioral] task [we use] is designed so that good performance depends on signals of the kind carried by direction-selective cortical neurons. We asked three basic questions during the course of the investigation: (1) Is performance on the direction discrimination task impaired following chemical lesions of [area] MT [the cortical area in which motion-sensitive neurons are located]? (2) Are cortical neurons [in area MT] sufficiently sensitive to the motion signal in the random-dot [motion] display to account for psychophysical [ly measured behavioral] performance? (3) Can we influence [the monkey's] perceptual judgements of motion by manipulating the discharge [or neural activity] of directionally selective neurons with electrical micro-stimulation? The answer to each of these three questions is yes. (Newsome et al., 1990)

Newsome and his colleagues were interested in understanding how the brain generates the perception of motion, so they began by training rhesus monkeys to watch a visual display that humans perceive as moving in a particular direction. They then asked their monkey subjects to report the direction in which the display appeared to move. They accomplished this by having monkeys look through a circular window at a cloud of moving white dots. Critically, whenever the dots appeared, not all of them moved in the same direction. During any given 2-sec display, many of the individual dots were moving in different, randomly selected, directions. Only a small fraction of the dots actually moved in a coordinated direction, and it was this coordinated direction of movement that the monkeys were trained to detect. (See figure 5.3.)

When human observers view a display of this kind, they report that the display looks like a chaotic blizzard of randomly moving white dots with some of the dots drifting in a particular direction. Consider a case in which 7 percent of the dots move in coordinated fashion to the left, and the remaining 93 percent of the dots move randomly. Under these

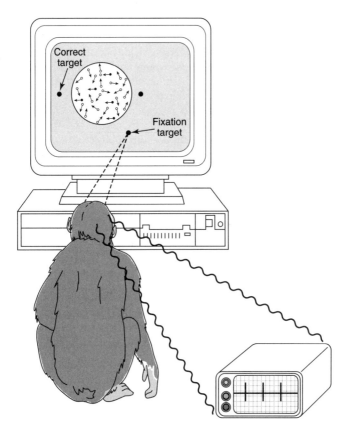

Figure 5.3
Monkey performing Newsome task with oscilloscope showing the activity of a single neuron in area MT.

circumstances humans report that they see a blizzard with a weak tendency for the dots to drift toward the left. In contrast, if 20 percent of the dots move in a coordinated fashion, humans report an overwhelming sense that the blizzard is moving to the left. If only 1 percent of the dots move in a coordinated fashion, human observers have a tremendous amount of difficulty determining the direction in which the dots are moving, and they perform on the task almost as if they were guessing. Thus, by varying the percentage of dots moving in a coordinated fashion, Newsome could effectively control how accurately humans could report, and presumably perceive, the direction of dot motion.

Newsome's goal was to teach monkeys to perform this same task and then to determine whether particular neurons in monkey visual cortex were causally responsible for the monkeys' judgments about the direction of dot motion. While the monkeys stared straight ahead, a patch of moving dots was presented for 2 sec. Either a small and variable fraction of the dots were moving in a coordinated manner to the left or they were moving in a coordinated manner to the right. Across hundreds of these 2-sec. presentations, both the direction of dot motion and the fraction of dots moving in a coordinated manner were varied randomly. At the end of each 2-sec. display the monkey was asked whether the dots had moved to the left or to the right. He indicated this by making an eye movement that shifted his line of sight either toward a spot of light to the left of the circular window or toward a second spot of light to the right of the circular window.

The monkeys agreed to learn this task, and then to perform it after learning was complete, because each time they selected the correct response, they received a small drink of fruit juice as a reward.

When Newsome began these experiments, he already knew that there is a small area in the brains of monkeys and humans highly specialized for processing moving visual stimuli, cortical area MT. Newsome hypothesized that activity in this area might be causally responsible for the perceptual experience we have when we see an object move. In fact, quite a bit was known about the activity of individual neurons in area MT at the time these experiments were performed. Each MT neuron was known to become active whenever a visual stimulus moved in a particular direction across the portion of the visual world scrutinized by that cell. Each neuron thus had an idiosyncratic preferred direction. And because each neuron preferred motion in a different direction, the population of neurons in area MT could, in principle, discriminate motion in all possible directions.

What Newsome was trying to determine was whether the activity of the cells that preferred leftward motion was the physical embodiment of the perceptual experience we have when we see a visual stimulus moving to the left. He developed an answer to that question by performing dozens of experiments, only two of which I will describe. In the first of these two experiments (Newsome, Britten, and Movshon, 1989), he and his colleagues Ken Britten and Tony Movshon had the monkeys evaluate a variety of moving dot stimuli as *left* or *right* while monitoring the activity of individual neurons in area MT that preferred either leftward or rightward motion. Newsome found that if 15 percent of the dots in the display moved to the right, the monkeys always reported that they saw rightward motion and MT cells that preferred rightward motion also always reported that rightward motion had been detected. Much more interesting was the observation that as the percent of rightward dots was decreased, both the probability that the monkey would report that he had seen rightward motion and the probability that the neurons would report that they had seen rightward motion decreased at *exactly the same rate*. Newsome realized that it was very unlikely that this was due to chance, and it raised the possibility that the perceptually based report of the monkey, *left* or *right*, might reflect the activity of these particular cells.

A second series of experiments was then conducted with Dan Salzman using the same basic strategy (Salzman, Britten, and Newsome, 1990). In these experiments, however, monkeys were shown a display in which all the dots moved in random directions. While the animals were being presented with this ambiguous stimulus and asked to evaluate it as *left* or *right*, Newsome and Saltzman activated leftward-preferring neurons in area MT by direct electrical stimulation. Under these conditions, amazingly enough, the monkeys reported that they had seen leftward motion even though there was no leftward motion in the display.

These experiments revolutionized sensory physiology because they demonstrated that the activation of neurons in a specific brain area can produce a perceptual experience. Newsome and his colleagues showed that the activity of a small group of neurons in the visual cortex is sufficient to generate the percept of motion and to elicit the leftward eye movement that was its marker in these experiments. Although revolutionary in this sense, it is also important to note that Newsome's experiments were very conservative in another sense. In his task a visual stimulus is used to trigger an eye movement, a direct sensorimotor linkage of the type we encountered in NetTalk. This is exactly the type of behavioral response that reflex theory was designed to model.

At about the time that these experiments were being completed, a young scientist named Michael Shadlen joined Newsome's laboratory at Stanford University. In order to better understand how activity in leftward-preferring neurons might be used to produce leftward eye movements, Shadlen and Newsome began an extensive program of computer analysis that yielded a mathematical model describing how sensory neurons in area MT might produce leftward eye movements.

At the time that they began to develop their model, Newsome and Shadlen were well aware of extensive research on how shifts in the line of sight were accomplished. It was widely held that structures at the base of the brain seemed to act as eye-movement command structures, as a final common path for the control of eye movements. Shadlen and Newsome reasoned that the minimally complex circuit that could account for the left or right eye movement responses which the monkeys produced in the Newsome sensorimotor task was one in which the neurons sensitive to leftward motion activated the neurons of the final common path for leftward eye movements. Similarly, sensory neurons specialized as receptors for rightward movement would activate the final common path for rightward eye movements. (See figure 5.4.)

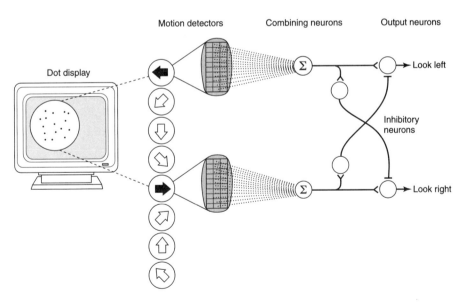

Figure 5.4
Shadlen's network.

With this insight in hand, Shadlen had to sift through mountains of cellular data and to explain, mathematically, how information was combined across populations of MT neurons, how ambiguous stimuli competed for access to the final common path, and how stimulation could bias the reports of Newsome's monkeys. In the end, Newsome and Shadlen produced a computer model that used the activity of simulated MT neurons to produce behavioral judgments just like those produced by real monkeys (Shadlen et al., 1996). In their model, small groups of rightward-preferring neurons combine their signals and compete with small groups of leftward-preferring neurons for access to a final common path that executes either a rightward or a leftward eye movement. At the time the motion display is turned off, whichever population of neurons is more active controls the final common path and produces the eye movement that it specifies.

The real beauty of Shadlen and Newsome's model was its simplicity and mathematical rigor. They had developed a model sensory-to-motor system that could completely account for the behavior of Newsome's monkeys in the moving dot task. It did so by incorporating only those elements which were necessary to account for that behavior. You may recall from chapter 3 that Pavlov had said of Descartes: "He regarded every activity of the organism as a necessary reaction to some external stimulus, the connection of the stimulus and the response being made through some definite nervous path." Shadlen's model was, I would argue, the closest anyone had come to realizing the goal of Descartes and Pavlov to clearly identify that "definite nervous path" for a complex behavior in a primate.

Despite this obvious success, it seems reasonable to examine the Shadlen model and to ask how it differs from a model Sherrington might have built to account for these same data. To do that, let's begin by examining the circuit that produces the leftward movement. This circuit begins with a group of sensory neurons that function as a receptor for leftward movement in the visual stimulus. Activity in the sensory neurons is summed across time in an internuncial neuron. The internuncial neuron connects, in turn, to the final common path for producing a leftward eye movement.

A similar circuit is presumed to produce rightward movements. Sensory receptors specialized for detecting rightward movement project to internuncial neurons that sum the rightward activity and activate the final common path at the end of the trial. The left and right responses are, however, mutually exclusive. The animal must produce either a leftward or a rightward eye movement, never both. Sherrington had faced exactly this problem in designing the reflex circuits for stepping:

When two receptors are stimulated simultaneously, each of the receptors tending to evoke reflex action that for its end-effect employs the same final common path but employs it in a different way from the other, one reflex appears without the other. The result is *this* reflex or *that* reflex but not the two together.... These reflexes may in regard to one another be termed antagonistic; and the reflex or group of reflexes which succeeds in inhibiting its opponents may be termed "prepotent" for the time being. (Sherrington, 1906)

Shadlen and Newsome proposed that the internuncial neuron in their circuit which was most active effectively became "prepotent" at the end of the 2-sec display. To achieve this prepotency, the internuncial neurons were designed to inhibit each other at a specific point in the circuit, one that lay just upstream of the final common path.

Like NetTalk, the Shadlen model does not seem to employ any of the determinate extrareflexive mechanisms—for example, reafference—that Von Holtz and others argued must exist within the nervous system.[1] Also like NetTalk, Shadlen's model *does* teach us quite a bit about the nervous system. Shadlen's model, for example, has taught us quite a lot about how information is pooled across neurons and about how pools of neurons might compete for access to a final common path. And finally, it is important to note that in order to account for this behavior, Shadlen's model does not require any of these extrareflexive mechanisms. Those components are not necessary.

So why is it that the reflexological nature of NetTalk and of the Shadlen model seems to me to be a problem, or to reflect a conceptual limitation? For me the biggest limitation which these models imply is that we select particular behaviors for study, and ignore others, because

1. Although in fairness it does employ the mathematic operation of integration, a determinate operator that lies outside the Sherringtonian tradition.

the reflexological tool kit we all carry around with us makes some behaviors tractable to analysis and leaves others incomprehensible.

Consider what happens when Newsome begins to train a monkey. From the experimenter's point of view, the monkey is learning how to perform a new task, left versus right motion discrimination. Only after the monkey has fully learned this new behavior can the experiment begin. From the monkey's point of view, however, the process he participates in looks quite different. The monkey comes to the laboratory already knowing that he wants to maximize the amount of juice he obtains. Slowly he learns to do that by performing the motion discrimination task more and more efficiently. For the monkey there is no new experimental task per se, just a change in the environment within which he can obtain juice. This may be an important distinction, because we have already seen that the Sherringtonian framework often provides explanatory power only within the limited context of the experimenter's view of the task.

The risk posed by reflexology is essentially this: Are we developing a theory of individual trees that is testable and verifiable but that does a very poor job of describing an entire forest? If we forced ourselves to employ the much more complicated extrareflexological tools that were available to us, might we be able to extend our descriptive theories of the brain to a broader range of behaviors? Might the identification of simple behaviors as *reflexes* come to seem an artificial distinction? As Von Holtz said:

The sooner we recognize the fact that the [higher functions] which leave the reflex physiologist dumbfounded in fact send roots *down to the simplest basal functions of the CNS*, the sooner we shall see that the previously terminologically insurmountable barrier between the lower levels of neurophysiology and higher behavioral theory simply dissolves away. (Von Holtz and Mittelstaedt, 1950)

6

Global Computation: An Alternative to Sherrington?

Why is the Sherringtonian paradigm so robust, and so obviously useful, if so much evidence indicates that the paradigm is limiting neurobiological research today? One answer to this question may be the simplicity of the logical approach that Sherrington pioneered: (1) Begin by identifying an elementary behavior, like the withdrawal of a foot from fire, (2) determine a priori the minimal set of neurobiological components that could account for that behavior, and (3) look for evidence that those components exist.

This approach has two enormous advantages. First, each of the components that you identify is absolutely necessary for the behavioral response that you hope to explain. Second, the neural hardware that you propose has been reduced to the smallest and simplest component set possible. For this reason Pavlov called Descartes's idea of the reflex a "truly scientific" notion; as Pavlov put it, it embodied the notion of "necessity." Every component included in a reflex circuit is necessary. It is this property of the Sherringtonian paradigm that has made it both so useful and so limiting for studies of the brain.

In the preceding chapters I have described a number of the constraints imposed by the logical building blocks that the Cartesian-Sherringtonian paradigm employs. For example, the paradigm leads investigators to ignore the possibility that autonomously active neural elements shape behavior. Instead, it favors passive elements that conduct sensory activity toward a motor output. It also shies away from feedback loops and corollary discharge. But the real problems with the reflexological approach go much deeper than the limitations imposed by the use of passive conducting elements. One of the most critical problems with the reflexological paradigm is that the behaviors we call reflexes may in actuality be only tiny parts of much more complex and complete behavioral systems. We may run the risk, by studying these reflexes in isolation, of learning very little about the relationship between behavior and brain as a whole. Instead we may learn only about tiny behavioral reactions that may teach us very little about how the brain functions. Nickolai Bernstein made this point in the 1960s when he wrote:

The classical physiology of the last hundred years is characterized by ... the study of the operation of the organism under quiescent inactive conditions ... under conditions of maximal isolation from the external world. This analytical approach to the study of the quiescent conditions derived from the attempt to study every organ and every elementary process in isolation, attempting to exclude side effects or mutual interactions.... The absolutism of that point of view led to the conviction that the whole is the sum of its parts and no more than this, and that the organism is a collection of cells, that all behavior is a chain of reflexes, and that a sufficient acquaintance with the individual bricks would be enough for the comprehension of the edifice constructed from them. (Bernstein, 1961)

Bernstein was suggesting that classical physiology proceeded from an erroneous assumption. He believed that in order to understand how the brain as a whole functions, one would simply have to study how the brain as a whole functions. It may not be possible, he suggested, to build a complete understanding of the relationship between behavior, brain, and mind by studying in isolation the tiny and perhaps arbitrarily selected pieces of behavior that we call reflexes.

To take Bernstein's comment about the limitations of the reflexological paradigm's focus on "individual bricks" to an extreme, consider the following example. I am writing this book on a computer in my office. When I leave the computer alone for more than 15 min, the machine goes to sleep; the screen and disk drives shut down, and other components go into a power-saving mode. This powered-down mode is what Bernstein or Sherrington would have called a baseline state. It is a repeatable experimental condition that I can arrive at simply by waiting 15 min. Now I observe that when my computer is in this baseline state, if I touch the spacebar, the screen illuminates after a 1-sec delay. How does my computer do this? What is the hardware by which it achieves this reflexive linkage between the spacebar being depressed and the screen re-illuminating?

The simplest possible hardware that could achieve this would be a sensory pathway from the spacebar that, when the machine is in the appropriate state, is used to activate the power-up line on my monitor. If we began to perform a physiological investigation of my computer, we would indeed find that there is a distinct pathway from the keyboard into the center of my computer. We would also find a power-up line that connected the center of my computer to my monitor. With much more sophisticated tools we could even work out the discrete route by which electrons mobilized when I depress the spacebar trace a path through the maze of silicon inside the machine and then travel out to the monitor.

How much would we have learned about how my computer works? We would not, for example, know that it had a central processing unit that could execute about 100 different kinds of logical operations, even though our electron tracing would take us through the heart of that processor. We would not know that the processor included an internal clock used to time the 15-min delay. We would not know anything about the little program with which I configured the sleep mode and specified how the computer should behave. In fact, what we would have learned would be something fairly trivial, something that offered very little insight into how a computer's sleep circuit works, let alone any insight into how a computer itself works.

The problem with trying to understand my computer by studying its sleep circuit in isolation is that there is no guarantee a complex system like a computer, or a brain, can be fully described by studying its smallest parts in isolation. As I quoted Bernstein: "the attempt to study every organ and every elementary process in isolation ... led to the conviction ... that a sufficient acquaintance with the individual bricks would be enough for the comprehension of the edifice constructed from them." While highly useful, an acquaintance with the individual bricks may not provide an adequate insight into how the mammalian brain functions as a neural edifice.

David Marr

A number of scholars have raised this objection to the level at which classical physiology, rooted in the Cartesian-Sherringtonian tradition, attempts to dissect the relationship between brain and behavior. These scholars have argued that trying to conceptualize complex behaviors as enormous chains of interconnected reflexes will fail. Bernstein and Weiss made this point in their writings. Bernstein, in particular, engaged this issue when he suggested that to study coordinated movement, one would have to begin by defining the problem-of-coordination. He was proposing that in order to understand the physiology of the nervous system, one had to begin by understanding the computations the nervous system performed. Unfortunately, Bernstein's work came at a time, and in a place, where it had very little immediate impact on working physiologists.

The contemporary scholar who presented the clearest and most influential formulation of this alternative to the reflexological paradigm was probably the English computer scientist David Marr. (See figure 6.1.)

Figure 6.1
David Marr. (Courtesy of Eric Grimson and Ellen Mildreth)

Marr was born in 1945, just a few years before Alan Turing would take his own life, and was raised in the same intellectual environment that had shaped Turing's worldview. Marr was an English boy genius who worked on his doctoral degree at Trinity College, Cambridge, in the late 1960s, producing a theory of how the brain as a whole might work at a mathematical and computational level. Although this early work was fairly naive, it drove Marr to think about how global mathematical theories of computational processing might be used to understand the relationship between brain and behavior.

Perceptrons and Computation

You will recall from chapter 5 that during the late 1950s Frank Rosenblatt had begun to explore the functional properties of small networks of neurons, perceptrons (Rosenblatt, 1962). In a typical experiment Rosenblatt would hook together, either in hardware or in a computer simulation, a set of sensory neurons, a set of internuncial neurons, and a set of output neurons. Using a learning rule based on Hebb's theories, Rosenblatt would then explore what computations his networks could and could not learn to accomplish.

Rosenblatt's approach represented a huge theoretical advance because it allowed one to ask what specific computations small networks of neurons were capable of performing. The work was, however, limited by Rosenblatt's empirical focus on the neuron-to-neuron architectures of his perceptrons. When, for example, Rosenblatt found that a particular architecture could not perform a particular computation, he often proceeded by simply adding or subtracting interneurons until the desired computation could be achieved. Using this approach, Rosenblatt examined literally hundreds of different perceptron architectures, one at a time. The empirical results of these kinds of experiments convinced him that these simple networks of sensory, integrative, and motor neurons could be constructed to solve almost any problem, to perform almost any computation.

More formal mathematicians, however, were skeptical of both Rosenblatt's theoretical claim that these architectures could solve nearly any problem and the largely empirical approach that had led him to this claim. At a theoretical level, Rosenblatt's machines performed what any mathematician would call determinate computations. The computations were determinate in the sense that every time you provided a fully trained perceptron with a given set of input data, it reliably and predictably produced exactly the same output. As determinate devices they could, of course, be simulated by any Universal Turing Machine. In fact, Rosenblatt and his students often did simulate new perceptron architectures on their general-purpose computers rather than taking the time to construct the perceptrons from parts. This meant that all of the limitations on computability which any Turing machine faces must necessarily have encumbered Rosenblatt's machines. So despite Rosenblatt's convictions, perceptrons had to be at least as limited in their abilities as the regular digital computers on which they were simulated.

At another level, many mathematicians were skeptical of Rosenblatt's conclusions because they were so empirically drawn. The great advantage of using small networks of simulated neurons, these mathematicians argued, was that their behavior *could* be described mathematically; their behavior could be *fully* understood. One could, in principle, develop a complete mathematical theory of the computations these networks could perform.

The two computer scientists who tried to make these objections clear, and in so doing made a tremendous impression on Marr, were the Massachusetts Institute of Technology's Marvin Minsky and Seymour Papert. In 1969 they published *Perceptrons*, a widely read mathematical theory of what many classes of Rosenblatt's machines could and could not do. In their book, Minsky and Papert developed equations that amounted to an impressive, although admittedly incomplete, computational theory of perceptrons. They presented a theory that rigorously defined the boundaries within which these architectures could perform calculations efficiently. Minsky and Papert's book made it clear that perceptron architectures were much more limited in what they could accomplish than had been obvious from Rosenblatt's own writing. They showed that the architectures they described in mathematical detail were, in fact, a good deal more limited in capability than the digital computers on which they were simulated. For better or worse, the book had the effect of quickly damping the interest of scientists in perceptron-like machines.

At a more conceptual level, however, *Perceptrons* had a second and much wider-ranging effect on young scientists like Marr. The formal analysis presented in the book demonstrated unequivocally that computational theories of brainlike architectures were possible. Minsky and Papert had stayed within the formal mathematical approach to computation that Turing had pioneered, and had shown that this strategy could be used to study and describe entire networks of neurons. What they were pioneering was nothing less than the formal mathematical study of neural computation. Given this accomplishment, it was only natural that the young David Marr would choose to travel from Cambridge, England, to Cambridge, Massachusetts, in order to begin his mathematical study of the brain in earnest.

Marr's Approach

Marr seems to have been struck early on by the idea that formal computational studies of the nervous system were the only way to achieve a deep understanding of brain function. At Cambridge, and later at MIT, Marr completed a number of influential mathematical studies of everything ranging from how the cellular structures of the human cerebellum might learn to produce skilled movements accurately, to theories of how neural architectures might achieve concept learning. By the mid-1970s, however, he began to focus his attention on the problem of understanding the mammalian visual system. Huge strides were being made at that time by traditional physiologists in their studies of the visual system. Marr became convinced that the time was ripe for applying something like Minsky and Papert's approach to the problem of understanding the neurobiological basis of vision. This approach would, he hoped, yield a depth of understanding that would have been impossible within the narrow confines of the traditional physiological paradigm.

In a famous paper published in 1976 (Marr and Poggio, 1976), Marr and Tomaso Poggio argued that in order to understand any neurobiological architecture, one had to begin by understanding exactly what it was that the architecture was attempting, as a whole, to accomplish. First, they argued, one had to understand the computational goal of the neurobiological system one was studying. Only when one started by understanding what the whole system was "trying" to accomplish could one attempt to understand the structure of the neurobiological hardware which achieved that goal.

This was an approach that flew directly in the face of traditional strategies. Rather than isolating a tiny piece of behavior, figuring out what "definite nervous path" produced that behavior, and trying to build a theory of the brain out of these tiny pieces, Marr and Poggio argued that one had to start from an overview, to start from the top. One began at the top by describing what the whole system was trying to do, as formally and mathematically as possible, and then one began to ask how the biological hardware achieved that goal, or computation.

As this new programmatic approach to the very process of neuro-science was beginning to take form in the minds and laboratories of Marr and Poggio, disaster struck. In the winter of 1977–1978, Marr was diagnosed with a fatal form of leukemia. Although he was only in his mid-thirties, it became clear that there was little possibility he would live long enough to really develop this new approach to neurobiology. Both Marr and Poggio were, however, committed to the idea that this top-down approach to neurobiology would revolutionize the way the brain was studied. As a result, Marr made a critical decision after his diagno-sis; from that moment on, he would devote a significant amount of his remaining time to completing a single book. That book, which he titled *Vision*, became a last-ditch effort by Marr, his students, and his col-leagues to put in writing this new philosophy. In the summer of 1979, with his death just over a year away, Marr wrote the preface to a draft of *Vision*:

In December 1977, certain events occurred that forced me to write this book a few years earlier than I had planned. Although the book has important gaps, which I hope will soon be filled, a new framework for studying vision is already clear and supported by enough solid results to be worth setting down as a co-herent whole.... William Prince steered me to Professor F. G. Hayhoe and Dr. John Rees at Addenbrooke's Hospital in Cambridge, and them I thank for giving me time.

The book was largely completed by the time of Marr's death in Novem-ber 1980, and the continued work of Marr's colleagues and students after his death finally led to its publication in 1982 (Marr, 1982).

There is no doubt that Marr was brilliant and that he was arguing for a fundamental shift in the neurobiological paradigm. He was arguing for a shift away from the logical calculus of reflexology and toward broader systematic mathematical approaches. There is also no doubt that Marr's program contributed critically to the birth of a new kind of neurobiology which we now call computational neuroscience. But the influence of *Vision* on younger neurobiologists, people who were graduate students and postdoctoral fellows at the time of Marr's death, cannot be overstated. Marr's terrible and dramatic death at the age of thirty-six, as he completed a manifesto for this new approach, led *Vision* to be almost uncritically accepted by this generation of young neuroscientists. Of course there were flaws in the logic of *Vision,* and by the mid-1980s a revisionist period followed in which *Vision* was widely attacked. Still, it is critical to understand what Marr was trying to say and why his ideas captivated a generation of young scientists.

Vision

In the introduction to *Vision,* Marr recounts the history of modern neurobiology and argues that a critical limitation is faced by traditional reflex-based approaches. While these reflex-based approaches were clearly producing data about synapses and reflexes, "somewhere underneath, something was going wrong.... None of the new studies succeeded in elucidating the *function* of the visual cortex."

When studying the relationship between brain and behavior, it is the function of the nervous system, Marr argued, that should be the target of investigation.

It is difficult to say precisely why this [failure to elucidate function] had happened, because the reasoning was never made explicit and was probably largely unconscious. However various factors are identifiable. In my own case, the cerebellar study [one of Marr's early papers] had two effects. On the one hand, it suggested that one could eventually hope to understand cortical structure in functional terms, and this was exciting. But at the same time the study had disappointed me, because even if the theory was correct, it did not much enlighten one about the motor system—it did not, for example, tell one how to go about programming a mechanical arm. It suggested that if one wishes to program a mechanical arm so that it operates in a versatile way, then at some point a very large and rather simple type of memory will prove indispensable. But it did not say why, nor what that memory should contain.

The discoveries of the visual neurophysiologists left one in a similar situation. Suppose, for example, that one had actually found the apocryphal grandmother cell.[1] Would that really tell us anything much at all? It would tell us that it existed—[Charlie] Gross's [studies of] hand-detectors [neurons in monkey cortex] tell us almost that—but not *why* or even *how* such a thing may be constructed from the outputs of previously discovered cells. Do the single-unit recordings—the simple and complex [classes of] cells [found in the visual cortex]—tell us much about how to detect edges or why one would want to, except in a rather general way through arguments based on economy and redundancy? If we really knew the answers, for example, we should be able to program them on a computer. But finding a hand detector certainly did not allow us to program one.

The message was plain. There must exist an additional level of understanding at which the character of the information-processing tasks carried out during perception are analyzed and understood in a way that is independent of the particular mechanisms and structures which implement them in our heads. This was what was missing—the analysis of the problem as an information processing task. Such analysis does not usurp an understanding at other levels—of neurons or of computer programs—but it is a necessary complement to them, since *without it there can be no real understanding of the function of all those neurons*. [my italics]

Marr then goes on to make Bernstein's argument that a sufficient acquaintance with the "individual bricks" of the nervous system will not be adequate for an understanding of the relationship between behavior, brain, and mind:

Almost never can a complex system of any kind be understood as a simple extrapolation from the properties of its elementary components. Consider, for example, some gas in a bottle. A description of thermodynamic effects—temperature, pressure, density, and the relationships among these factors—is not formulated by using a large set of equations, one for each of the particles involved. Such effects are described at their own level, that of an enormous collection of particles; the effort is to show that in principle the microscopic and macroscopic descriptions are consistent with one another. If one hopes to achieve a full understanding of a system as complicated as a nervous system, a developing embryo, a set of metabolic pathways, a bottle of gas, or even a large computer program, then one must be prepared to contemplate different kinds of explanation at different levels of description that are linked, at least in principle, into a cohesive whole, even if linking the levels in complete detail is impractical. For the specific case of a system that solves an information-processing problem, there are in addition the twin strands of process and representation, and both these ideas need some discussion.

---

1. A cell that fires only when one's grandmother comes into view. [Marr's note]

Figure 1-4
The three levels at which any machine carrying out an information-processing task must be understood.

Computational theory	Representation and algorithm	Hardware implementation
What is the goal of the computation, why is it appropriate, and what is the logic of the strategy by which it can be carried out?	How can this computational theory be implemented? In particular, what is the representation for the input and output, and what is the algorithm for the transformation?	How can the representation and algorithm be realized physically?

Figure 6.2
Marr's figure 1-4.

Marr goes on to argue that in order to successfully understand the function of the brain, neurobiological studies must be conducted simultaneously at three levels of complexity.

The Three Levels

We can summarize our discussion in something like the manner shown in Figure 1-4 [see figure 6.2], which illustrates the different levels at which an information-processing device must be understood before one can be said to have understood it completely. At one extreme, the top level, is the abstract computational theory of the device, in which the performance of the device is characterized as a mapping from one kind of information to another, the abstract properties of this mapping are defined precisely, and its appropriateness and adequacy for the task at hand are demonstrated. (It is this level at which the *function* of the device is defined. [*Marr's note*]) In the center is the choice of representation for the input and output and the algorithm used to transform one into the other. And at the other extreme are the details of how the algorithm and representation are realized physically—the detailed computer architecture, so to speak. These three levels are coupled, but only loosely. The choice of algorithm is influenced, for example, by what it has to do and by the hardware in which it must run. But there is a wide choice available at each level, and the explication of each level involves issues that are rather independent of the other two.

Marr then suggests that in many ways the most important of the three levels, and the one most clearly missing from the traditional Cartesian-Sherringtonian approach, is the computational theory.

Importance of Computational Theory

Although algorithms and mechanisms are empirically more accessible, it is the top level, the level of the computational theory, which is critically important from an information-processing point of view. The reason for this is that the nature of the computations that underlie perception [recall that Marr is focused here on the study of vision; *my note*] depends more upon the computational problems that have to be solved than upon the particular hardware in which their solutions are implemented. To phrase the matter another way, *an algorithm is likely to be understood more readily by understanding the nature of the problem being solved than by examining the mechanism (and the hardware) in which it is embodied.* [my italics]

In a similar vein, trying to understand perception by studying only neurons is like trying to understand bird flight by studying only feathers; It just cannot be done. In order to understand bird flight, we have to understand aerodynamics; only then do the structure of feathers and the different shapes of birds' wings make sense. More to the point, we shall see, we cannot understand why retinal ganglion cells and lateral geniculate neurons have the receptive fields they do just by studying their anatomy and physiology. We can understand how these cells and neurons behave as they do by studying their wiring and interactions, but in order to understand *why* the receptive fields are as they are—why they are circularly symmetrical and why their excitatory and inhibitory regions have characteristic shapes and distributions—we have to know a little of the theory of differential operators, band-pass channels, and the mathematics of the uncertainty principle.

The Cartesian–Sherringtonian approach had been focused on reducing behavior to its smallest possible components. These elementary components were presumed to be the building blocks from which all behavior must be built. Support for this notion had come from the work of the mathematicians and logicians who attempted to demonstrate that all of mathematics could be constructed from elementary components in a similar manner. Marr had made a different suggestion: In order to understand the relationship between behavior and brain, one had to begin by understanding the goals or functions of a behavior. Then one could begin to ask how the brain accomplished a specific goal. For Marr it was the mathematical analysis of function, an understanding of the process of computation, that would have to be the centerpiece of any theory of behavior, brain, and mind.

These ideas that Marr and his colleagues proposed had at least two important impacts in neuroscience during the 1980s and 1990s. At a purely practical level, he convinced many neurobiologists that mathematical analyses and computer models were a critical part of the neuro-scientific enterprise. The two models I presented in chapter 5 reflect the strong mathematical tradition that Marr helped to import from computer science into the physiological mainstream. But at a philosophical level Marr was making a claim that was much more controversial and one that continues to be widely challenged. Neuroscientists must begin their work, he argued, by defining the function of the neural system they hope to study.

Unresolved Problems with Marr's Approach

To understand the relationship between behavior and brain one has to begin by defining the function, or computational goal, of a complete behavior. Only then can a neuroscientist determine how the brain achieves that goal. After *Vision* was published, this larger philosophical claim became controversial because two critical flaws were identified in the new paradigm. First, people realized that it was unclear how one could determine, a priori, what size of computation constituted the goal of a complete behavior. Second, there was a growing feeling that evolution, which had produced the mammalian brain, could not be viewed as a process that would necessarily organize the brain around computational goals, regardless of the size of those computational goals.

Defining the size of a computational goal, and thus the conceptual boundaries of the system one hoped to study, was quickly acknowledged to be critically important to the new paradigm. Marr had realized this when he had suggested that the traditional view of reflexes as computational objects was much too narrow. In his own research Marr had argued, somewhat arbitrarily, that the perceptual experience of vision should be viewed as the product of a single computational system, but he had provided little guidance for others in determining how large or small a suite of behaviors constituted the framework within which a computational goal would be achieved. For Marr as a computer scientist, this may not have seemed an overwhelming problem, but to most biologists it seemed critical. Biologists would be interested in studying mathematically defined computational goals only if there was evidence that the real neural architecture was organized around biologically discrete modules that performed each of those computations. If goals were arbitrary suites of computations rather than a reflection of something endemic to the brain, then the computational approach would be of little interest.

Marr had also assumed, completely implicitly, that evolution would necessarily drive biological systems toward efficiently achieving theoretically defined computational goals. There was, however, little evidence that this was true. *Vision* itself provided no compelling reason to believe that evolution would necessarily produce computational systems organized around functional goals. If evolution did not force modular chunks of neural hardware to achieve theoretically defined goals, then Marr's approach would have even less applicability to the biological world.

Perhaps because both of these issues were already the subjects of intensive investigation, many neuroscientists quickly identified them as devastating to Marr's philosophical program. Psychologists and cognitive neuroscientists were struggling to determine whether empirical grounds existed for breaking down behavior, and mind, into a set of independent computational systems, or modules. Biologists were working to determine empirically whether the evolutionary process tended to produce systems that achieved functional goals or whether evolution simply produced haphazard agglomerations of traits. These questions were critical, because a global mathematical approach could only succeed if the brain itself employed an efficient modular architecture.

In the early 1990s the available evidence seemed to suggest that Marr's approach was in trouble with regard to both neural modularity and evolutionary theory. As a result, many of the young neuroscientists who had been shaped by *Vision* in the 1980s became convinced that Marr's approach, although valuable, was doomed to failure as a complete paradigm. In order to understand why that conclusion was often drawn, and what limitations psychology and evolutionary biology placed on Marr's approach, we have to turn next to an examination of theories of modularity and evolution.

7

Modularity and Evolution

At MIT, Marr was a member of the Psychology Department. In that context, he formulated the notion that in order to understand the brain, one had to understand, at a global level, the computations it was performing. Within departments of psychology there had been a long tradition of thinking in this global manner about mind and brain. Indeed, many psychologists have argued that *all* of behavior should be viewed as the single coherent product of a unitary mental system. If we were trying to understand the relationship between behavior and brain at this global level, using Marr's approach, we might ask: What is the computational goal of behavior *in general?*

In physiology and neuroscience departments, by contrast, the focus had always been on reflexes. Scientists in these departments had asked questions about the goals of behaviors, but they had studied the simplest behaviors possible. This approach had undoubtedly provided significant traction on reflex-level behaviors, but Marr argued that lessons learned at this level simply could not be used to understand behavior or physiology at a functionally meaningful scale.

So how should one select the scale at which the goals, or functions, of neural processing are defined for study? Marr himself at least occasionally approached this issue by selecting an entire sensory-perceptual system as the framework within which he would define goals and functions. What, he asked, is the goal of visual perception? But this selection seems arbitrary. Why pick *visual* perception and not all sensory perception in general? Or why pick visual perception instead of something much more specific, like stereoscopic depth perception?

It seems obvious, when the problem is phrased this way, that the scale at which we seek to understand functionality should reflect the scale at which the architecture of the brain actually achieves functional goals. But at what scale is the architecture of the mammalian brain organized? Many people believe that this reduces to both an empirical question in neuroscience and a theoretical question in evolutionary biology. The empirical question is whether we can find evidence that the mammalian brain manages behavior in functional modules. The evolutionary question is much larger; it asks whether there is reason to believe that the brain evolved modules through the mechanism of natural selection, and whether these modules can be thought of as achieving definable goals.

Modules

When considering brain modules, it is important to remember that reflexology does postulate the existence of processing modules, reflexes are a type of module. As a result, one of the innovative aspects of Marr's program was his theoretical argument that the modules neuroscientists study have to be much richer and more sophisticated than those employed by the Cartesian–Sherringtonian approach.

Consider a specific example. Take a stick and glue a sharp tack to the end of the stick. Next hold the palm of your right hand out in front of you at waist level with the palm facing up. Close your eyes and have an assistant lightly strike the palm of your hand with the tack. Your assistant will observe that at a very short latency the palm of your hand will move downward away from the tack, a cutaneous withdrawal response. Reflex theory allows us to propose a hypothetical neural circuit that could produce this response at a totally atomistic level, at the level of this particular connection between sensation and action. A neuron that senses the tack makes an excitatory connection with the motor neurons of the triceps muscle and an indirect inhibitory connection with the motor neurons of the biceps muscle. (At the synaptic level these connections are almost certain to exist.) Obviously, this sensorimotor pair serves in reflex theory as a functional module.

Now consider a closely related response that the reflexological level of analysis requires us to think of being produced by a separate module. Rotate your wrist 180° so that your palm is now facing downward.

Close your eyes and once again have your assistant bring the tack into contact with exactly the same patch of skin on the palm of your hand. Now note that the hand moves quickly upward, a cutaneous withdrawal response, triggered by stimulating exactly the same pain receptors, a stimulation that now causes an activation of the biceps muscle and an inhibition of the triceps muscle.

Finally, look at a third response. Rotate your hand to an intermediate position so that your palm faces to the left. Repeat the experiment here, and note that neither the biceps nor the triceps contracts significantly; instead, muscles along your back, including the infraspinus, contract, causing a rotation of the upper arm that moves the hand laterally away from the tack.

According to reflex theory, which classifies behaviors according to patterns of muscle activation, these are necessarily three different functional elements, or modules. Neurons that sense the angle of the wrist can be thought of as gating elements which potentiate and depotentiate these three modules. With the palm up, the module that pulls the hand downward is active; the connection between the pain receptors in the skin and the triceps motor neurons is maximally excitatory, and the connection between the skin and the biceps motor neurons is maximally inhibitory. In contrast, when the palm faces to the left, the module that pulls the hand to the right is active. When the wrist is rotated palm down, the upward module is active. Three independent and discrete neural systems are turned on and off by a gating element. What happens when the wrist is rotated to any intermediate position and contact with a tack causes the hand to be withdrawn along a particular diagonal? Does every possible withdrawal of the palm along a specific diagonal represent a functionally independent reflex?

Marr would have argued against conceptualizing each of these many different withdrawal responses as an independent module, or reflex. Instead, he would have argued that the goal of the cutaneous withdrawal response was to move the palm away from the tack. The overall response accomplishes this by varying the strength of connections between the tack detector and the biceps, triceps, and infraspinus muscles as a function of wrist angle. If we were to arbitrarily refer to the strength of each connection between the tack detector and a particular muscle as having a value that ranged from +1 to −1 (where +1 refers to a maximally excitatory connection and −1 refers to a maximally inhibitory connection), then we could plot the strength of the palm-to-biceps connection as a function of the rotational position of the wrist. We would propose that the strength, or gain, of this connection was +1 when the palm was facing down and that the gain of the connection would drop steadily as the palm was rotated, reaching a value of 0 as the palm came to face left. If the palm was rotated further, the sign of the strength of the connection would reverse. An inhibitory connection would now engage, and this inhibitory connection would steadily gain in strength until it reached a peak value of −1 when the palm was facing up. Of course similar curves would describe the gain of the palm-to-triceps and palm-to-infraspinus connections.

In an example like this, Marr would argue that the set of different arm movements which we observe simply should not be considered unrelated reflexes. Rather, this suite of behavioral responses should be viewed at a theoretical level as a single module that achieves the computational goal of removing the hand from a sharp object. The gain curves represent a hypothetical implementation of this computational goal in a way that the Sherringtonian strategy of modularizing the response at the level of individual sensorimotor pairs (reflexes) does not. I find this a fairly convincing argument that at a theoretical level Marr must have been right. One does not have to model the cutaneous withdrawal response as a suite of many independent reflexes. Instead, one can think about the cutaneous withdrawal response as a single system working toward a larger goal, at least in this case. How far can one take this logic? As I pointed out at the beginning of this chapter, taken to the extreme, one can even argue that all of human behavior must serve a single computational goal. Almost by definition that goal must be to maximize the evolutionary fitness of the organism. But what is the natural scale at which the architecture of the human brain is organized?

Two contemporary scientists have worked very hard to define the functional modules of human behavior and of the human brain in this regard: the philosopher and psychologist Jerry Fodor, who has argued that psychologists have often failed to recognize the existence of behaviorally defined modules, and the neurobiologist Michael Gazzaniga, who has argued that the human brain can be viewed as a set of fairly large computationally independent subsystems. Working from very different starting points, these two scientists and their colleagues seem to be reaching a consensus about the general properties of the modules that Marr's approach requires.

Psychological Modules

Jerry Fodor was a professor at the Massachusetts Institute of Technology at the same time as Marr. He played a central role in arguing, within psychological circles, against the widespread belief that all of behavior should be viewed as the product of a single system in his 1983 book *The Modularity of Mind*. Instead, he argued that the mind should be conceived of as a set of related, but often independent, organs that function together to produce behavior. Many behavioral and cognitive abilities, he argued, should be conceptualized as the product of a multitiered processing system that must include within its hierarchical structur some functionally independent subprocesses which receive distinct inputs, produce distinct outputs, and communicate with other systems only via these fixed inputs and outputs.

In a number of experiments that examined how the human mind processes language, Fodor and his colleagues were able to provide compelling evidence for the existence of some of these independent modules. They were, for example, able to show that the process of understanding and analyzing language seems to involve a series of completely independent stages, or modules, that parse the meaning of sentences in a step-by-step fashion. These *Fodorian* modules are psychologically defined independent processes that achieve a defined computational goal and pass the information they produce on to other (often more global) systems for further processing. Fodor's ideas described, in a very real sense, exactly the class of modules for which Marr was searching.

Fodor, however, argued that this insight could be applied *only* to the psychological study of behavior, not to physiological studies of the brain. As a philosopher and psychologist, Fodor believed that the study of psychology was an endeavor which had to be conducted in complete independence from brain sciences; he adamantly asserted that his ideas were never directed at the questions Marr was asking. Nonetheless, his argument did gain a significant audience in the neurobiological community and clearly had something to say about the level of analysis at which Marr's paradigm could be conducted.

Neurobiological Modules

Long before Fodor began to examine these issues both neurologists and psychologists had flirted with the idea that modules might exist for the control of complex cognitive functions. As early as the late eighteenth century in Vienna, Franz Josef Gall had argued that the brain could be conceptualized as a set of anatomically distinct faculties, an idea that served as the forerunner of modern neurobiological theories of modularity.

At the time that Marr began to examine these issues, the work of Michael Gazzaniga was beginning to dominate discussions of functional modularity among neurobiologists. At that time, Gazzaniga was studying humans with split brains: patients in whom the left and right hemispheres of the cerebral cortex had been surgically separated as a treatment for severe epilepsy. In those experiments, Gazzaniga and his mentor, the Nobel laureate Roger Sperry, attempted to determine whether the left and right halves of the brain contained functionally independent modules.

To achieve that goal, Gazzaniga developed experimental techniques that allowed him to communicate independently with the right and left halves of these patients' brains. When he did that, he was able to show that the right and left hemispheres were highly specialized, often performing particular tasks in complete independence. He demonstrated, in essence, that if one separated the brain into two subbrains, different behavioral goals were being achieved by the independent modules of the two half-brains.

Literally hundreds of studies have confirmed and extended these findings. Just as Gall had proposed, specific abilities (for example speech) appear to reside in identifiable modules that have discrete neurobiological locations in the brain. While it is not yet clear how each of these modules is constructed, the evidence suggests that modules are typically composed of a few square millimeters or centimeters of brain tissue and perform very specific functions. As Kathleen Baynes, Gazzaniga, and their colleagues put it (Baynes et al., 1998):

> One of the central challenges to cognitive neuroscience is to unmask the apparent unitary nature of perceptual, memorial, and cognitive systems. Neuropsychological analyses, functional brain imaging methodologies, and analyses of normal reaction times have contributed to revealing how seemingly unitary processes are made up of multiple components. Frequently these multiple components are distributed across the hemispheres but appear unified because of the integration that is possible through the corpus callosum [the neural pathway that connects the left and right hemispheres of the brain].

The available psychological and biological evidence thus seems to favor the idea that neural processing can be usefully conceptualized as modular. While the precise scale at which the architecture of the brain operates remains a subject of experimental inquiry, we can conclude with some certainty that neural processing is neither completely global nor as local as reflex theory implies. For neurobiologists this naturally raises the question of how modules arise, how circumscribed are the problems that they engage, and what defines the goals they accomplish. In part the answer to those questions can be obtained only by asking them in an evolutionary context: How did any given neurobiological module evolve and what computational goals did it evolve to achieve? This is an absolutely critical question because the computational approach starts by defining an a priori goal for a neurobiological module, a biological structure that is the product of evolution. We turn, therefore, to the question of evolution and whether we can even consider the notion of a computational goal as an organizational principle for module production in an evolved biological system.

Evolution

What, exactly, is the computational goal of a neurobiological module, and is it meaningful even to posit the existence of goals for systems developed by the haphazard process of evolution? Debate over this question may be the most contentious legacy of Marr's paradigm. For a computer scientist or an electrical engineer designing or studying a man-made system, this issue never arises. A human engineer designed the system to achieve a goal. But we really think of biological systems that have evolved over millions of years as having goals in this same way? If we can, are there general principles that describe the kinds of goals evolved systems accomplish?

In 1859 Darwin wrote: "This preservation of favorable variations and the rejection of injurious variations I call Natural Selection." Darwin argued that by the gradual accretion of favorable variations, animals would evolve toward what he called "more perfect forms." "When we see any structure highly perfected for any particular habit, as the wings of a bird for flight, we should bear in mind that animals displaying early transitional grades of the structure will seldom continue to exist to the present day, for they will have been supplanted by the very process of perfection through natural selection" (Darwin, 1859). Darwin realized that the processes by which variations accrue would be fairly random, and the need for animals bearing the "transitional grades" of structures reflecting random changes favored by natural selection meant that evolution could not guarantee that optimal forms (in our terms, modules that achieve computational goals perfectly) could be produced in real animals. He found this a frustrating paradox. Many animal forms appeared nearly "perfect," but it seemed impossible that perfection could be achieved by natural selection. As Darwin put it with regard to the very problem Marr would later address:

To suppose that the eye, with all its inimitable contrivances for adjusting the focus to different distances, for admitting different amounts of light, and for the correction of spherical and chromatic aberration, could have been formed by Natural Selection, seems, I freely confess, absurd in the highest possible degree. (Darwin, 1859)

Nonetheless, the eye does exist, and it does seem in many ways to capture light in a very efficient manner. Indeed, there is clear evidence that the retina is a nearly optimal detector of photonic energy and that the limits of retinal sensitivity are imposed more by the properties of quantum physics than by constraints on evolution. Still, it seems impossible to believe that evolution drives animals toward optimal and complete solutions to specific computational problems that can be defined in abstract terms. Even Darwin would have found this hard to believe. On the other hand, there are examples in which animal forms do seem to have adopted solutions to physical problems that function with nearly perfect efficiency, or at least it appears so at first blush.

Gould and Lewontin

In the late 1970s the Harvard biologists Steven J. Gould and Richard Lewontin addressed this issue directly, arguing that biological systems simply could not, on logical grounds, be conceptualized as optimally or nearly optimally achieving any abstractly defined goal. In the absence of that conceptualization, they argued, one should never even think of a biological system as achieving a goal of any type. They developed this idea in a now famous analogy to Renaissance architecture:

The great central dome of St. Mark's cathedral in Venice presents in its mosaic design a detailed iconography expressing the mainstays of Christian faith. Three circles of figures radiate out from a central image of Christ: angels, disciples, and virtues. Each circle is divided into quadrants, even though the dome itself is radially symmetrical in structure. Each quadrant meets one of the four spandrels in the arches below the dome. Spandrels—the tapering triangular spaces formed by the intersection of two rounded arches at right angles—are necessary architectural by-products of mounting a dome on rounded arches. Each spandrel contains a design admirably fitted into its tapering space. An evangelist sits in the upper part flanked by the heavenly cities....

The design is so elaborate, harmonious and purposeful that we are tempted to view it as the starting point of any analysis, as the cause in some sense of the surrounding architecture [or *goal* of the design, in Marr's terms]. But that would invert the proper path of analysis. The system begins with the architectural constraint: the necessary four spandrels and their tapering triangular form. They provide a space in which the mosaicists worked; they set the quadripartite symmetry of the dome above.

. . .

We wish to question a deeply ingrained habit of thinking among students of evolution.... It is rooted in a notion popularized by A. R. Wallace and A. Weismann ... the near omnipotence of natural selection in forging organic design and fashioning the best among possible worlds. The programme regards natural selection as so powerful and the constraints on it so few that direct production of adaptation through its operation becomes the primary cause of nearly all organic form, function, and behavior.

An organism is atomized into "traits" [or *computations*, in Marr's terms] and these traits are explained as structures optimally designed by natural selection for their functions. For lack of space, we must omit an extended discussion of this vital issue "what is a trait [or a *module*]?"

. . .

[In fact] constraints upon evolutionary change may be ordered into at least two categories. All evolutionists are familiar with *phyletic* constraints, as embodied in Gregory's classical distinction between habitus and heritage. We acknowledge a kind of phyletic inertia in recognizing, for example, that humans are not optimally designed for upright posture because so much of our *Bauplan* evolved for quadripedal life. We also invoke phyletic constraint in explaining why no molluscs fly in the air and no insects are as large as elephants.

The German paleontologist A. Seilacher ... has emphasized what he calls architectural constraints. These arise not from former adaptations retained in a new ecological setting, but as architectural restrictions that were never adaptations, rather the necessary consequences of materials and designs selected to build the Bauplan. (Gould and Lewontin, 1979)

In neurobiological terms, Gould and Lewontin made two critical points that cannot be overlooked. First, animals simply were not designed to achieve computational goals. A computational goal is a logical end point, the complete solution to a problem that could in principle be solved by the animal. For all we know, phyletic and architectural constraints may prevent natural selection from attaining computational goals even if achieving those goals would maximize the evolutionary fitness of the animal. If Gould and Lewontin are correct in this assertion, it may be very difficult for us to use the computational goal as a starting point for the kind of analysis Marr proposed, even if we understand the relationship between a computational goal and evolutionary fitness. Second, this analysis relies upon a knowledge of the level at which a computational goal should be specified. It requires that we be able to identify the boundaries of a neurobiological module, or trait, in order to bound the computational problem it solves.

The Need for an Optimal Benchmark: Defining the Evolutionary Goals of Neural Computation

It seems clear that at a logical level this is a critical problem with any approach that stresses function. In order to employ a functionalist approach, it is necessary at some level to be able to estimate the function of the system under study. One way to do that is to complete a full characterization of the system under every possible condition. Exhaustively measuring, in a purely empirical way, all possible functions of the system. But this approach is almost always impractical and as a result it is almost always necessary to rely on a theoretical analysis of function. One cannot, for example, hope to characterize the goal of vision by showing a human subject all possible visual images and asking what perceptual experience each image produced. The other possibility, and the one implicitly advocated by Marr's approach, is to assume that the system was evolved to achieve a specifiable, and theoretically defined, mathematical goal so as to maximize the fitness of the organism.

I should, however, point out that while one cannot hope to characterize all of behavior by using a strategy of exhaustive measurement, this strategy does work well for very small systems. Reflexology is, at some level, an approach of this type. It relies on constraining the subject of study to a tiny deterministic linkage, fully characterizing that system, and identifying the minimal set of connections that can produce that linkage as if it were a goal. Marr's effort to characterize human vision lies near the other extreme. He assumed that the goal of the visual system could be defined as "a process that produces from images of the external world a description that is useful to the viewer and not cluttered with irrelevant information" (Marr, 1982). Unfortunately, he had no specific evidence to support this functionalist assertion that vision produces a useful description of the external world. In order to make that assertion, Marr had to assume that natural selection had forced the visual system to achieve this goal. The problem is that we simply cannot assume a priori that natural selection does force the visual system to a complete and correct solution to every computational puzzle which bears on an organism's survival. In fact, the mere existence of phyletic and architectural constraints strongly suggests that no actual neural system could ever achieve any computational goal with 100 percent efficiency.

Marr's recognition of the value of stated computational goals, combined with the fact that biological systems probably cannot achieve computational goals perfectly, raises an empirical question upon which the computational approach hinges. Given that we cannot assume a priori that evolved systems achieve evolutionarily defined computational goals on theoretical grounds, we need to ask empirically just how close these systems come to achieving those goals in practice. If, in practice, evolved systems do even a fair job of approximating what we humans can define as a computational goal, then the strategy Marr advocates will be useful. If evolutionary systems are forests of spandrels in which phyletic and architectural constraints do far more to shape organisms than do the problems these organisms face in the external world, then Marr's approach will be largely useless.

For this reason it is critical to examine the efficiency with which computational goals related to evolutionary fitness are achieved or approximated in real biological systems. The utility of the computational approach hinges on this empirical point. Because this question is so important to deciding whether a functionalist strategy can be of any use to neurobiologists, the remainder of this chapter examines this question from two vantage points. First, we look at systems for which a computational goal can be clearly and quantitatively specified and ask, in a mathematical sense, how closely the solution achieved by a well-studied biological module approximates this goal. The second approach is much more inferential but also of value. We ask whether a large number of unrelated organisms employ a similar strategy when they face a common problem; we look for evidence of convergent evolution. Convergent evolution, when animals with different phyletic and architectural constraints converge to a common solution, suggests the existence of a common end point for the process of evolution. Such an end point, if it exists, may constitute evidence that a single evolutionarily relevant computational problem is being solved with high fidelity by the convergent organisms.

Achieving a Defined Goal: Phototransduction

When an organism relies for survival on vision in a dimly lit environment, it faces a problem that can be clearly defined. Under dim conditions a very small number of photons are being reflected by objects surrounding the organism. These photons carry information about the objects off of which they were reflected. Under these conditions, photons are extremely rare, and only by efficiently capturing and analyzing these rare photons can a system derive visual information about objects in the outside world.

So what is the computational goal of a module specialized to gather visual information under low-light conditions? Almost by definition, the goal of such a system would be to achieve an efficient counting of the number of photons reflected by each object in the environment. How efficient is "efficient"? A perfect system would have to be able to detect even single photons, the tiny packets of energy that are the elementary quantum mechanical particles of light. But trying to count individual photons seems an almost herculean task for a biological system. Is there any reason to believe that an evolved system could detect, let alone count, a single photon? Surely we have to assume that architectural and phyletic constraints would prevent any real system from achieving that goal. Despite this logic, our best estimates of the performance of the vertebrate phototransduction system seem to indicate that single photons can be detected, and accurately counted, by the rod cells of the retina.

The rod cells themselves are tiny tubes about 10 micrometers in diameter and the first step in photon counting is for these cells to detect photons. This occurs when a photon strikes one of the many *rhodopsin* molecules in a rod, causing a change in the conformational structure of the molecule. Of course the amount of energy in a single photon is truly tiny, only 1.3×10^{-27} joules at the frequency to which the rhodopsin molecule is *most* sensitive. Despite the tiny amount of energy this represents, physiologists and chemists have been able to show that the rhodopsin molecule is so sensitive that interaction with a single photon causes it to radically change shape almost instantaneously. Surely if a molecule has evolved to be this sensitive to such a tiny amount of energy, phyletic or architectural constraints will force that molecule to be highly unstable. It cannot possibly simultaneously achieve the computational goals of sensitivity to a single photon and tremendous stability in the absence of photons. Empirical studies, however, suggest that rhodopsin actually does achieve both of these goals. Despite the fact that rhodopsin isomerizes readily when it interacts with a single photon, a single molecule of rhodopsin will spontaneously isomerize only once every 300 years. The rhodopsin molecule achieves the computational goal of efficient phototransduction even though it is the product of evolution.

Given the observation that the rhodopsin molecule achieves a computational goal that can be specified, perhaps this is an unusual example. Perhaps the larger system within which rhodopsin molecules are embedded is not nearly so efficient. After all, when a single photon isomerizes a single molecule of rhodopsin, only a single molecule within the brain has been altered. Can an evolved system detect the isomerization of a single molecule and pass this on to higher centers? Once again the answer turns out to be yes. The isomerization of a single rhodopsin molecule sets in process an almost perfectly reliable, low-noise biochemical amplifier that leads ultimately to the generation of a robust electrical current, a current whose strength is strictly proportional to the number of photons absorbed by the rod. This signal, which reports the number of photons counted, is then passed to the rest of the visual system for further analysis. (For an introduction to the biophysics of phototransduction, see Rieke and Baylor, 1998.)

It would be unfair to say that the phototransduction process achieves the goal of photon counting with anything like perfect efficiency. While it achieves this goal more efficiently than some of the most sophisticated man-made devices available today, it is clearly an imperfect system. For example, a fraction of the photons that stream toward the eye are absorbed by the tissue of the cornea rather than by the rods. This absorption, which reflects an imperfect transparency of the cornea, may be an architectural constraint. The cornea has evolved a high degree of transparency, but it may be impossible to use a cornea-like architecture to achieve 100 percent transparency. Constraints like those proposed by Gould and Lewontin probably do operate here, but at an empirical level these constraints seem to have only minor effects. What can we conclude from this? I think that we can conclude that Gould and Lewontin are right in principle: There are architectural constraints that make neurobiological processes imperfect. But it also seems very clear that in this case the computational goal does provide an effective tool for thinking about phototransduction. This neurobiological system may not actually achieve this goal, but it does seem to come close enough that Marr's approach can offer real value.

As one might expect, similar analyses have been conducted for a number of neural systems. The hair cells of the inner ear, for example, seem to be able to detect the collisions between individual water molecules in the fluid that surrounds them. As a result, the efficiency of auditory transduction seems to be limited primarily by the thermodynamic constraints of Brownian motion. Similar efficiencies have been measured in a number of other sensory systems as well. These data argue at an empirical level that at least when the computational goal is easy for us to define, evolved biological systems approximate those computational goals.

What about more complex systems? How closely do they achieve evolutionary goals? Although we may ultimately know the answer to this question, very few complex systems have been studied well enough for us to answer this question today. Studies of convergent evolution, however, may give us a hint that evolutionary goals exist and are approximated even in more complex systems. To develop that argument, we turn to one of the most studied groups of animals in the world, the cichlid fishes of the African Rift Valley.

Convergent Evolution: Cichlid Fishes

Along a line running from Lake Victoria in Kenya to Lake Malawi west of Mozambique lies one of the most complex river and lake ecologies in the world. Three enormous freshwater seas, Lake Victoria, Lake Tanganyika, and Lake Malawi, lie interconnected among a forest of rivers and smaller lakes. (See figure 7.1.) If you travel to any of these lakes and cast a net, you catch representatives from literally hundreds of species of small spiny fishes, most of which belong to the family Cichlidae.

For argument's sake, let us begin by examining the species we might find at a field station beside Lake Tanganyika. Along the rocky banks of this 1–2-million-year-old lake we would find a group of cichlid species specialized for scraping algae off the rocks. These fish would be easy to recognize by the shapes of their mouths and the structure of their teeth. Although we might find several species of algae scrapers at our field station, they would almost certainly fall into three main types: grazers, browsers, and tappers. Lake Tanganyika's grazers would be identifiable because their teeth and jaws are specialized to act as combs that brush through the filamentous carpet of algae at the water's edge. Browsers would be algal scrapers with rasps for mouths: mouths specialized for breaking off the tough algal carpet itself. Finally, the tappers could be identified by their sharp teeth and strong heads that cut and pull algae from the rocks. All three of these types would be quite similar in body shape: basically oval fish that can move efficiently among the algae but are not particularly fast or maneuverable in open water.

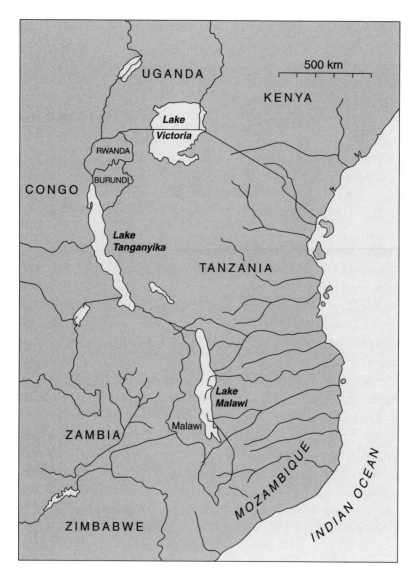

Figure 7.1
The Rift Valley Lakes of East Africa.

In the waters just off the rocky coast we might encounter a group of scale rippers. These are fish that wait in ambush for another cichlid to swim by. They then race toward their prey and, using a band of teeth shaped like a broad file, rasp scales from the tail, gaining all of their nutrition from these stolen scales.

Now imagine that we were to travel 1000 kilometers south to the shores of 10-million-year-old Lake Malawi. Once again we set about looking for fish of these four types. Once again we find three groups of fish specialized for algal scraping and fish specialized for scale ripping. Perhaps most amazing of all, we would see that each of these four groups of fish look almost identical in both Lake Tanganyika and Lake Malawi. (See figure 7.2).

How might we interpret this observation? What is the relationship between the scale rippers of Lake Tanganyika and the scale rippers of Lake Malawi? The simplest explanation for the similarity of these fish goes something like this: Once, millions of years ago, there was a single ancient species of scale ripper. The primordial scale ripper had developed a mouth that worked well at scale ripping. This ancient species of scale ripper diffused slowly through the many lakes of the Rift Valley, leaving progeny in both Lake Tanganyika and Lake Malawi. In time, through random variation, the ancient scale ripper species gave rise to a family of closely related subspecies within each lake. With more time each of these subspecies finally evolved into a full-fledged species. Speciation sprang, in each lake, from a common ancestor. If this were the case, it would hardly be surprising that the scale rippers in each lake were so similar; they would be similar mostly because they were derived from a common ancestor.

Since the 1960s a number of cichlid biologists have begun to question this explanation. How, they wonder, did each of the ancestral fish travel so readily among the lakes of the Rift Valley in order achieve such a uniform dispersal? How could such uniform dispersal patterns be achieved, given that Lake Malawi was already 8 million years old when Lake Tanganyika was formed?

Recently, both basic anatomical studies and molecular biological techniques have made it possible to ask the question directly: What is the

Tanganyika   Malawi

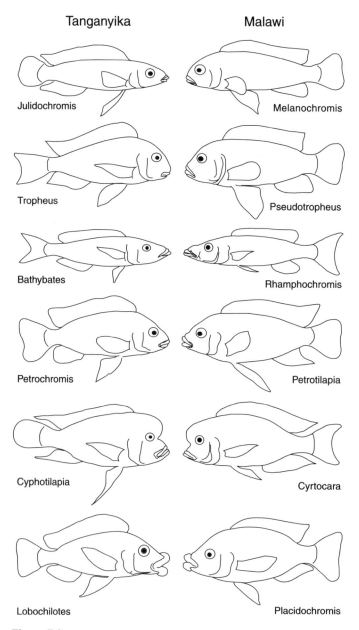

Figure 7.2
Convergent evolution in Lakes Tanganyika and Malawi. (Courtesy of Axel Meyer)

relatedness of the many species of cichlids that have been observed in Lake Tanganyika and Lake Malawi? When biologists began to do this work, they found a surprising result. They found that all of the many kinds of species *within each lake* are very closely related genetically, as if they had evolved from a single common ancestor cichlid species (or a small number of ancestor fish) that had populated only that lake. Surprisingly, the very similar-looking species found in different lakes are not at all closely related. Genetic data indicate that algae scrapers and scale rippers, to take only two examples, evolved separately in each lake, and they evolved from very different ancestor fish. The algae scrapers and the scale rippers in Lake Tanganyika are closely related *to each other* and are descended from a common ancestor. Similarly, the algae scrapers and the scale rippers in Lake Malawi are closely related to each other and are descended from a common ancestor, *but only distantly related to fish in Lake Tanganyika.*

In other words, the algae eaters in each lake seem to have evolved independently and from different ancestors. Despite this significant genetic difference, they appear to have converged on a similar jaw structure for algae scraping. The scale rippers in each lake also evolved independently, from different ancestors, and have converged on a similar mouth structure and body shape. This is a critical observation because it is exactly what you would expect if there was a nearly optimal body structure for surviving as an algae scraper or as a scale ripper, and if the jaws of cichlids had evolved again and again toward those goals irrespective of the species from which they started. (For an overview of the cichlid literature see Meyer, 1993; Goldschmidt, 1996; Stiassny and Meyer, 1999; Barlow, 2000.)

The cichlids are not the only example that we know of in which a flock of species seem to converge toward a particular set of traits even when they come from different genetic backgrounds. The anole lizards of the Bahamas are another example. On each Bahamian island there seems to be a set of four or five basic types of anoles that include a species specialized for living in trees and a species specialized for living in grasses. Across different islands the tree anoles all look alike, as do the grass anoles. Just as with the cichlids, genetic analyses suggest that all of the anole species on each island are almost always descended from a single common ancestor that varies from island to island. Just as in the case of the cichlids, it looks as if the specific details of the body plan of the organisms in each environment are specified more by the niche into which they evolved than by the differences among their many ancestors (Beuttell and Losos, 1999; Losos, 2001).

The data from the cichlids and the anoles hints that evolution can drive the features of organisms toward survival-related goals which are defined by the environment. Our neurobiological data also point in this direction when we examine processes like sensory transduction. But it is certainly true than these data are open to alternative interpretation and to criticism. First, it is important to remember that sensory transduction may be a very simple process compared with the more complex behavioral goals we hope to study with computational approaches. Second, the observation that jaw morphology and feeding behavior suggest convergent evolution in cichlids does not guarantee that cichlid algae scrapers approach perfect efficiency at food gathering or that cichlids are a typical group of species. Each of these conclusions needs to be examined in more detail. But even given these caveats, the pattern in this data is undeniably suggestive. These data and others like them raise the question of whether the lessons we learn about evolution's apparent ability to optimize an organism's simple traits can be generalized to the study of computational goals in complex neurobiological or behavioral systems.

Generalizing to Complex Systems?
In neurobiology, probably the first person to venture an answer to that question was the English physiologist Horace Barlow. In the 1950s Barlow was interested in whether the encoding of sensory data after phototransduction was complete was performed using a maximally efficient process. He assessed this by using the mathematical tool of information theory to determine coding efficiency.

[The tendency of sensory systems to respond only when a stimulus changes but not when a stimulus remains constant] may be regarded as a mechanism for compressing sensory messages into fewer impulses by decreasing the tendency for serial correlations in the values of impulse intervals. There must be many occasions when neighboring sense organs are subjected to the same stimulus, and this will lead to correlations in the values of impulses in neighboring fibres. This offers scope for further economy of impulses, and one might look for a mechanism to perform the appropriate recoding. [A form of recoding that] would ... diminish the correlations between impulse intervals spatially separated ... [and thus would, according to information theory, achieve a more nearly optimal encoding of the sensory event].

A mechanism which seems designed to do just this has been found in the compound eye of *Limulus* [the common horseshoe crab]. Light falling on an ommatidium causes a discharge of impulses in the nerve fibre connected to that ommatidium, but the number of impulses is reduced if light falls on a neighboring ommatidium at the same time. A mechanism which must have similar functional results is found in the frog's and cat's retina, but there is no possibility that this mechanism is related phylogenetically to that in *Limulus*, for the structures involved are totally different. [And the species involved are separated by more than 300 million years of evolution.] Evidence is also accumulating that [this process which is called] "lateral inhibition" ... [occurs] elsewhere in the nervous system [for example, in the cochlear nucleus of the ear and in the somatosensory cortex]. (Barlow, 1961)

Barlow was arguing that mechanisms in the eyes of horseshoe crabs, and in the brains of frogs and cats, achieved a highly efficient encoding of incoming data, using an almost identical computational strategy. He went on to argue that the technique by which this encoding was accomplished was defined more by the mathematical constraints of information theory than by the phyletic or architectural constraints of the organism. In essence, Barlow was arguing that he could both define a clear computational goal for sensory encoding on a priori grounds and find evidence of convergent evolution around that computational goal. As a result, Barlow's example comes very close to demonstrating that complex computational goals can be both defined theoretically and achieved biologically. Barlow's data suggest that Marr's computational approach may work. But even Barlow's example is fairly simple. Sensory encoding is a simple process when compared with something as complicated as finding a mate or searching for food. Can processes as complicated as these be modeled and studied with an evolutionarily based computational approach? Can we define a priori goals when considering computational tasks that are this complete? As we will see in the second half of this book, there is growing evidence to suggest that this approach may be applicable to even the most complex of behavioral processes.

Marr, Evolution, and Modules: The Road Ahead

David Marr suggested that an alternative to studying how local neural circuits operate was to attempt a more functionalist approach. One should, he argued, define modular goals that the brain ought to accomplish and then try to develop mathematical descriptions of those goals. These modular mathematical descriptions could then serve as guides for behavioral and physiological investigations.

Two critical objections have been raised to this approach. First, it is not yet clear how to modularize neural function. Searching for mechanisms that achieve modular computations may fail if one selects a scale other than the one the architecture of the brain employs. I believe that this is a very reasonable criticism, but one that can be resolved empirically. There is already a tremendous amount of evidence suggesting that the brain operates in a modular fashion. To be sure, we do need to learn how to identify modules more efficiently, but as long as modules exist, Marr's approach should empirically be possible. The second major criticism that Marr's approach has faced is that it has been unclear whether evolution can be conceived of as a process that structures nervous systems to accomplish goals with enough efficiency to make the computational goal a useful starting point for neurobiological analysis.

An analysis of many systems, however, seems to suggest that neural processing may often be very efficient at achieving computational goals. What we already know indicates that specified goals can at least begin to define what it is that animals actually do. In fact, one could even argue that it is when animals can be shown to deviate from these optimal goals that we have succeeded in identifying a phyletic or architectural constraint of the type Gould and Lewontin described. Viewed this way, the evolutionary definition of an optimal solution can be seen as a critical tool for identifying phyletic and architectural constraints. The major goal of computational neuroscience could, in a sense, be described as a search for the neurobiological mechanisms that produce these constraints.

René Descartes began *L'Homme* thus:

These men will be composed, as we are, of a soul and a body; and I must first describe for you the body; then, also separately, the soul; and finally I must show you how these two natures would have to be joined and united to constitute men. . . .

I assume their body to be but a statue, an earthen machine formed intentionally by God to be as much as possible like us. Thus not only does he give it externally the shapes and color of all the parts of our bodies; He also places inside it all the pieces required to make it walk, eat, breathe.... (Descartes, 1664)

Descartes tried to explain how the physical hardware of the material world could be used to construct an object that behaved like a human. Marr challenges us to invert that approach. Begin not with the hardware, but with the problem that the hardware solves. Then ask how the solution is accomplished. Only in this way can one truly understand how the nervous system functions.

The reason Marr even conceived of this approach was that at heart he was a computer scientist and not a biologist. For biologists, approaching form via function has always been problematic. How can we ever be sure that we understand the function of a biological process? But recently a number of biologists have begun to suggest that we can begin to study, and to understand, function in a meaningful sense. The goal of the nervous system is to maximize the inclusive fitness of the organism. And fitness is ultimately constrained by the same physical laws that govern the planetary motion Kepler, Galileo, and Laplace described. Rod cells must capture photons if animals are to see under dim illumination. The problem they face can be described by quantum mechanics, and rod cells actually seem to efficiently solve the quantum mechanical problem that they face.

For a cognitive neuroscientist, Marr's paradigm raises the question of whether we can use rigorous mathematical tools to define the global behavioral goals of an animal in evolutionary terms. It then asks whether we can use empirical approaches to separate and analyze the neurobiological modules that animals employ to achieve their evolutionary goals. As we will see in the second section of this book, many neurobiologists working today believe that this is possible. This is an approach that may even allow us to resolve the dualism of body and soul, or of reflex and volition, recasting the way we ask questions about the nervous system.

II

Neuroeconomics

8

Defining the Goal: Extending Marr's Approach

The Goal of Behavior

In the last chapter I quoted David Marr: "an algorithm is likely to be understood more readily by understanding the nature of the problem being solved than by examining the mechanism (and the hardware) in which it is embodied." In the first half of this book I tried to make two critical and related arguments. First, I argued that all classical approaches to understanding the relationship between behavior and brain derived from the work of Descartes, and focused more on defining a minimally complex mechanism for producing a behavior than on understanding the problem that the behavior engaged. Second, I argued that our notions of what would constitute a minimally complex neural circuit have been shaped by the development of determinate mathematics; mathematical systems developed for describing predictable cause-and-effect relationships in the physical world.

In the late 1970s the mathematician and neurobiologist David Marr explicitly questioned the first of these classical notions: the notion that physiological studies of behavior should seek to define the minimally complex neural circuits which could account for minimally complex behaviors. Marr argued that in order to understand the relationship between a behavior and the brain, we must first understand the goal of that behavior. Marr's approach was, however, fraught with problems. Two in particular stood out. First, it was unclear how neuroscientists could hope to define the goals of behavior in rigorous mathematical terms. Second, it was unclear how the presence or absence of processing modules within the nervous system would be related to goals defined on abstract mathematical grounds. In the preceding chapter I argued that there is some hope that we can address these problems by seeking to define the goals of behavior in evolutionary terms, and then can use physiological tools to identify, understand, and delimit the neurobiological modules that achieve these goals.

Replacing Minimal Complexity: Inclusive Fitness

At a very fundamental level the goal of all behavior must be to use sensory data and stored knowledge of the structure of the world to produce motor responses that are adaptive. The goal of the nervous system, ultimately, must be to produce motor responses that yield the highest possible inclusive fitness[1] for an organism. Of course phyletic and architectural constraints will limit both how high a level of inclusive fitness an animal can achieve and the mechanism by which that level of fitness is produced, but at an evolutionary level we *can* specify the goal of behavior and brain. The goal of behavior is to make the right choices; to choose the course of action that maximizes the survival of the organism's genetic code.

What are the right choices? How are behavior and Darwinian fitness related? This is a complex, but not necessarily intractable, problem. Often, simple, externally observable variables, like the efficiency with which photons are counted, will be tightly correlated with fitness. In other cases the link may be more obscure, but as I hope will become clear in the next several chapters, there is no conceptual barrier to identifying the fitness-related goals of behavior.

To make this clear imagine a simpler world, one fully described by a concise set of deterministic equations and populated organisms whose genetic fitness is easily computed, a world in which single living white billiard balls inhabit the surfaces of inanimate billiard tables. One living

---

1. The inclusive fitness of an organism is the rate at which its genes are propagated, and this rate of propagation specifically includes genetic propagation by brothers, sisters, and other relatives as well as self-propagation. For an overview of the concept of inclusive fitness as William Hamilton developed it, see either E. O. Wilson's 1975 book *Sociobiology* or Robert Trivers's 1985 book *Social Evolution*. Hamilton's original work on the subject is considered a major landmark in the development of evolutionary theory (Hamilton, 1964a, 1964b).

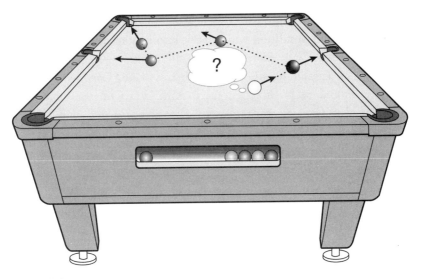

Figure 8.1
A determinate billiard ball world.

billiard ball inhabits each table. For argument, let us assume that the
surface of each table is also occupied by four inanimate billiard balls
that are distributed randomly across the table's surface. Imagine that the
reproductive fitness of our animate billiard balls is determined in a
straightforward fashion. The white billiard balls that produce the most
descendants are those which clear their tables of inanimate balls quickly;
the more quickly a white ball can clear its table of inanimate billiard
balls, the fitter the ball. Our billiard balls can even face architectural
constraints; balls may be able to propel themselves forward only at a
fixed initial velocity and along a straight line. (See figure 8.1.)

Because the movements of the balls must obey the laws of Newtonian
physics and because we posit a relationship between the behavior and
the fitness of these imaginary organisms, it is possible for us to fully
specify the evolutionary goal of any white billiard ball's behavior. The
nervous system of the white ball should use sensory input that specifies
the locations of each inanimate ball and a stored representation of the
laws of physics to compute a set of movements that will clear the table as
quickly as possible. The nervous system of the white ball should select an

initial movement, setting off in a single direction at a fixed initial velocity. That direction of motion will bring it into contact with one or more other balls, which will result in a fixed and entirely predictable set of collisions. By examining all possible first, second, third, and fourth moves, it should be possible for us, looking down on the table from above, to identify in advance an optimal solution to the white billiard ball's problem. As natural scientists studying living billiard balls behaviorally from this vantage point, we could ask how closely the white balls we observe come to achieving an optimal solution for any given configuration of inanimate balls. Studying the billiard balls at a physiological level, we could ask how the ball's sensorimotor nervous system achieves the precise level of performance we observed behaviorally.

Marr had recognized that nervous systems could be conceptualized as goal-driven in this way, but had devoted little energy to developing a schema for specifying behavioral goals. Evolutionary theory, however, provides just such a schema. It suggests that, in the end, there is only one goal for all of behavior—the maximization of inclusive fitness. The example of the billiard ball captures a part of this approach, allowing us to define and test a behavioral efficiency. Perhaps the most interesting thing that this toy example suggests is that the global function of the nervous system can be characterized as decision making with regard to evolutionary fitness. Of course it will not always be possible to specify the relationship between behavior and fitness on a priori grounds, as we have done here. In some cases—for example, when examining the efficiencies with which animals gather food—we may be able to make strong inferences about the relationship between fitness and behavior. In other cases the link may be indirect and require experimental validation. But, as we will see in the next chapter, the techniques for obtaining that validation are becoming well developed.

Darwin suggested that natural selection shapes animals toward a more fit state. It acts to push surviving organisms toward a state of maximal fitness. Behavior, the product of the nervous system, contributes to fitness, and so must also be shaped by evolution. The evolutionary process therefore defines a goal for the nervous system: the maximization of inclusive fitness. The function of the nervous system can be defined as the selection and execution of behaviors that maximize inclusive fitness as much as possible.

Marr said that "an algorithm is likely to be understood more readily by understanding the nature of the problem being solved than by examining the mechanism (and the hardware) in which it is embodied." I want to suggest that at a global level we can characterize the function of the nervous system as *decision making*. Deciding how to withdraw a hand from a sharp tack. Deciding what direction to move. Deciding whether to look to the left or to the right after viewing a field of moving dots. These are all decisions that the nervous system makes, decisions that are the product of evolutionary, developmental, or moment-to-moment processes. In these terms, even Descartes's reflexes can be seen as the simple functional decisions that the nervous system makes when it is faced with very simple problems that define an obvious goal for the organism.

Replacing Determinate Models: Probability Theory

If we can characterize the function of the nervous system in evolutionary terms as decision making, then it seems essential to develop a conceptual benchmark based on this idea, to rigorously define optimal decision processes for the maximization of inclusive fitness. These are the benchmarks against which empirical measurements of behavior should be made.

Unfortunately classical examples in which the benchmark relies on determinate mathematics, like the example of the white billiard ball, may be quite atypical of the kind of decision making that real nervous systems must face. One reason that stating the goal of our white billiard ball's nervous system was easy was that we assumed the white ball lived in a predictable Newtonian world and had complete knowledge of the state of that world. Given those constraints, we could use simple determinate equations to identify an optimal motor response. Do real animals often face problems like these? How often can we, when studying the organisms we hope to understand, use determinate mathematical formulas to identify a behavioral goal with the mathematical precision that Marr employed? (See figure 8.2.)

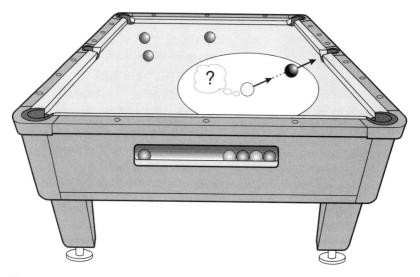

Figure 8.2
Epistemological uncertainty in a billiard ball world.

Imagine that our white billiard ball had a limited knowledge of the world around it. Imagine that it could only detect inanimate balls that lay on the table surface within a foot of its current position. Incomplete knowledge makes identifying the optimal response considerably more difficult. There is no way for the white ball to use simple determinate tools to compute an optimal solution if it does not know where all the inanimate balls are located. In any world where significant uncertainty exists, determinate tools, no matter how sophisticated, simply fail to identify optimal responses. And without a way to identify goals under real-world conditions like these, how can we ever hope to apply Marr's approach to the study of behavior?

In the next several chapters I will argue that in practice this has been the crucial problem for Marr's approach, an even more crucial problem than those imposed by modularity and evolution (or inclusive fitness theory). It is easy enough to specify a computational goal if you have full knowledge of a deterministic world, but we rarely have full knowledge of the state of the world. The real challenge faced by the nervous system is to select a motor response (to make a decision) that maximizes evolutionary fitness under conditions of uncertainty.

The remainder of this chapter explores this problem. It asks what tools mathematicians and philosophers have developed for identifying solutions to problems that involve uncertainty. As we will see, identifying optimal solutions under conditions of uncertainty has been a central problem faced by economic theorists since the seventeenth century. As a result, the mathematical techniques of economists will become a focus as we seek to derive tools for defining the goals of behavior in an uncertain world.

Uncertainty, Value, and Economics

When Descartes developed the idea of the determinate reflex, he led us to focus our neurobiological efforts on the study of determinate responses to determinate phenomena. But at the same time that Descartes and his colleagues selected determinate mathematics as the central tool by which neurobiology would be shaped, a second branch of mathematics was being born—a branch which, perhaps because of Descartes's focus on the determinate reflex, would have almost no influence on physiology for the next three centuries. This was a branch of mathematics that was initially focused on simply describing uncertain events but soon came to be a general-purpose tool for modeling decision making in an uncertain world. It was a set of ideas that would become the central components of modern economic theory.

The thesis of this book is that the fundamental limitation which neurobiology faces today is a failure to adequately incorporate probability theory into the approaches we use to understand the brain. In the mid-seventeenth century mathematics branched into two related but independent areas: determinate mathematics and probability theory. Descartes identified determinate mathematics as the central tool for the study of behavior and brain, and since then neurobiology has largely followed his lead. While probability theory became the central tool for understanding efficient decision making by humans, markets, and corporations, the relationship between probability theory and neural function has, until recently, remained largely unexplored.

The rest of this book makes the case that mathematical theories of decision making that include probability theory must form the core of future approaches to understanding the relationship between behavior and brain, because understanding the relationship between behavior and brain is fundamentally about understanding decision making. To explain why I and many others believe that is the case, we have to examine the history of probability theory and the close relationship between probability theory and decision making.

The Birth of Probability Theory

When I throw a six-sided die, I do not know in advance which side will land upward, but I do know that there is one chance in six that I will throw a 2. Surprisingly, before the Enlightenment this was not a fact that everyone knew. While there is no doubt that dice and other games of chance have been played since antiquity, as late as the seventeenth century neither mathematicians nor common folk seem to have had any ideas about how uncertain events could be formally characterized, quantified, or predicted.

Even while Galileo and his colleagues were making huge strides toward understanding deterministic astronomical phenomena, no one was studying the relationship between mathematics and chance—or *hazard*, as it was then called (from Arabic). At one level, this makes tremendous sense. The entire premise of the early scientific method was that when a natural phenomena appeared unpredictable, it was only because scientists had failed to understand the underlying physical process adequately. For Bacon and his colleagues, science was the process of discovering natural laws that reduced the unpredictable world to mathematical order and strict determinism.

Optimal decision making in a strictly determined world reduces to selecting the available option that maximizes one's gain. Whether it is selecting a job with a higher rate of pay or adopting a system for stereoscopic vision that yields a higher level of accuracy, efficient decision making is straightforward in a fully determined world. Sum the costs and benefits of each behavioral option, find the best available option, and produce that behavior. By working to reduce the unpredictable world to a fully determined place, Descartes and his colleagues were simply broadening the scope within which intelligent decisions of this type could be made.

At the time that the young Descartes was being educated by Jesuits in northern France, ideas about the determinate nature of the world were still very much in play. Martin Luther had died just 50 years before René Descartes was born in 1596, and Luther's call for a reformation of Christianity had shaken the foundations of Western society. Luther and other Protestant thinkers had argued, among other things, that if God was truly all-powerful and all-knowing, then he must have complete knowledge of the future. If any being had a complete knowledge of all future events, then it seemed incontrovertible to these Protestant theologians that future events must be predetermined, that the world must be a fundamentally deterministic place. Most Protestant groups took this hypothesis to its natural end point, arguing that God must know in advance which living people will achieve salvation in heaven and which will be punished with damnation.

While the notion that the world was a determinate place began to influence the Europeans who were developing the scientific method, the Church responded to the Protestant reformation with a massive sweep of reforms that were largely the product of the Council of Trent, convened by Pope Paul III in 1545. In the course of this Counterreformation, a religious order calling itself The Society of Jesus, or Jesuits, rose to prominence as one of the driving intellectual forces of the Catholic world. The Jesuits sought to provide an intellectual center for Catholicism during the Enlightenment and to respond to what they saw as the anti-authoritarian excesses of the Protestant reformation. With regard to determinism, the Jesuits argued that each man's fate should not be viewed as predetermined, but as uncertain. The divine grace of God, they argued, permitted each man to determine his own fate by his own actions. For the Jesuits, the notion of a determinate world flew in the face of free will, the exercise of which they saw as critical for salvation.

Against this Jesuit notion that each man's fate was the product of his own free will, some theological factions within the Catholic Church began to raise an objection, suggesting that in combating the Protestant reformation, the Jesuits had gone too far. Central to this philosophical debate was the Flemish theologian Cornelius Jansen. Jansen argued in the early seventeenth century that the Jesuits had driven the Church away from the theology of St. Augustine. The Church should return to its Augustinian roots, Jansen argued, and this included Augustine's belief that God, not man's free will, determines who will be saved. For the Jansenists, the Protestants had been right. The world was a determinate place. So within the Church itself a debate was raging in the late sixteenth and early seventeenth centuries about the determinate nature of the universe. During the early part of the seventeenth century, this conflict between the Jansenists and the Jesuits reached a fever pitch in France, and it was against this backdrop that Descartes was educated in the Jesuit tradition.

Descartes left this controversy largely behind when he decided to spend the bulk of his life in the Netherlands, but his own work must have been influenced by this theological battle. Descartes had argued throughout the early seventeenth century that the universe could be seen as an elaborate clockwork, a huge, determinate machine. All natural phenomena, even the behavior of animals, could be seen as expressions of clocklike lawful behavior that was subject to study by determinate mathematical law. In *L'Homme* he had argued that only the human soul possessed the ability to express the unpredictable freedom that his Jesuit teachers argued was essential for human salvation.

In France, the center of Jansenist thought was the monastery of Port Royal, a community centered around the seventeenth-century French intellectual family of Antoine Arnauld. Together, this brilliant family and their friends at Port-Royal tried unsuccessfully to defend Jansenism from suppression by the Jesuits throughout much of the seventeenth century. Their greatest and most lasting effect, however, may have been that as defenders of Jansenism they became a center for anti-establishment thinking.

The first half of the seventeenth century was a period of tremendous political and intellectual upheaval in France. While the Jesuits, who favored an indeterminate worldview, sought to have determinate Jansenism branded a heresy, France was rocked by the instability caused by Cardinal Richelieu's rise to power and by the uprisings of the Fronde that followed his death. It was against this background of sociopolitical instability and a fundamental debate about the determinate nature of the universe that the mathematics of probability theory were first developed by a young Jansenist mathematician, Blaise Pascal. (See figure 8.3.)

Figure 8.3
Blaise Pascal (Hulton Archive, IH000636).

Pascal was born into an upper-middle-class French family and demonstrated his mathematical brilliance as a teenager by publishing a treatise on conic sections at the age of sixteen. Years later, Pascal's sister Jacqueline would become a nun at Port-Royal, and it was she who would draw this iconoclastic young mathematician into the inner circle there. However, even by his mid-twenties, before Pascal had become an intimate of the Jansenist community of Arnauld and his followers, he had begun to grapple with mathematical approaches to uncertain events.

In September 1653 Pascal was invited to travel with a company of gentlemen: the Duc de Roannez (a patron of the young Pascal), the

Chevalier de Mere, and Monsieur Minton, a popular figure at court. Over the course of the journey, the Chevalier de Mere introduced Pascal to a gambling conundrum known as the "point problem" or the "division of stakes problem." Consider two gentlemen who wager 50 gold louis each on a series of coin flips. If four heads are thrown first, the Chevalier wins all 100 louis. If four tails are thrown first, the Duc collects all 100 louis. Suddenly the game is interrupted after five flips, two flips having shown tails and three flips having shown heads. The Chevalier thus lacks one head to win and the Duc lacks two tails. How should the 100 louis be divided?

It seems natural to us that the 100 louis should be divided between the players as a function of the probability that each would have won the game. In 1653, however, the word *probabilité* had not even come to mean "probability" in the sense that we use the word today. In 1653 an event was called probable if it was the opinion of someone in authority. That the blood is expanded by heating in the heart was probable in the sense that Descartes had argued this was the case. In fact, it was fairly common for an idea to be accepted as both probable and false. Even lacking the word "probability" in our sense, the Chevalier, when he proposed the problem to Pascal, shared our intuition about how to divide the 100 louis. The coins should be divided according to how likely it was that each player would win on subsequent tosses. How could one possibly know how likely it was that either player would win a game of chance?

At the time that the Chevalier posed this question, a number of approaches had been proposed to the division of stakes problem, but no one had actually been able to derive a mathematical solution. Certainly no one had been able to explain how you might actually predict the numerical likelihood that each player would win. Almost 400 years later, long after the Counterreformation and the political upheavals of the Fronde, the problem seems absurdly simple. On the next coin toss there would be two equally probable outcomes: heads, and the Chevalier wins all 100 coins; and tails, the score is tied at 3 and a second flip is made. In this case there is an even chance of either player winning. In sum, then, there must be a 75 percent chance of the Chevalier winning and a 25 percent chance of the Duc winning; they should split the coins 75/25.

Regardless of how obvious this logic is to us today, it was unavailable, even unthinkable, for the Chevalier and his friends.

Pascal seems to have been fascinated by this problem, and hoped both to solve it and to develop a mathematical method rooted in classical geometry for solving the general form of the problem. In 1654, still interested in the problem after almost a year, Pascal began a correspondence with Pierre de Fermat, a mathematician who would soon die in a duel and centuries later would became most famous for his last, unsolved, theorem. Fermat and Pascal corresponded about the points problem, and it is Pascal's letters to Fermat during that year which are almost always cited as the birth of probability theory.

July 29, 1654
Sir:
I have become just as impatient as you, and although I am still in bed I cannot refrain from telling you that last evening I received through Monsieur de Carcavi your letter on division of stakes which I admire more than I can say....

I admire the method of the points much more than that of the dice. I have seen several persons find that of the dice, among them Monsieur le Chevalier de Mere who is the one that proposed these questions to me. Also Monsieur de Roberval, but Monsieur de Mere had never been able to find the exact value of the points [Pascal really means the exact value of the probabilities, but he lacks even the words to write this idea], nor any way of arriving at it, so that I found that I was the only one who had known this proportion....

This is approximately how I determine the share of each player when, for example, there are two players engaged in a game of three points [three heads or three tails], and each player has staked 32 pistoles on the match.

Let us suppose that the first player has won two points and the second has one point; they now play for a point on the condition that if the first player wins it, he takes all the money at stake, namely 64 pistoles; if the other wins it, the games are two and two, and consequently if they wish to quit, each one ought to take out his original stake, namely the 32 pistoles apiece.

Now consider, Sir, that if the first one wins, 64 belong to him; if he loses, 32 belong to him. Hence if he does not wish to risk this point and wants to quit without it, the first player must say: "I am sure of 32 pistoles, for even if I lose this point, I shall have them; but as for the 32 others, perhaps I shall have them, perhaps you shall have them; the chances are even. So let us divide these 32 pistoles equally, and in addition you give me the 32 pistoles of which I am sure." Then he will have 48 pistoles and the other will have 16. (Pascal, 1623–1662)

In the pages that follow, Pascal goes on to develop a mathematical approach to this problem, even going so far as to include a table listing the relative probabilities under certain conditions. The single most important thing that can be gleaned from this letter, however, is what a very different starting point Pascal works from than we do. Pascal makes his argument in the same way I have, but without ever referring to probabilities per se. Instead, everything is reduced to a set of certain outcomes or even chances. The more complex probabilities that follow are all constructed from these simple building blocks. From these simple building blocks Pascal works out a set of rules that describe how events of equal probability combine to produce uneven compound probabilities. It is this notion that probabilities can be combined and compared mathematically which completely revolutionized Western thought.

Pascal's idea was immensely and immediately influential throughout Europe. Within a decade the Dutch astronomer Christiaan Huygens had completed a rudimentary textbook on probability. Within 50 years everything from life insurance to lotteries had been transformed by Pascal's insight. Insurance came to be associated with actuarial tables and mathematical measures of risk rather than with arbitrary policy values that often proved disastrous for the insurers. Pascal, however, recognized that an understanding of probability would influence more than just the teaching of mathematics and computations of risk; it would have to influence everything from theology to human decision making. His recognition that probability must influence decision making may have been Pascal's greatest contribution.

Speaking with Antoine Arnauld and the other members of Port Royal, Pascal developed what is now known as Pascal's wager on the existence of God. Although *The Wager* was not published until after Pascal's death (as part of his Christian apologia *Pensées*), the gentlemen of Port-Royal must have been familiar with Pascal's probabilistic argument by the later 1650s:

"Either God is or he is not." But to which view shall we be inclined? Reason [based on the tools of determinate mathematics] cannot decide this question ... a coin is being spun which will come down heads or tails. How will you wager? Reason [by determinate methods] cannot make you choose either, reason cannot prove either wrong.

... but you must wager. There is no choice, you are already committed. Which will you choose then? Let us see: since a choice must be made, let us see which offers you the least interest.... Let us weigh up the gain and loss involved in calling heads that God exists. Let us assess the two cases; if you win you win everything, if you lose you lose nothing. Do not hesitate then, wager that he does exist.

"... but perhaps I am wagering too much [by giving up a life of sin]." Let us see. Since there is [or perhaps, rather, if there were] an equal chance of gain and loss, if you stood to win only two lives [of heavenly bliss] for one [lived in licentious sin on earth] you could still wager [be unsure how to choose], but supposing you stood to win three?... it would be unwise of you, once you are obliged to play, not to risk your life in order to win three lives at a game in which there is an equal chance of losing and winning. But there is an eternity of life and happiness. That being so, even if there were an infinite number of chances, of which only one were in your favor you would still be right to wager one.... Thus our argument carries infinite weight, when the stakes [or losses] are finite in a game where there are even chances of winning and losing and an infinite prize to be won. (Pascal, 1670)

What Arnauld and the people around him realized was that Pascal was doing nothing less than developing a calculus for how to make decisions in an uncertain, or probabilistic, world. Pascal was trying to understand how estimates of gain and loss could be coupled with estimates of the likelihood of future events to determine what course of action would yield an optimal outcome. This is an idea that Arnauld and his coauthor Pierre Nicole developed (probably with Pascal's direct assistance) at the very end of their textbook on logic, *La Logique ou L'Art de Penser*, which was published in 1662, about the same time as Descartes's *L'Homme*.

But with respect to accidents in which we play a part, and that we can bring about or prevent in some sense by our care in exposing ourselves to them or avoiding them, many people happen to fall into an illusion that is all the more deceptive as it appears reasonable to them. This is that they consider only the greatness and importance of the benefit they desire or the disadvantage they fear, without considering in any way the likelihood or probability that this benefit or disadvantage will or will not come about.

The flaw in this reasoning is that in order to decide what we ought to do to obtain some good or avoid some harm, it is necessary to consider not only the good or harm in itself, but also the probability that it will or will not occur, and to view geometrically the proportion all these things have when taken together. This can be clarified by the following example.

There are games which, if ten persons each put in a crown, only one wins the whole pot and all the others lose. Thus each person risks losing only one crown and may win nine. If we consider only the gain and loss in themselves, it would appear that each person has the advantage. But we must consider in addition that if each could win nine crowns and risks losing only one, it is also nine times more probable for each person to lose one crown and not to win the nine. Hence each has nine crowns to hope for himself, one crown to lose, nine degrees of probability of losing a crown, and only one of winning the nine crowns. This puts the matter at perfect equality.

These reflections appear trivial, and in effect they are if we go no further. But we can make them useful for more important things. The main use that we ought to derive from them is to make us more reasonable in our hopes and fears. Many people, for example, are exceedingly frightened when they hear thunder. If thunder makes them think of God and death and happiness, we could not think about it too much. But if it is only the danger of dying by lightning that causes them this unusual apprehension, it is easy to show that this is unreasonable. For out of two million people, at the most there is one that dies in this way. We could even say that there is hardly a violent death that is less common. So, then, our fear of some harm ought to be proportional not only to the magnitude of the harm, but also to the probability of the event. Just as there is hardly any kind of death more rare than being struck by lightning, there is also hardly any that ought to cause us less fear, especially given that this fear is no help in avoiding it. (Arnauld and Nicole, 1662)

Earlier in this chapter I pointed out that for any nervous system which operates in an uncertain world, identifying the behavior that maximizes inclusive fitness is problematic. Pascal would have said that there is no way for "reason" to decide these questions; there is no way for determinate mathematical tools to define an optimal course of action. Pascal and his colleagues at Port Royal were the first Europeans to fully understand this fact. Unlike previous thinkers who had simply acknowledged the existence of uncertainty, they had proposed that uncertainty could be quantified and then the likelihood of each possible outcome could be combined with the gain expected from that outcome. The result was an expected value for any possible course of action. An optimal course of action, these men suggested, is one that yields the greatest expected value.

This was one of the most critical insights of the Enlightenment. Even when significant uncertainty exists, it is possible to identify an optimal course of action. Although one must rely on a theory of probabilities to identify an optimal choice under indeterminate conditions, it is possible.

Extending this insight to Marr's problem is almost trivial. If the goal of the nervous system is to produce motor responses that yield the highest possible inclusive fitness for an organism, then under conditions of uncertainty the goal of the nervous system must be to yield the highest possible expected inclusive fitness.

Over the course of the century that followed the publication of the *Port Royal Logic*, probability theory made steady advances. Notions of how to compute, measure, and combine probabilities were advanced and developed. This advancing mathematical corpus could be used to describe uncertain future events, whether they were the date on which an individual would die or the probability of winning at roulette. Jakob Bernoulli codified much of this knowledge in his masterwork *Ars Conjectandi* (The Art of Conjecture), which was published posthumously (Bernoulli, 1713). The "calculus of probability," as Leibniz had called Pascal's advance, was fast becoming a tool both for describing the likelihood of uncertain future events and for selecting an optimal course of action given that uncertainty.

Pascal's Idea: Combining Value and Probability

During this first century, probability theory became a tool for assessing the likelihood of future events whose outcomes were uncertain. This represented a quantum leap for thinking about how one selects an optimal outcome under conditions of uncertainty because it made it possible to place numerical values on the likelihood of future events. Pascal and Arnauld had, however, gone a step beyond this; they had begun to think about how decision making must combine information about the likelihood of an event with the value of that event to a chooser. Pascal's formula for accomplishing this combination was simple: One multiplied the probability of an event by its value in currency—gold louis, for example—to determine an expected value. Optimal decision making could then be reduced to the art of identifying the course of action that yielded the highest possible expected value.

To make this formulation clear, consider a lottery that costs $50 to play and in which you have a 50 percent probability of winning $100. To compute the expected value of the lottery, one simply multiplies the probability that you will win, in this case 50 percent (or 0.50) by the amount that you would win, in this case $100. The lottery thus has an expected value of $50. Since the lottery actually costs $50 to enter, the net expected value of the lottery is zero. If you were to play the lottery an infinite number of times, on half those times you would win $100 and on the other half you would lose $50. Overall you would end up with exactly as much money as you started with. Now consider a situation in which you have to choose between playing the lottery described above and a lottery in which you must also wager $50 but in which there is a 6 percent chance that you will win $1000. In this case the expected value is $60. Since the lottery costs only $50 to play, it represents, on average, a gain of $10 per play. Expected-value theory reveals that players who pick the second lottery over the first will be richer on average, and it tells us exactly how much richer. Expected-value theory provides a clear mathematical method for combining the probabilities of future outcomes with the gain they offer in order to estimate a value for those choices in currency. That is true whether that currency is gold louis, pistoles, or units of inclusive fitness. This is one of the central insights, if not *the* central insight, around which modern economic theory is structured.

As expected-value theory came to be widely used and understood, an odd paradox produced by the theory came to light that was first formally described by Nicholas Bernoulli, nephew of Jakob (and son of the equally important Swiss mathematician Johann).[2] Consider the following: I have a fair coin and I agree to allow you to pay me for a turn at the following game. If, on the first flip of the coin, the coin lands heads, I will pay you $2; if it lands tails up, I pay you nothing. The expected value of this flip is thus $2 multiplied by 0.5, or $1. But if you lose (the coin lands tails up), I agree to throw the coin for you again. This time, if the coin lands heads up, I will pay you $4. Now the probability of throwing first a tail, and then a head, is 0.25 and the gain I offer under these conditions would be $4, so the expected value for this second flip is also $1. Now imagine that the coin had again landed tails up on the second throw. I would then agree to throw the coin again. If heads, I would pay you $8 (an event with a probability of 0.125), and again the expected value would stay constant at $1. Assuming that I agree to flip the coin for you an infinite number of times or until you win, whichever comes first, anyone can conclude that the expected value of this game must be infinite. Each flip has an expected value of $1. One dollar plus $1, plus $1, plus $1, ad infinitum comes to an infinite expected value.

2. In fact, it was the casino operators of St. Petersburg who first discovered the paradox.

Put in other terms, you should be willing to pay me any amount of money at all in order to play this game with me. If I say to you that for $500 you can play this game with me, then according to expected-value theory, you should say yes. Of course you may win only $1, losing $499. But on some rare plays, say when 20 tails are thrown before a heads comes up, you stand to win quite a lot (in that case about a million dollars). In fact, there is no reason why I should limit your entry fee to $500. I should be able to charge you any amount of money to play this game that yields an infinite expected value.

As the casino owners of St. Petersburg discovered, however, only a handful of people are willing to pay more than a few dollars to play such a game. In fact, if you ask people how much they are willing to pay to enter such a lottery, the amount is usually about $4. How can this be? Expected-value theory predicts that a rational decision maker should be willing to wager all of the money that he has on this game. In practice, few will pay more than $4. How could expected-value theory and human decision making be so different?

A Critical Advance in Valuation: Bernoulli

This paradox, which has come to be known as the St. Petersburg problem, became a subject of tremendous inquiry in the study of probability theory during the early part of the eighteenth century. Mathematicians all over Europe tried to understand how this could be, and whether it implied that probability theory itself, the mechanism by which we compute the likelihoods of each sequence of coin flips, could be wrong. It was not until 1738 that this paradox was resolved by Nicholas's brother, Daniel Bernoulli.

Daniel made an interesting and novel suggestion. Yes, he agreed, expected-value theory does predict the *mathematical* expected value. It does this by correctly computing the probability of future outcomes and by correctly computing the gain in currency. But this argument, he believed, made an unreasonable claim about humans. Expected-value theory implicitly assumes that decision makers are insensitive to risk. Consider the following choice between two lotteries. In lottery A you have a 100 percent chance of winning $1 million; in lottery B, a 50 percent chance of winning $2 million. Expected-value theory says that both of these lotteries are worth $1 million. Since they both have the same expected value, the theory assumes that any decision maker will consider them equally desirable. Almost all humans, however, report a preference for lottery A. Daniel reasoned that this was because humans are rationally prudent, and thus averse to taking the risks associated with the $2 million lottery.

To continue along Daniel's line of thought in a more typical situation, imagine that you are hungry, that it is late at night, and that you are given a choice between a 100 percent chance of winning 50 potato chips and a 50 percent chance of winning 100 potato chips. Under these conditions my friends pick the sure win of 50 potato chips, expressing an aversion to the risk of winding up with no chips at all. One can assess exactly how risk-averse my friends are by raising the payoff on the 50 percent lottery until they find the two offers equally attractive: A 100 percent chance of gaining 50 is as attractive as a 50 percent chance of winning how many potato chips? 150? 200? 400? My friends mostly agree that a 50 percent chance of winning 200 chips is slightly preferable to a sure bet on 50 chips. As Bernoulli would have put it, the moral value of 200 chips seems to be roughly twice the moral value of 50 chips.

Now let us go a step further, reducing the value of both lotteries. Which would you rather choose, a 100 percent chance of winning 5 chips or a 50 percent chance of winning 20 chips? 15 chips? 12 chips? Almost all people here strongly prefer even the 12-chip gamble to the 5-chip sure bet. The moral value of 12 chips is twice the moral value of 5 chips even though the moral value of 200 is only twice the value of 50. Bernoulli noted this and concluded that the moral value of any gain grows more slowly than its mathematical value.

Then Daniel made one final observation. Wealthy individuals, in our case people who have several bags of potato chips, are more willing to take risks than people without any potato chips. Someone with five bags of chips is much more likely to risk the 50 percent chance of winning 150 chips described above, than a person with no chips.

For Daniel all of these observations pointed toward the idea that the moral value of a gain and the mathematical value of a gain were different but related concepts. Bernoulli proposed that humans do not make decisions based on the expected value of a choice, as Pascal, Arnauld, and his uncle Jakob had proposed, but rather that they make decisions based on the expected utility of a choice. Expected utility was, according to Daniel, computed as the product of the probability of a gain and the utility (not the value) of a gain. The relationship between value and utility, in Daniel's formulation, accounted for the differences between mathematical and moral value that the St. Petersburg paradox highlighted.

Given that set of observations, Daniel needed to develop a simple formalism that associated value and utility; a two-dimensional graph that showed how value and utility were related. First, Daniel's formalism had to account for the fact that twice the moral value of 50 was 200 (in the example of our potato chip lottery). Second, Daniel had to account for the fact that rich people seemed more likely to take risks with a given amount of money than did poor people. To explain all of this, Daniel proposed that the relationship between value and utility in a two-dimensional graph formed a concave curve and that prospective gains are effectively prorated for the chooser's net worth. Later work has challenged Daniel's conclusion that the human utility curve looks exactly like this one, but his insight remains very much a feature of decision theory and is at the core of modern economics. The utility of a dollar is not, and should not be, a truly constant thing for humans. Instead, utility seems to increase in a more complex fashion and to reflect the net worth of the chooser. (See figure 8.4.)

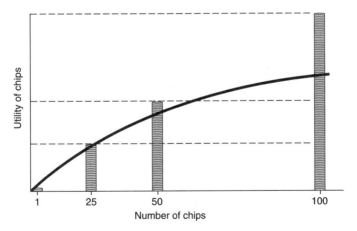

Figure 8.4
A human utility function for potato chips.

Bernoulli's utility theory represented a quantum leap, but not really in the realm of pure probability. In terms of pure probability, Daniel Bernoulli's utility theory continued to rely on combinations of coin flips, or actuarial tables about births and deaths, to model the probabilities of events that would take place in the future. But Daniel had proposed that when humans make a choice, they always evaluate an opportunity with regard to the fraction by which it will improve their current circumstances rather than by its absolute value. This seems intuitively true to us: One potato chip more or less makes little difference until the bag is almost empty.

A Critical Advance in Probability: Bayes and Laplace

Until the mid-1700s, the theory of probabilities (as distinct from theories of valuation like expected-utility theory) was focused almost entirely on estimating the likelihood of uncertain future events: lotteries, coin flips, life expectancies. This class of probability estimate is often called aleatory probability, from the latin *aleator*, meaning gambler. In law, aleatory contracts are those in which the signatories to the contract both risk loss or gain in the face of future uncertainty. A life insurance policy is an example of an aleatory contract.

Aleatory uncertainties are exactly the kind of probabilistic events that Pascal had envisioned as the subject of a calculus of probabilities. Regardless of whether or not the world is as truly deterministic as Descartes and Galileo hoped, we often do not know what will happen in the future. We do not know when a particular individual will die or whether a particular coin will land heads or tails up if it is flipped. Pascal's probability theory was designed to model events of this type. In the second half of the eighteenth century, two men revolutionized the calculus of probability when they realized that one could apply this probability theory not just to assess the likelihood of future events, but also to assess the likelihood of past events. While this may seem a small thing, it changed the way Europeans thought about the mathematics of probability and opened the way to a more formal theory of decision making.

Consider an uncertain situation that was of tremendous interest to both the English clergyman Thomas Bayes and the French mathematician Pierre-Simon Laplace. An astronomer measures the angular altitude of Jupiter six times in rapid succession and gets six slightly different numbers. Jupiter has a single altitude, but we have six imperfect observations of that altitude, all of which differ. What, we might ask, was the most likely actual altitude of Jupiter at the time that we made our observations? It was Thomas Bayes's insight, published posthumously in 1763, that probability theory could be extended to answer questions of this type. Bayes reasoned that if one knew the distribution of errors induced by the astronomer's instruments, one could mathematically infer the most likely true altitude of Jupiter when the observations were made. It is important to note that there is nothing aleatory about this kind of probability. At the time the measurement was made, Jupiter certainly had an altitude. The only uncertainty derives from our own lack of knowledge. The limitation that we face in this example is entirely epistemological. Bayes was suggesting that probability theory could be used to describe epistemological uncertainty as well as aleatory uncertainty.

Thomas Bayes

Unfortunately, little is known about the historical Thomas Bayes. We do know that he was a rural Protestant theologian and minister who was a Dissenter, not a member of the Church of England. He published only two works during his life: a theological work titled *Divine Benevolence, or an Attempt to Prove That the Principal End of the Divine Providence and Government Is the Happiness of His Creatures*, and a mathematical work: *An Introduction to the Doctrine of Fluxions, and a Defence of the Mathematicians Against the Objections of the Author of The Analyst*, in which he defended Newton's calculus against an attack by the philosopher Bishop George Berkeley. After his death, Bayes's friend and executor Richard Price discovered among his papers a manuscript titled "Essay Towards Solving a Problem in the Doctrine of Chances." Price presented that paper at the Royal Society in 1763, and it is entirely upon that work which Bayes's quite considerable fame rests.

Today Bayes is such a towering name in mathematics that it seems astonishing we know so little about him. We do not, for example, know why he was elected a fellow of the Royal Society before his death. In fact, the only picture of Bayes that we have may not even be a portrait of him. The historical Bayes is an almost total mystery. To his contemporaries that may not have been terribly surprising; the posthumous publication of Bayes's essay in *Philosophical Transactions of the Royal Society* had almost no impact until Laplace rediscovered it about 10 years later.

Bayes's insight was profound. He realized that there are many events about which we have only partial or inaccurate knowledge, events that truly happened but about which we, because of our limited knowledge, are uncertain. It was Bayes who first realized that a mathematically complete kind of inverse probability could be used to infer the most likely values or properties of those events.[3]

The Bayesian theorem provides the basis for a fundamentally statistical approach to this kind of epistemological uncertainty. It does this by putting the process of predicting the likelihood of all possible previous states of the world, given one's available observations, on rigorous mathematical footing. Put in English, Bayes's theorem allows us to ask the following question: Given my knowledge of how often I have observed that the world appeared to be in state x, and my knowledge of how well correlated my current sensory data are with the actual world state x, then precisely how likely is it that the world was actually in state x?

Bayes's theorem is so important that I want to digress here to present a fairly complete example of how the mathematics of the theorem work. Imagine that you are a monkey trained to fixate a spot of light while two eccentric spots of light are also illuminated, just as in the example presented in chapter 5. In this experiment, however, the central fixation light changes color to indicate which of the two eccentric target lights, the left one or the right one, will serve as your goal on this trial. If you can decide which target is the goal, and look at it, you receive a raisin as a reward. However, the color of the central fixation light (or, more precisely, the wavelength of the light emitted by the central stimulus) can be any one of 100 different hues (or wavelengths). We can begin our Bayesian description of this task by saying that there are two possible world states. One state in which a leftward eye movement will be rewarded and one state in which a rightward eye movement will be rewarded. (See figure 8.5.)

3. As Stephen Stigler has pointed out, Thomas Stimpson was really the first mathematician to propose the idea of inverse probabilities, but it was Bayes who developed the mathematical approach on which modern inverse probabilities are based (Stigler, 1989).

A: Likelihood of Seeing a Given Wavelength

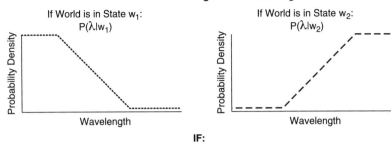

If World is in State w_1:
$P(\lambda|w_1)$

If World is in State w_2:
$P(\lambda|w_2)$

IF:

Total Probability of w_1 = 0.25 **Total Probability of w_2 = 0.75**

**B: Probability of Seeing a Given Wavelength
and Seeing It in a Given World State:**

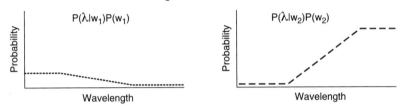

$P(\lambda|w_1)P(w_1)$

$P(\lambda|w_2)P(w_2)$

**C: Prior Probability of Seeing a Given Wavelength
Regardless of World State:**

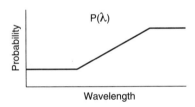

$P(\lambda)$

THEN:

**D: The Posterior Probability that You Are in a Particular World State
As a Function of Wavelength Is:**

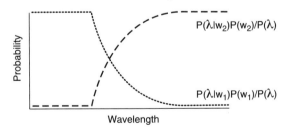

$P(\lambda|w_2)P(w_2)/P(\lambda)$

$P(\lambda|w_1)P(w_1)/P(\lambda)$

Figure 8.5
Bayes's theorem.

In mathematical notation we designate these two world states as w_1 and w_2. State w_1 is when a leftward eye movement, or saccade, will be rewarded, and state w_2 is when a rightward saccade will be rewarded. After observing 100 trials we discover that on 25 percent of trials a leftward movement was rewarded, irrespective of the color of the fixation light, and on 75 percent of trials the rightward movement was rewarded. Based upon this observation, we can say that the prior probability that world state w_1 will occur (known as $P(w_1)$) is 0.25, and the prior probability of world state w_2 is 0.75.

To make these prior probabilities more accurate estimates of the state of the world, we next have to take into account the color of the central fixation stimulus and the correlation of that stimulus color with each of the world states. To do that, we need to generate a graph that plots the probability that we will encounter a particular stimulus wavelength (which we will call λ) when the world is in state w_1. Figure 8.5A plots an example of such a probability density function[4] showing the likelihood of each value of λ when the world is in state w_1, and when in state w_2. We refer to this as the conditional probability density function for λ in world state w_1, or $P(\lambda \mid w_1)$.

Next, in order to get the two graphs in figure 8.5A to tell us how likely it is that we see a given λ *and* the world is in a given state, we have to correct these graphs for the overall likelihood that the world is in either state w_1 or state w_2. To do that, we multiply each point on the graphs by the prior probability of that world state. The graph on the left thus becomes $P(\lambda \mid w_1)P(w_1)$, where $P(w_1)$ is the prior probability for world state w_1 as described above. Note in figure 8.5B that this has the effect of rescaling the graphs that appeared in figure 8.5A.

Finally, we have to determine how likely it is that any given value of λ will occur regardless of world state. To do this, we need simply to count up all the times we have seen λ at a specific value, and then plot the probability density function for all values of λ (irrespective of which movement was rewarded), as shown in figure 8.5C.

---

4. I should point out that $P(\lambda)$ in this specific example is actually a probability function, not a probability density function, because wavelength is treated here as a discrete variable. This makes little difference to my exposition but it is, in fairness, an abuse of notation that more mathematical readers may find annoying.

Now we are ready to ask, when we see a given wavelength of light, what the probability is that on this trial a leftward movement will be rewarded (that we are in world state w_1) and what the probability is that a rightward movement will be rewarded (world state w_2). To compute these likelihoods, we divide the curves shown in figure 8.5B by the curve shown in figure 8.5C to produce the curves shown together in figure 8.5D. This essentially corrects the probability that one would see a particular λ in a particular world state for the overall probability that one would ever have seen that wavelength λ. This is the essence of the Bayesian theorem given by the equation

$$\text{Probability of } w_1 \text{ given the current value of } \lambda = \frac{P(\lambda \mid w_1)P(w_1)}{P(\lambda)}.$$

To restate this in English, one could say, The best possible estimate of the probability that a leftward movement will be rewarded is equal to the probability that the central stimulus would be this color on a leftward trial, times the overall probability of a leftward trial, divided by the probability that this particular color would ever be observed. The result is usually referred to as a posterior probability, and it reports, in principle, the best estimate that you can derive for this likelihood. Therein lies the absolute beauty of Bayes's theorem: It provides a mechanical tool that can report the best possible estimate of the likelihood of an event. No other method, no matter how sophisticated, can provide a more accurate estimate of the likelihood of an uncertain event. The Bayesian theorem is a critical advance because no decision process that must estimate the likelihood of an uncertain outcome can ever do better than a Bayesian estimate of that probability. The Bayesian theorem is a tool for reducing epistemological uncertainty to a minimal level and then assigning probabilities to world states.

Pierre-Simon Laplace

Unaware that Bayes had already derived an optimal method for computing the likelihood of a past event, Laplace became interested in inverse probability in 1772. At that time, Laplace was in the process of developing much of modern probability theory at the same time that he was hard at work developing celestial mechanics. You may recall from chapter 2 that Laplace had what may have been the most completely deterministic worldview of any major thinker during his time. His own studies of celestial mechanics were leading to the conclusion that every aspect of the universe was governed deterministically. A superintelligence, Laplace would later conclude, could in principle survey the complete state of the universe at an instant in time, and from this survey, and a complete knowledge of the mathematical laws of physics, predict with absolute accuracy the state of the world at any time in the future. In short, Laplace was coming to believe that there was nothing uncertain about the future.

This was probably a critical step for Laplace, because it allowed him to assume an unusual stance with regard to aleatory and epistemological probabilities. While it is certainly true that one does not know whether a coin tossed in the air will land heads or tails up, this reflected, in Laplace's view, the epistemological limitations of human knowledge rather than anything fundamentally aleatory. Laplace's superintelligence would know the position of every molecule in the coin as it was thrown. We have to assume, he might have argued, that from this data the superintelligence would be able to predict how the coin would land. If the world is in fact totally deterministic, future events that we think of as aleatory are uncertain because of our own ignorance about the state of the world and about physical laws. For Laplace there was nothing fundamentally aleatory about future uncertainties, there were just greater or lesser degrees of epistemological uncertainty about both the past and the future. This is a critical idea because it meant that for Laplace, uncertainties about past events were really not that different from uncertainties about future events. Both forward and inverse probabilities represented epistemological problems of a philosophically similar type.

Starting from this base, Laplace also attempted to derive an optimal system for estimating the likelihood of past *or future* events, and he derived a closely related set of conclusions before coming across Bayes's paper in the *Philosophical Transactions of the Royal Society*. Although Laplace may not have been the first to derive Bayes's theorem, his uniquely deterministic worldview may have allowed him to see the importance of the theorem. It was in Laplace's hands that modern probability theory and decision theory were born from, among other things, Bayes's insight.

Valuation, Probability, and Decision: Foundations of Modern Economic Theory

I suggested that the goal of the nervous system, in evolutionary terms, must be to make decisions that maximize the inclusive fitness of the organism. Putting that another way, we can ask, What is the best possible way to combine sensory information and a stored representation of the structure of the environment in order to identify an optimal motor response when we know how motor responses and inclusive fitness are related? The work of Pascal, Bernoulli, Bayes, and Laplace, interpreted through the lens of modern economic theory, gives us an answer to this question. To identify the goal, one needs to be able to compute the utility, in evolutionary terms, of each of the courses of action available to a behaving organism. Then the probability of each of those outcomes must be evaluated with Bayes's theorem. When those data points are combined, one can identify *the* optimal motor response in any given situation.

For an economist, tools like Bayesian probability estimation and utility functions allow one to identify ideal, or what economists call *rational*, courses of action. Many economists have proceeded from the assumption that these tools can be used not only to identify optimal solutions but also to predict the behavior of humans making economic decisions in the real world. Unfortunately, global rationality (as this approach is called) often seems to do a poor job of explaining human decision making in the economic world. There are probably many reasons for this, all of which are the subjects of contemporary economic research. Humans often, for example, seem to evaluate their options with a utility function that is quite different from the one Bernoulli proposed. It also seems that humans often do a poor job of estimating probabilities correctly, although this assertion is more controversial. All of these observations have led some economists to suggest that human decision makers may show only a bounded rationality, as the economist Herbert Simon has put it. (For an overview of this work, see Simon, 1997.)

I began this chapter by arguing, like David Marr, that "an algorithm is likely to be understood more readily by understanding the nature of the problem being solved than by examining the mechanism (and the hardware) in which it is embodied." One of the great problems that Marr faced, however, was trying to define exactly what problem animals were trying to solve. Defining the problem was particularly difficult for Marr for two reasons. First, it was not clear how the determinate mathematics Marr was using could deal with the uncertainty that exists in the real world. Second, it seemed equally uncertain that the twin challenges of modularity and evolution would allow the nervous system to compute solutions to real problems. Indeed, the observation of economists that humans perform as suboptimal decision makers in many abstract situations seems proof to many that evolution fails, in a global sense, to achieve the goal of producing efficient behavior.

I believe that this response misses the point of what it is that evolution and economic theory can be used to accomplish. The economics of rational choice allow us to identify an optimal solution to any problem that involves uncertainty and for which the utility function can be defined. The Bayesian theorem gives us, in principle, a mathematical tool for optimal statistical estimation. The theory of natural selection gives us a theoretically complete, if empirically difficult, utility function. Natural selection works toward a maximization of the survival of fit individuals. From the point of view of biological economics, units of inclusive fitness are units of utility. At an evolutionary level, then, the idealized problem of relating behavior and brain reduces to this: Given my current knowledge of the state of the world and any current uncertainty, what is the course of behavioral action that maximizes my fitness? As we will see in the following chapters, computational approaches that have employed this economic logic have been very effective tools in the hands of behavioral biologists. There is every empirical reason to believe that animals evolve nervous systems which allow them to solve the problems they face with startling efficiency in these evolutionary terms. If that is true, then economic theory may well be a tool for defining the goals against which nervous systems evolve functional abilities.

Evolving Optimal Solutions or Optimal Brains?
At this point it is important that I make something clear. I am not arguing that any brain can solve any problem optimally. Instead, I am argu-

ing that animals produce behaviors, within their environments, which fairly efficiently achieve the goal of maximizing fitness. Economics is a tool for defining the problem that an animal faces or the goal that it should achieve. It is the functioning of the nervous system which achieves that goal within the animal's environment.

To make this clearer, let me borrow an example from the cognitive psychologist Gerd Gigerenzer and his colleagues (Gigerenzer, Todd, and ABC Research Group, 2000). Consider a bacterium that lives in a large world where food is randomly distributed and constantly in motion. What is an optimal solution to the problem of finding food under these uncertain, but *uniformly uncertain*, conditions? The answer is for the bacterium to head off in a random direction in search of food. Because of the structure of this environment, any randomly selected path that the bacterium takes is as good as any other randomly selected path. So searching randomly is, for this organism, an optimal solution to the for- aging problem it faces: Gather food as efficiently as possible to maximize fitness. An organism evolved to achieve this goal could be constructed very simply. An internal random process could select a direction for movement and then initiate that movement. Nothing more would be needed to achieve an optimal strategy defined by this organism's envi- ronment. Of course, in an environment in which food was distributed in patches, this organism would function poorly. Under these conditions we might see the bacterium feed briefly in a patch and then head off in a random direction rather than adopting the strategy of staying in the vi- cinity of the food-rich patch. There is no doubt that in a patchy envi- ronment the bacterium is solving this problem of finding food poorly, and would be less fit than a bacterium that solved this problem well. In the randomly distributed environment in which this animal lives, how- ever, it may indeed solve the foraging problem optimally.

The bacterium serves as a prototype for using economic theory to think about how organisms solve the problem of producing efficient be- havior at an evolutionary level. In this case we can think of the evolu- tionary utility function as a process that maximizes the rate at which the bacterium reproduces when it maximizes the amount of food the bacte- rium eats. In a world where food is distributed uniformly and randomly, random search is an optimal behavior and yields an optimally fit bacterium. Of course our bacterium knows nothing about Bayesian estimation or fitness-utility functions. There is no reason for it to know anything about these mathematical models. These models describe properties of the environment, and organisms that reflect these properties more accurately are more fit than organisms that reflect these properties of the environment poorly.

Summary

At a deep level, Marr's proposal that we need to understand what the brain is trying to do can be recast. In an uncertain world, Bayesian estimation theory is a mathematical tool for defining the best estimate of the properties of the world that any organism *could* have. Utility functions are mathematical tools for describing the best way an animal can react to the uncertainties of that environment from an evolutionary perspective. Economic theory allows us to define the behavioral problems that the environment poses, and it allows us to determine how accurately real animals solve those problems.

Of course it can be argued that real animals do such a poor job of solving these problems that understanding the environmental goals animals must face will be of no help in understanding how the nervous system functions. In chapter 7 I provided an initial response to that problem by arguing that there is a significant amount of evidence suggesting that when we can identify what constitutes an optimal solution, animals come remarkably close to achieving those optimal solutions. In the chapters that follow, I will provide a number of specific examples of neural processes that can be well understood if one begins by defining a fitness-related goal for the nervous system, using economic tools.

In this chapter I want to suggest that the basic instruments of economic theory may be promising tools for a study of the relationship between behavior and brain. Using economic approaches, we can define the problems animals face in the way that Marr suggested. As he put it: "trying to understand perception by studying only neurons is like trying to understand bird flight by studying only feathers; it just cannot be done. In order to understand bird flight, we have to understand aerodynamics." I want to make a similar claim for behavior in general: Trying to understand the relationship between behavior and brain by studying reflex arcs simply cannot be done. In order to understand how the brain solves sensorimotor problems, we have to understand, we have to have a theory of, the sensorimotor problem posed by the environment to the organism. Bayesian economic mathematics is that theory.

9

Evolution, Probability, and Economics

In the 1650s, when Pascal and Descartes would meet after dinner to discuss mathematics in the salons of Paris, they were defining the two principal directions in which mathematics would develop for the next century. Pascal argued that in order to understand and model the world, a calculus of probability was required. Descartes stood against this assertion, arguing that when the physical world was truly understood, only determinate models would be required.

A century and a half after Descartes and Pascal argued politely in the company of the French nobility, Bayes, Laplace, and Bernoulli had finally succeeded in showing that a calculus of probability could be used to represent uncertainty and to identify optimal solutions to complex problems in a probabilistic world. While their work did not make probability theory the centerpiece of nineteenth-century mathematics, it did make probability theory important and influential in European intellectual circles. Despite this, Descartes's vision continued to dominate European thought about the nervous system. Even today, Pascal's insight makes only occasional appearances in the world of biology.

Take as an example the nineteenth-century work of Marshall Hall, who relied on a deterministic vision of the brain in the construction of his own physiological models. In the 1830s he proposed the reflex arc as the embodiment of Descartes's notion that the nervous system achieved a form of sensory-to-motor *reflection*. The nervous system was a clockwork in which reflection served the role played by the determinate mechanical gears of machines. In retrospect, this overwhelming emphasis on determinate behaviors seems odd. All animals, like Pascal's gambling patron the Chevalier de Mere, must generate behavior that interacts with the probabalistic machinery of an uncertain world.

Outside of the disciplines of biology, however, it is an uncontested fact that probability theory grew and achieved many successes over the course of the nineteenth and twentieth centuries. Mathematical theories of probability and valuation became the centerpieces around which nearly all quantitative thinking in the social and behavioral sciences was organized. Probability theory thus served as the foundation for economics and the constellation of behavioral sciences that grew to encircle it.

In this chapter I want to show you how one group of biologists has begun to recover Pascal's legacy by using economic theories to better understand the behavior of animals and to explicitly test the hypothesis that evolution acts to produce behaviors which maximize inclusive fitness. These scientists, behavioral ecologists, form a small but growing group who use theories of probability and valuation to identify the evolutionarily defined goals that animal behavior should, in principle, attempt to achieve. They then examine behavior to determine how closely real animals approximate theoretically defined goals.

Most behavioral ecologists are, perhaps surprisingly, adamant that they do not study physiology, neurobiology, or the brain. As a group, these behavioral scientists have made an effort to distance themselves from the mechanisms that underlie behavior, and as a result their work says very little about the function of the brain. But they have made tremendous progress in an area that is critical to neuroscience. They have begun to describe the goals of behavior in mathematical terms, and they have done this by using an evolutionary approach to studies of probability and valuation.

Behavioral Ecology as a Theoretical Approach

Since the 1950s behavioral ecologists have tried to understand why animals behave as they do by developing quantitative models that describe optimal behavioral strategies. Their goal has been to understand why animals foraging for nourishment select one food type rather than another. Or why animals looking for a mate select one individual over another. In trying to understand why animals behave as they do, it has been their working premise that animals must generate efficient solutions to the problems their environments present in order to maximize the rate at which their genes are propagated. They recognize that efficient solutions in a uncertain world can be described only by using probability theory, and as a result these scientists have employed economic formulations as a starting point for their work. One sees this reliance on economic theory everywhere in behavioral ecology. For example, in the third edition of John Krebs and Nicholas Davies's classic textbook *Behavioural Ecology*, Krebs and Alejandro Kacelnik begin their chapter titled "Decision Making" with the following statement:

If you spend a few minutes watching a small bird such as a European robin in the spring, you will see it performing a variety of activities. Perhaps when you first see it, it is searching for food on the ground. Soon it flies into a tree and sings, then after a short period of singing it stops and preens or simply sits "resting." If you extend your observations to cover a series of whole days, daily patterns will emerge. For example there will be more singing in the early morning and more resting in the middle of the day. If, on the other hand, you focus your observations on just one kind of activity, for example, foraging, you will discover that it can be broken down into a series of components. The robin may sometimes forage on lawns, sometimes on flower borders, sometimes it captures worms and sometimes it captures flying insects. In this chapter we will present a framework for describing, understanding, and predicting those sorts of patterns. We shall use the metaphor of the animal as a "decision-maker." Without implying any conscious choice, the robin can be thought of as "deciding" whether to sing or feed, whether to feed on worms or insects, whether to search for food on the grass or on the flower bed. We shall see how these decisions can be analyzed in terms of the costs and benefits of alternative courses of action. Costs and benefits are ultimately measured in terms of Darwinian fitness (survival and reproduction), and may, in many instances, be measured in terms of some other more immediate metric such as energy expenditure, food intake, or body reserves. As will become apparent later on, analyzing decisions in terms of their costs and benefits cannot be done without also taking into consideration physiological and psychological features that might act as constraints on an animal's performance. The fitness consequences of decisions, and the various constraints that limit an animal's options, can be brought together in a single framework using optimality modeling.

Optimality Modeling

The main tool for helping us to analyze decisions in terms of their costs and benefits is optimality modeling. The logic of this approach in biology (as opposed to economics or decision theory) is a Darwinian one. Selection, it is argued, is an

iterative and competitive process, so that eventually it will tend to produce outcomes (phenotypes) that represent the best achievable balance of costs and benefits. These adaptations are often so exquisite (an obvious example being the
match of many cryptic [camouflaged] insects to their background) that in pre–
Darwinian days they were taken as evidence for a divine creator. Nowadays they
are seen as the outcome of natural selection and as suitable material for some
kind of optimality analysis. (Krebs and Davies, 1991)

The field of behavioral ecology is a fusion of classical economics (of
the kind described in the last chapter) and behavioral biology, a fusion
that has been extremely fruitful in the study of many kinds of behavior.
For example, in his classic work on how baboons make decisions about
whom to mate with in order to maximize their inclusive fitness, Robin
Dunbar (1984) used economic tools to revolutionize the way ecologists
think about reproduction. Even his title, *Reproductive Decisions: An
Economic Analysis of Gelada Baboon Social Strategies*, reflects the fundamental fusion of behavioral studies and economics that underlies this
growing field of study. But the initial triumphs of this economic approach to animal behavior came from studies of the decisions animals
make when foraging for food.

Foraging Theory

Ecological biology began as a field in the mid-1960s, when a number of
researchers began to explicitly consider the linkage between economic
models and the decisions animals make about what they should eat.
These biologists reasoned that if one could economically define an optimal strategy for finding and eating food, then one could study the behavior of actual animals both to test the hypothesis that evolution shapes
behavior toward definable optima (in this case maximizing feeding efficiency) and to test the hypothesis that economic tools could be used to
model behavior. This idea made its debut in 1966 in two simultaneously
published reports. As Robert MacArthur and Eric Pianka put it in one of
these two landmark papers:

There is a close parallel between the development of theories in economics and
population biology. In biology, however, the geometry of the organisms and their
environment plays a greater role. Different phenotypes have different abilities at
harvesting resources, and the resources are distributed in a patchwork in three

dimensions in the environment. In this paper we undertake to determine in which patches a species would feed and which items would form its diet if the species acted in the most economical fashion. Hopefully, natural selection will often have achieved such optimal allocation of time and energy expenditures, but such "optimum theories" are hypotheses for testing rather than anything certain. (MacArthur and Pianka, 1966)

MacArthur and Pianka's paper, "On Optimal Use of a Patchy Environment," was published in *The American Naturalist* as a companion to J. Merritt Emlen's paper "The Role of Time and Energy in Food Preference." As Emlen put it in his report:

Let us assume that natural selection will favor the development (by whatever means—innate or learned) of feeding preferences that will, by their direction and intensity, and within the physical and nervous limitations of a species, maximize the net caloric intake per individual of that species per unit time. (Emlen, 1966)

Together, these two papers launched the field of foraging theory and the larger discipline of behavioral ecology. The papers drew on economic theory to define ecological goals toward which, they hypothesized, natural selection should drive animal behavior.

Over the ten years that followed the publication of these papers, a number of critical advances were made, both theoretically and empirically, which seemed to validate the hypothesis that economic approaches of this type could revolutionize the ecological study of behavior. In the 1970s Eric Charnov and Gordon Orians, then both at the University of Washington, made the next quantum leap, developing a much more advanced approach to the questions MacArthur, Pianka, and Emlen had raised.

The basic premise of Charnov and Orians's approach (Charnov, 1973), like that of MacArthur, Pianka, and Emlen, was that animals who are more efficient gatherers of food will enjoy a higher level of fitness than animals who are less efficient gatherers of food. If two species of similar animals compete for access to the same food resources, Charnov and Orians presumed that the species which is more efficient at gathering food will be "preserved" as a favorable variation while the less efficient animals will be "rejected" by the process Darwin called natural selection. The goal of any foraging animal, Charnov and Orians reasoned, is to gather food efficiently. This meant that an animal should, in principle, spend as little energy as possible to gather as much food as possible.

Over the course of the 1970s, Charnov and Oriens suggested that the process of foraging for food could be broken down into two subproblems,[1] each of which could be described with a distinct economic model. The first problem that an animal faced, as they saw it, was to decide whether or not to try to eat an edible object once it was encountered. A lion might, for example, see many potential prey before it decides to attack and attempt to eat one. The lion might encounter a water buffalo, a hyena, and a fox before it encountered a warthog, which it decides to attack. The size of the potential prey, the time required to catch it, and the scarcity of that type of prey might all influence this decision. An herbivore like a zebra faces a similar problem when it decides in which patch of grass to browse. The zebra may encounter grass patches of different sizes and different qualities before it selects one patch to eat. Charnov and Orians described this entire class of problem as prey selection. Given what I know about the current state of the world, and the potential food that I see before me, should I try to eat this thing I have found?

Once an animal has begun to eat an object, Charnov and Orians reasoned that a second decision would eventually have to be made, a decision about when to stop eating. Consider our zebra again. After encountering a series of grass patches, the zebra selects one and settles down to browse. At some point, as the zebra consumes the grass in the area, grass becomes scarce. A moment-by-moment analysis reveals that the amount of food the zebra ingests per minute decreases as the patch of grass becomes depleted. When should the zebra stop eating and begin to look for another patch? This is a decision that must be influenced by, among other things, the quality of other available patches and the likely distance to the next acceptable patch. In a similar way, the lion must decide when to stop gnawing on the carcass of a dead warthog so it can

---

1. Today, most behavioral ecologists identify about six mathematically discrete problems that foraging animals can face. Graham Pyke has written an excellent critical review of these problems (Pyke, 1984). The general insights around which solutions to these six problems are built, however, are largely captured by the two original problems Charnov and Orians examined.

start looking for another meal. Charnov and Orians described this class of decision as the patch residence problem. As my rate of energy intake drops, given what I know about the world around me, when should I stop eating and start looking for a new patch?

When Charnov and Orians began to develop equations describing optimal strategies for patch residence and prey selection, they quickly realized the two problems had very different solutions. Defining the ideal patch residency time requires an analysis of the rate at which energy is gained while feeding in a patch. Charnov therefore based his patch model on a set of equations that described how decisions alter the rate at which calories are acquired, a set of equations known as the marginal value theorem. The prey model was based on an existing piece of early foraging theory, Holling's disc equation (Holling, 1959), which had been developed to model the hunting behavior of praying mantises. Both because it has been well tested empirically and because it is an example of how deterministic reflexlike models can be superseded by economically based models, we now turn to an examination of the prey model.

The Prey Model

Imagine a hungry spider sitting quietly at the center of its web. Suddenly a housefly becomes entangled in a far edge of the web. Vibration-sensitive neurons in the feet of the spider become active and the spider rotates, aligning its body axis with the axis of the vibrating thread. The vibration continues. The spider walks outward along the vibrating thread until it encounters the fly. As an image of the fly falls on its retina, the spider begins to encircle the fly in silk, tying it to the web. Once the prey is fully encircled, the spider penetrates the silk pouch and begins to liquefy and consume its prey. Surely this is exactly the kind of behavior for which reflex theories were designed.

Later, we observe a tiny fruit fly strike the net, producing a vibration that this time the spider ignores. In fact, we observe that every time a fruit fly strikes the net *on this day* the spider ignores it, taking only the much larger houseflies. If we make additional observations of this spider on different days and under different environmental conditions, we notice something extraordinary. On some days the spider will take every fruit fly that strikes the net, but only on days when the houseflies are rare. What we notice is that the probability the spider will attack a fruit fly seems to depend almost exclusively on how often it encounters houseflies.

If we try to understand this observation with regard to a behavioral goal, it makes obvious sense. The spider is trying to get enough to eat, and it must do this in an efficient manner that takes the prevalence of houseflies into account. No doubt one could devise a complex set of interlocking reflex mechanisms that would yield this behavior. We could postulate that the rate at which the housefly-attack reflex was activated controlled the threshold for activating the fruit fly-attack reflex. Using reflexes as building blocks, we could generate this behavioral pattern. But what would this tell us about the functional capabilities of the spider nervous system? If we discovered that the spider ignored houseflies on days when dragonflies were common, we would have to postulate yet another complete set of interconnected reflexes to account for this observation.

Foraging theorists have argued that behaviors like these cannot be understood in this piecemeal fashion, but instead require a theory of predation. Optimal predation is the process of achieving a maximum rate of energy intake with a minimal expenditure of effort in a random and unpredictable world. In Charnov's original formulation (1973) the prey model was developed to specifically determine the most efficient predation strategy for any animal. It was meant to be a quantitative mathematical tool for understanding the decisions animals like our foraging spider make when selecting prey. As an economically based optimality model, it is also meant to be parsimonious. It seeks to describe all of the prey selection behavior an animal produces within a single framework rather than attempting to account for behavior in a piecemeal fashion.

The complete prey model has been presented a number of times, and has been developed fairly independently by several researchers. Within the field of behavioral ecology, however, the definitive presentation of the prey model was made by two close colleagues of Charnov's, David Stephens and John Krebs. In the mid-1980s Stephens and Krebs compiled a book called *Foraging Theory*, which has come to serve as a handbook and a manifesto for much of behavioral ecology (Stephens and Krebs, 1986). In the presentation of the prey model that follows, I employ most of the conventions Stephens and Krebs developed when they presented the Charnov model, but without as much mathematical detail as they employ.

Imagine, Charnov proposed, the process of looking for appropriate food as an endless cycle that proceeds in the following manner. The first step in looking for food is to begin searching. Searching in this sense is any activity that takes time and during which the foraging animal may encounter something edible. For a spider, one might think of search time as the time spent waiting silently for an insect to strike the web. For a lion, search time might be the interval spent prowling the savanna looking for prey. In both cases this first phase of the cycle involves searching for prey.

Charnov assumed that searching costs animals something, the energy that it takes to search. The search cost per hour for a prowling lion is probably a good deal higher than the search cost for a quiet spider, but searching costs both of these organisms something. Recognizing this, Charnov individualized the cost of search time for each kind of animal. In his equations, searching costs s units of energy per minute, and s is different for each forager.

After a period of searching, it is assumed that the animal eventually encounters a possible prey item. For the spider, this phase of the prey cycle occurs whenever an insect strikes the web. For the lion, this phase begins when another animal is detected on the savanna. Once a potential prey item is encountered, the forager has to make *the* critical decision around which the prey model is structured. It has to decide whether to take the time and spend additional energy to attempt to capture and eat the prey item, or whether to pass up this prey item and wait for another, perhaps more valuable one, to come along. In Charnov's conceptualization, the process of predation is thus a cycle: search, encounter, decide, search, encounter, decide....

The goal of the model is to characterize the decision-making phase, the decision about whether to eat this item or to continue searching. In order to make that decision efficiently, Charnov reasoned, a forager needs to know four things about every possible prey item:

1. The energy gained from eating a typical prey item of this type. For the lion this is tantamount to knowing that a water buffalo has 20 times as much meat as a warthog. For the spider, it means knowing that the housefly is 20 times the size of a fruit fly.

2. The average time it will take to acquire and consume this particular type of prey, the handling time. For the spider, handling time reflects how long it will take from the moment that the web begins to vibrate until the prey is consumed. For the lion this is the time of the hunt and the period of consumption.

3. The cost, in energy spent, during the handling process. Obviously the energy cost incurred by a hunting lion is greater when pursuing a water buffalo than when pursuing a warthog.

4. The rate, in encounters per day, at which a prey of each type is detected.

Each of these four variables is set by properties of the environment, by properties of the prey, and by features of the forager. These four variables define the problem that a foraging animal must face. The forager, in turn, directly controls one variable: the probability that it will attack a prey object of any particular type. The goal of an efficient forager is to select an attack probability for each type of prey that maximizes the rate at which energy is obtained. The goal of the animal is to be as efficient a forager as possible whenever it is in the prey cycle. By being the most efficient forager it can be, it effectively minimizes the time that it spends in the prey cycle, leaving it free for other activities.

Charnov argues that we can characterize the rate of net energy intake in any environment, and for any possible prey attack strategy, in the following way. First, we need to characterize the total energy gained or lost in association with each type of prey. To accomplish that characterization, we multiply the probability that the forager will attack that prey type (the variable controlled by the forager, which we will call p) by the frequency with which that prey is encountered (which we will call λ). This tells us, on average, how often an attack on that prey type actually occurs. We multiply this quantity by the total search time to yield the average number of prey attacked. Finally, we multiply this quantity by the energy gained from the prey (the value of the prey minus the energy lost during handling). This calculation tells us how much energy the forager can expect to gain for each prey type.

"average" gain per prey type $= p * \lambda *$ total search time

$$* \text{(energy gained} - \text{energy lost).} \qquad (9.1)$$

Next, we need to know what attacking each type of prey costs in terms of time diverted from searching for other, potentially better, prey items. To determine that cost, we multiply the probability of an attack by the frequency of an encounter and the total search time for that prey type to find the average number of prey attacked. This product is multiplied by the total handling time for that prey type. This calculation tells us how much time is lost as a result of handling this type of prey if one adopts this particular attack strategy:

"average" time taken per prey type $= p * \lambda * \text{(total search time)}$

$$* \text{(handling time).} \qquad (9.2)$$

Finally, one performs this calculation for every possible prey type and then totals all of these gains to give the total energy gain for a particular set of attack strategies, P. This total energy gain is then divided by the sum of the times spent searching and the time spent handling. This calculation thus yields a measure of how much energy is gained, for a given set of attack strategies, per unit time:

$$R = \frac{[(\text{sum over all prey types: average gain})}{\text{total search time} + [\text{sum over all prey types: average handling time}]}$$

$$(9.3)$$

This equation describes the problem faced by the spider and the lion alike. For any given set of prey types with a known value, handling time, handling cost, and encounter rate, we can plug in an attack strategy and then compute the average energy gain per hour associated with that strategy.

Of course the goal of the animal in evolutionary terms is to select an attack strategy that maximizes the rate of energy gain. One way for us to figure that out would be to systematically try all possible attack strategies and then compare the results. Or we could adopt some more random and competitive search strategy that might approximate the way evolution would approach this problem. Thanks to the invention of the calculus, we, as mathematical biologists, can do something much more elegant: We can figure out directly which specific attack strategy maximizes the rate of energy intake. To do that, we perform a bit of calculus on equation 9.3 and create a new equation that allows us to compute the set of attack strategies that maximize R.[2]

Once this new equation has been derived, an interesting, and unexpected, observation emerges. In order to maximize the rate of energy intake, R, the probability that a particular prey type will be attacked should be either 1 or 0. That is, one should either *always* attack a particular prey type or one should *never* attack a particular prey type, an observation known as the zero-one rule. Under no conditions should one ever attack any type of prey only *sometimes*.

Which prey types should be attacked? The model reveals that a prey type should never be attacked if the energy gained from eating it divided by the handling time (this is the net rate of energy gain for that prey type) is less than the probability of encountering each other prey type times the rate of energy gain from those other prey types. In other words, attack something only if attacking it will yield greater value than spending that time looking for something better.

When the zero-one rule and the observation that one should attack something only if one cannot do better by looking for something else are derived, the forager's goal becomes clear. Rank order all prey items in terms of profitability (the ratio of energy gained to handling time invested) and then set a cutoff point in the rank order. Any item more profitable than the cutoff point should always be attacked, and any item less profitable than the cutoff should never be attacked.

Whether or not an item is above or below the cutoff depends on (1) how profitable that item is and (2) the profitability and encounter rates for all better (more profitable) prey. Surprisingly, this means that whether or not you attack a particular item is independent of how likely or unlikely it is that you will encounter that prey type or any less profit-

2. Readers interested in the actual derivations should see Stephens and Krebs (1986) for a full presentation.

able prey type. Stephens and Krebs refer to this as the independence of inclusion from encounter rate principle.

Now let me explain why I have taken the time to present this model in so much detail. First and foremost this is an example of how economically based models of likelihoods and gains can be used in biological research. Charnov is trying to develop a full mathematical description of the problem that evolution engages when foragers develop. Efficient foragers, by definition, gather more food in less time than inefficient foragers. Charnov's prey model is an effort to describe what makes a forager efficient. It is our hypothesis that this is, as Marr might have said, the computational goal, or perhaps more accurately, the computational constraint that evolution must operate within as foragers evolve. In the next section we begin to test that hypothesis by asking how good the prey model is and how well it predicts the behavior of real animals.

Empirical Tests of Foraging Economics

The classic test of the prey model and the assumptions on which it is based was made by Krebs, Charnov, and two of their colleagues, Jonathan Erichsen and Michael Webber, in the mid-1970s (Krebs et al., 1977). Krebs and his colleagues' goal in designing the following experiment was to test two specific predictions of the prey model. First, they wanted to test the independence of inclusion from encounter rate principle, the hypothesis that whether or not you attack an item is independent of how frequently you see it (or how frequently you see any less valuable item). This seemed to them to be a bit counterintuitive, and thus an interesting thing to test. Second, they wanted to test the zero-one rule, the principle that you either attack a particular prey type every time you see it or you never attack it, that you become deterministic about attacking a prey type once all the other variables and likelihoods have been considered.

To perform an experimental test of the prey model in the laboratory, Krebs and his colleagues needed to find an animal that could forage in a very controlled setting where they could precisely regulate the encounter frequency for two or more prey types. They would also have to be able to control, or at least measure, the value, handling time, and handling cost associated with each prey type. With these values in hand, the prey model could then be used to make specific predictions about the behavior of the actual animal during foraging.

Krebs and his colleagues settled on a small bird, *Parus major*, which goes by the English common name of great titmouse, as the subject of their experiments. Tits are a genus of the order Passeriformes, which includes the finches, larks, and swallows, among others. The great titmouse is a 5-inch-tall bird distributed throughout Europe that in the wild eats mostly insects in the summer and seeds and fruit in the winter. In captivity, a favorite food of titmice is mealworms, and it was on this prey that Krebs and his colleagues focused.

In order to create two prey items of known value, these scientists artificially created what they called large and small mealworms. Large mealworms were cut from the centers of whole mealworms and were exactly eight mealworm segments long. Small mealworms were half this length. (See figure 9.1.)

Next, an artificial foraging environment into which a hungry titmouse could be placed was constructed. The environment was a 1-cubic-meter cage. Near the floor of the cage was a perch placed just over a black

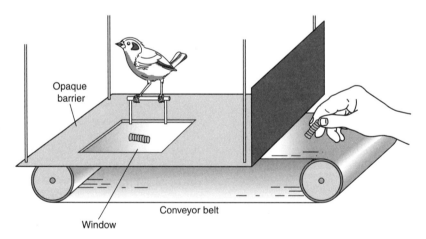

Figure 9.1
Krebs's mealworm foraging experiment.

rubber conveyor belt. The bird could view the belt through an open $2\frac{1}{2}$-in. window cut into the floor beneath its perch. Beneath this window the conveyor belt could be seen moving along at about 5 in. per second. A large or small mealworm placed on the conveyor belt by the hidden hand of an experimenter was visible for about half a second as it rushed by the waiting bird.

In order to make the prey model of this situation quantitative, Krebs and his colleagues assumed that the value of the large mealworms was twice the value of the small mealworms. To make the small mealworms even less profitable, a strip of paper tape eight segments long was attached to each small mealworm. Because the titmice would have to remove the tape before eating the smaller prey, this would increase the handling time for small mealworms significantly. To determine the exact handling times for each individual titmouse, the authors gave each bird prey items of both types and timed how long it took each individual to grab, handle, and eat each type of prey. Large mealworms were handled at about the same speed by all five subject birds, but each bird handled the small prey items at different speeds ranging from 5 to 12.5 sec per small mealworm. From these data the authors were able to compute the precise mathematical profitability, *for each individual bird*, of each prey type.

In order to present the two kinds of prey items under different conditions, the authors designed five foraging situations. In condition A, large and small mealworms were placed on the conveyor belt independently, but both appeared about once every 40 sec; large and small mealworms were encountered at a rate of 1.5 per minute. In condition B, again the two kinds of prey appeared with equal frequency, about once every 20 sec. In conditions C, D, and E the large prey always appeared once every 6.5 sec but the small prey appeared at rates ranging from once every 20 sec to once every 3.5 sec.

With these data in hand, the prey model made very specific predictions about what each bird should do under each experimental condition. First, the equations predicted that the two birds who handled the small prey fastest should, over the range of encounter frequencies tested, always take all prey. These two birds should take all prey because the profitability of the small prey (to these particular birds) was high enough that a maximal rate of energy intake would be achieved when both large and small mealworms were taken. For the three other birds, in contrast, the prey model predicted that as soon as the large prey were encountered more frequently than once every 7 or 8 sec, the birds should become selective. Under these conditions, the three slow birds should take only the larger mealworms, ignoring the smaller ones. The independence of inclusion from encounter rate principle meant that they should take only the large mealworms under these conditions, regardless of how frequently the small mealworms appeared. In other words, in conditions C, D, and E they should be selective even though the rate of encounter with the small prey was varied over a sixfold range.

In fact, this is exactly what Krebs and his colleagues observed. The two fastest small mealworm handlers remained unselective under all conditions. As predicted from their rate maximization equations, they took any worm that appeared on the conveyor belt under any condition that was examined. The three other birds, however, showed a preference for large worms only after the large worms were encountered at a frequency of once every 6.5 sec. This selectivity was, as predicted by theory, unaffected by the frequency with which the small worms were encountered.

These data thus seem to support one of the hypotheses that Krebs and his colleagues had derived from the prey model, the independence of inclusion from encounter rate principle. But Krebs had also set out to test a second idea derived from the prey model, the zero-one rule. The zero-one rule states that if a prey item is worth eating, eat it all the time. If it is not worth eating, eat it none of the time. This all-or-none selection of prey was one of the most interesting and counterintuitive predictions of the prey model. A particularly relevant point here is that the model predicts that for a given encounter frequency and prey value, foragers should behave deterministically.

Translated into a prediction for the behavior of the birds, this principle suggested that under conditions C, D, and E (when the three slow-handling birds should have been selective for large mealworms), the three slow birds should have completely ignored the small mealworms. Surprisingly, this was not exactly what Krebs and his colleagues observed. While the birds were selective, only about 85 percent of the worms that they took under these conditions were large worms, not the 100 percent predicted by theory. The birds seemed to persist in behaving probabilistically even when the prey model said that they should have been a good deal more deterministic.

Conclusions from Testing the Prey Model

I think that a number of important conclusions can be drawn both from the existence of the prey model and from this empirical test of its applicability to real animals. The prey model was designed both to describe the problems that a foraging animal faces and to define an optimal solution to that problem. The model faces a real-world problem and has to identify a solution by assuming that foragers who are more efficient are more fit. It does this by using theoretical tools from economics. Probabilities (in the form of encounter frequencies) and utilities (in the form of profitabilities) are combined in the prey model to describe the computational goal of the organism under these conditions.

In terms of describing the basic behavior of the animals, it also seems clear that this economic model does a good job of describing what the birds decide to eat. The time that it takes each bird to handle the small worms, the frequency with which the large worms are encountered, and the relative profitability of the two prey types all seem to influence the decisions that the birds make in a simple and mathematically tractable fashion. This is exactly the result that we would expect to obtain if models based on standard economic theories did describe the computations that the brains of these birds performed.

The model, however, does make a prediction that is not fulfilled. The model predicts an all-or-none selectivity by the birds (the zero-one rule) that is not observed. In their paper, Krebs and his colleagues offer an interesting explanation for this observation. They suggest that the birds occasionally select a small worm in order to update an internal estimate of the relative profitability of the two prey types. Their argument is that the birds cannot risk the possibility that the small worms might become more profitable while they go unsampled. So the birds always sample the small worms at a low frequency. In essence, what the authors are saying is that the birds probably are behaving optimally; it is the mathematical model that is in error. The values of prey change in the real world, and the nervous systems of the birds recognize this fact. As a result, they sample the small worms occasionally because within the global environment, the environment that extends outside the laboratory setting in which the prey model was tested, this is an optimal strategy.

There are, however, at least two other possible explanations for the failure of the zero-one rule that are quite interesting. The first is that the birds may be unable to behave optimally. Phylectic or architectural constraints in the brains of the birds may prevent them from adopting the presumably optimal zero-one strategy. For a neurobiologist this would be one of the most exciting outcomes because it would mean that some portion of the neural circuit which selects prey should show this interesting and very characteristic limitation. Another possibility is that being unpredictable may be a more essential feature of animal behavior than we have so far realized. This is a point that we will return to when we discuss the theory of games and competition between animals for limited resources.

Summary

Many tests have been made of the prey model with species ranging from insects to mammals (and tests have been made of many other economically based models of behavior as well). Most of these tests of the prey model have yielded similar results: The independence of inclusion from encounter rate principle seems to be widely supported, whereas the zero-one rule seems not to be precisely observed.[3] I picked the titmouse experiment because it is the most famous and well-studied example of this type.

The most important point that these models make is that it *is* possible to extend Marr's approach both into an uncertain world by using probability theory and into the broader domain of complex behavior by using assumptions from evolutionary biology. These models and experiments seem to me to be an empirical proof that economically based optimality

---

3. The observation that the zero-one rule has never really been observed in tests of many species of animals from many different evolutionary lineages does seem to suggest that it may be a feature of convergent evolution. That lends credence to the idea that it may be an optimal strategy in a way we do not yet understand.

modeling can be used to identify the computational goal of a behavior and that the behavior of real animals can be understood in terms of these goals. And from a neurobiological perspective there is, of course, no doubt that these behaviors are produced by brains. Predatory behavior represents sensorimotor processing as surely as does the cutaneous withdrawal response. So why, I think we need to ask ourselves, has modeling of this type been almost completely absent from the field of neurophysiology? Nickolai Bernstein foreshadowed this question in 1961 when he wrote:

That important form of cerebral modelling which was only recognized by investigators after the arousal of interest in the physiology of activity—that is, the *modelling of the future* to which we now turn—is logically possible only by means of extrapolation from whatever the brain is able to select from the current situation, from the fresh traces of immediately preceding perceptions, from the entire previous experience of the individual, and finally from those active trials and assays belonging to the class of actions which have so far been summarized briefly as orientational reactions and whose fundamental significance has certainly been underestimated.

. . .

In sharp distinction to the model of the present, the model of the future has *a probabalistic* character. The anticipation or expectance of the possible outcome towards which the current situation is moving is only possible by means of the extrapolation and never, generally speaking, can be brought to a categorical result. At any phase of this process the brain is only in a position to survey a sort of table of probabilities for possible outcomes.

. . .

In this way the organism's activity is directed against the probabalistic model of the future ... (Bernstein, 1961)

Although the behavioral ecologists, as a group, have shied away from neurobiologial explanations, this need not necessarily be the case. Economic models could be used to define behavioral goals that could serve as starting points for physiological studies of brain function. Physiology could be used to identify computational modules that achieve economically defined goals. To make it clear just how this might be accomplished, we turn next to a case study in physiology, the study of sensorimotor processing in the primate eye movement control system.

10
Probability, Valuation, and Neural Circuits: A Case Study

This chapter is a case study. It describes how a number of research groups, including my own, have struggled to understand a very specific neural circuit. For about 50 years, neurophysiologists have tried to understand the role that parietal cortex plays in the generation of movements that are guided by sensory events. Among these researchers, a debate has raged over whether parietal cortex should be considered the last link in a hierarchically organized set of structures specialized for sensory processing or whether it should be considered the first step along the final common path for movement production. Despite dozens of clever experiments, no one has ever been able to answer this question convincingly. Indeed, many young researchers have argued that this debate poses an unanswerable, and perhaps even unimportant, question. What I want to argue in this chapter is that the question of what parietal cortex does in this context is neither unanswerable nor unimportant. I want to argue, instead, that the computations around which parietal cortex is organized are missing from the questions which classical approaches *can* ask. I will suggest that if the debate were refocused around concepts like probability and valuation, experiments that try to determine the computational function of parietal cortex would become more fruitful undertakings.

My goal for this chapter is therefore threefold. First, I want to show how modern physiological studies of sensorimotor processing in parietal cortex have tended to stick with traditional reflex-based conceptualizations. The second goal of this chapter is to show that probability theory and theories of valuation can be applied to the physiological problems encountered in parietal cortex which are usually thought to be the exclusive province of determinate reflexlike theories. The final goal of this chapter is to demonstrate that when these economically based approaches are applied, surprising and illuminating results about the computational structure of the brain can be derived.

To accomplish these goals, I want to describe research on the control of eye movements that is closely related to the work of Newsome and Shadlen described in chapter 5. As those experiments attest, tremendous strides have been made toward understanding how animals gather visual data from the outside world and use that data to plan and execute eye movements. The primate visual system is, without a doubt, the most heavily studied neural system in any vertebrate brain. The primate eye movement control system is undebatably the movement control system that we understand best. For this reason, studies of the pathways that connect visual-sensory systems with eye movement control systems in the monkey brain have served as models for understanding the sensory-to-motor process in general. It is the study of these pathways, and their interconnections in parietal cortex, that is the subject of this chapter.

To understand how research on the sensory-to-motor functions of the parietal cortex has progressed, one has to begin with an outline of the visual and eye movement control circuitry in the primate brain. Only after this basic ground plan is clear can we move on to examine studies of the connections between these two sets of areas and to challenge conceptual approaches to the problem of how sensory and motor areas *ought* to be connected.

An Overview of Visual-Saccadic Processing

Visual Processing in the Primate Brain

Monkeys, like all mammals, receive their visual information from the right and left retinas. Lining the inner surface of the eyeball like a sheet of photographic film, each retina is a mosaic made up of about 1 billion photoreceptors.[1] The activity of these photoreceptors is processed within the retina and passed, by a class of neurons called retinal ganglion cells,

1. In humans.

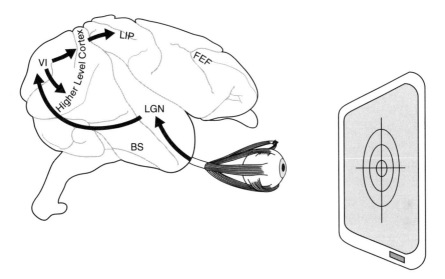

Figure 10.1
The principal pathways for visual processing.

through the optic nerve to the neurons of the lateral geniculate nucleus, or LGN. (See figure 10.1.)

The lateral geniculate nucleus in monkeys is a laminar structure, composed of six pancake-like sheets of neurons stacked on top of each other. Each sheet receives a topographically organized set of projections from one of the two retinas. This topographic organization means that at a particular location in, for example, the second layer of the lateral geniculate, all the neurons receive inputs from a single fixed location in one of the two retinas. Because individual locations in a retina monitor a single location in visual space (like an individual location on a photographic negative), each location in the geniculate is specialized to monitor a particular position in the visual world.

It has also been shown that adjacent positions within any given geniculate layer receive projections from adjacent positions within the referring retina. This adjacent topographic mapping means that each layer in the geniculate forms a complete and topographically organized screen on which retinal activity is projected. Each geniculate neuron thus has a receptive field, in the sense that Sherrington might have used the word.

Activation of that neuron occurs when a stimulus of the right kind falls on the topographically appropriate place in the retina.

These geniculate maps project, in turn, to the primary visual cortex. Lying against the back of the skull, the primary visual cortex, also called area V1, is composed of about 4 million neurons. These 4 million neurons form their own complex topographic map of the visual world; each square millimeter of tissue is specialized to perform a basic analysis on all the patterns of light that could fall on a specific region of the retina. Within these 1-mm-square chunks of cortex, individual neurons have been shown to be highly specialized. Some neurons become active whenever a vertically oriented boundary between light and dark falls on the region of the retina they monitor. Others are specialized for light-dark edges tilted to the right or to the left. Some respond to input exclusively from one retina; others respond equally well to inputs from either retina. Still others respond preferentially to colored stimuli. This complex pattern of sensitivities, or of receptive field properties, in area V1 is of tremendous conceptual importance. It suggests that information coming from the retina is sorted, analyzed, and recoded before being passed on to other visual areas.

The topographic, or retinotopic, map in area V1 projects, in turn, to a host of areas that also contain topographically mapped representations of the visual world. Areas with names like V2, V3, V4, and MT construct a maze of ascending and descending projections among what may be more than thirty mapped representations of the visual environment.[2] These networks of maps are the neural hardware with which we perceive the visual world around us.

While significant disagreement exists about the exact functions of each of these areas, nearly all neurophysiologists would agree that these are regions specialized for sensory processing. These areas may be heavily interconnected. They may do a tremendous amount of computational analysis. But what they do is to represent properties of the visual world. They serve as huge arrays of receptive fields, some of which are active only for the most specific combinations of visual events, but they are without a doubt sensory structures, or so most of us argue today. (For an overview of the primate visual system, see Reid, 1999.)

---

2. As measured in monkeys.

Eye Movements and the Primate Brain

At the other end of the sensorimotor connection lies the circuitry that controls movements of the eyes, circuitry that activates and deactivates the six muscles that rotate each eyeball in its bony socket. Although all movements of the eyes are produced by these six muscles, eye movements can be broken into two fairly discrete classes. *Gaze-stabilization* movements shift the lines of sight of the two eyes to compensate precisely for an animal's self-motion; these movements stabilize the visual world on the retina as we move about in the world. *Gaze-aligning* movements point a portion of the retina specialized for high resolution, the fovea, at objects of interest in the visual world. These are the movements we use when we look at something. Gaze-aligning movements can be further broken down into two subclasses: saccades and smooth pursuit movements. Saccadic eye movements rapidly shift the lines of sight of the two eyes from one place in the visual world to another at rotational velocities up to 1000°/sec. They are the orienting movements of the eyes we use to look back and forth when examining a picture or a landscape. Smooth pursuit eye movements rotate the eyes at a velocity and in a direction identical to those of a moving visual target, stabilizing that moving image on the retina. These are the movements we use when we track a car moving along a road.

The best understood category of eye movements is undoubtedly saccades. At this time we know a tremendous amount about the interconnected brain areas that play critical roles in saccade generation. For this reason the saccadic motor control system seems to be an ideal place to try to understand motor control in general. (See figure 10.2.)

When a saccade is produced, the six muscles that control the position of each eye are activated by six groups of motor neurons that lie deep in the brainstem (BS). These alpha motor neurons are, in turn, controlled by two other systems also located in the brainstem, one that regulates the horizontal position of the eye while a saccade is in flight and one that regulates the vertical position of the eye in flight. These two control centers receive inputs from two interconnected saccadic control areas, the superior colliculus (SC) and the frontal eye field (FEF). Like the visual areas described above, the superior colliculus and the frontal eye field are constructed in topographic fashion. In this case their constituent neurons

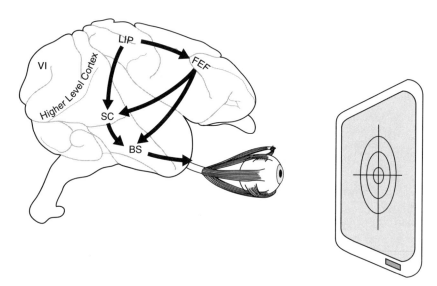

Figure 10.2
The principal pathways for saccade production.

form topographic maps of all possible eye movements. To understand how that works, imagine a photograph of a landscape. Now overlay a transparent coordinate grid that shows the horizontal and vertical eye movement that would be required to look directly at any point in the underlying photograph. Both the superior colliculus and the frontal eye fields contain maps very like these transparent coordinate grids. Activation of neurons at a particular location in the superior colliculus causes a saccade of a particular amplitude and direction to be executed. If this point of activation is moved across the collicular map, the amplitude and direction of the elicited saccade change in a lawful manner specified by the horizontal and vertical lines of the coordinate grid around which the map is organized. The neurons of the superior colliculus and the frontal eye field form topographically organized command arrays in which every neuron sits at a location in the map dictated by the direction and length of the saccade it produces.

I think that it would be uncontroversial (although not necessarily correct) to say that all of these saccadic control structures, from the frontal eye fields to the eye muscles themselves, are generally considered motor control areas. Many of them are interconnected in complex ways, and there is no doubt that each of these areas performs different and fairly complex computations, but most neurophysiologists would argue that these areas should be considered a final common path for saccade production. (For an overview of the eye movement control systems, see Glimcher, 1999.)

Linking Vision and Saccades

Consider the following fairly typical experimental situation. A thirsty monkey is staring straight ahead, fixating a tiny yellow spot of light projected onto a screen 3 ft in front of him. At an unpredictable time, a red spot appears 10° to the right of where the monkey is looking and then the original yellow spot is extinguished. If the monkey makes a saccade that shifts his line of sight toward the red spot, he receives a squirt of Berry Berry Fruit Juice (which monkeys love) as a reward. When we perform this experiment, and the monkey orients toward the red spot, he does it within about a quarter of a second. How does the monkey's brain use the visual stimulus of the red light to produce the 10° rightward saccade in a quarter of a second? (See figure 10.3.)

We know that a light illuminated 10° to the right of straight ahead will activate a specific location in each retina. This activation will propagate to specific topographic locations among the six maps of the lateral geniculate nucleus and then on to a specific region in the primary visual cortex. From there the activity will spread among many of the interconnected maps of the visual cortices. At corresponding positions on each of these maps, the red target will give rise to activity in small clusters of neurons.

We also know that just before the monkey makes his saccade, the position on the collicular and frontal eye field maps associated with a 10° rightward movement will become active. This activity, in turn, will lead to activation of the neurons of the horizontal saccadic control center in the brain stem. The horizontal control center will then activate the two clusters of alpha motor neurons that regulate the tension on the lateral and medial rectus muscles of each eye, causing the eyeballs to rotate.

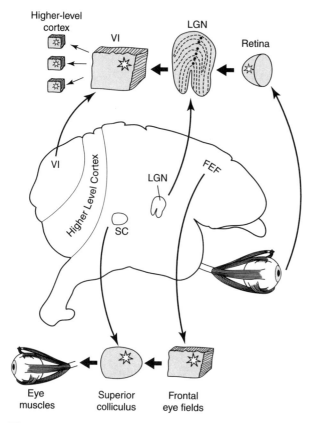

Figure 10.3
Patterns of neural activity when a target to the right elicits a rightward eye movement.

So how does the activity associated with the onset of the red light precipitate the eye movement? The simplest possible answer to that question is that the neurons of the motor system must be activated by the neurons in the visual system, via some "simple definite path." If we think of the saccadic control areas as the final common path for saccades and we conceive of the visual-sensory areas as a very elaborate Sherringtonian receptor, then the connection between them can be thought of as the product of an internuncial neuron (or neurons) connecting these two systems. Conceptualized this way, it seems reasonable to ask whether or not we can find evidence of a connection between the sensory and motor systems of the primate visual saccadic system that is active when this simple visual-saccadic response is produced. This linking connection must be the internuncial element that yields the sensorimotor response.

One way to begin looking for that connection would be to identify, at a purely anatomical level, those areas of the brain which actually connect the visual cortices with the frontal eye field and the superior colliculus. When one examines the anatomical connections between the visual and motor systems, a number of areas in posterior parietal cortex stand out. One in particular has been the subject of tremendous attention, the lateral intraparietal area, or area LIP.

The Visual-Saccadic Function of Parietal Cortex

By the 1950s most of parietal cortex had come to be called an association area in neuroscience textbooks. At that time, cortex came in essentially three flavors: sensory, motor, and association. The word *association* had come to neuroscience from the study of conditioned reflexes, where Pavlov had used it to refer to the process by which a stimulus comes to be associated with the production of a new response.

At that time, studies of neurological patients with damage to the association areas of parietal cortex had already made it clear that the bulk of the parietal lobe is not necessary either for sensory processing or for the production of movement. Patients with parietal damage were known to see and hear fairly well. They also could move their limbs and both eyes in a fairly normal manner. But these patients seemed to be impaired on tasks in which they needed to use one or more of their senses in order to plan a movement. These observations, and others like them made in monkeys, had led scientists to conclude that parietal cortex was something neither exactly sensory nor exactly motor. Inescapably, this led to the conclusion that it must be used to generate sensorimotor associations. Unfortunately, a more precise theory of what the parietal association areas did was lacking.

This almost complete ignorance about parietal association areas was, in large part, due to a serious technical limitation. In the 1950s it was possible to record the activity of single nerve cells within the brains of anesthetized animals. This was a critical technology for physiologists who wished to study sensory systems, because it allowed them to determine what role different groups of neurons played in the processing of sensory data. In a typical experiment these physiologists might stroke the forearm of an anesthetized cat while using microelectrodes to trace through the nervous system the pattern of activity produced by that stroking. In a similar way, physiologists could study motor control in anesthetized animals by electrically activating small groups of nerve cells with microelectrodes. This allowed them to determine how these cells influenced muscle tension. But association areas simply could not be studied in anesthetized animals because anesthetized animals could not make associations (or do anything else, for that matter). In the 1950s it was not possible to study single nerve cells in conscious animals. The technology simply did not exist, and this was a critical limitation because it meant that association areas could not be studied in a meaningful way.

In the late 1950s two researchers, Herbert Jasper at the Montreal Neurological Institute in Canada and Edward Evarts at the U.S. National Institutes of Health, took on this critical technical problem. Both men were convinced that neurobiologists had to be able to record the activity of single neurons within the brains of conscious, behaving animals without injuring the animals or disrupting their normal behavioral patterns. This seemed possible because it was known that the brain itself possesses no pain or touch receptors. Tiny wires inserted into the brains of conscious animals would therefore be undetectable by the animals. Jasper hoped to use this approach to study the activity of single nerve cells while monkeys formed memories in a normal fashion. Evarts hoped to understand how arm movements were produced by studying the activity of neurons in motor cortex.

In 1958 Jasper published the first report of this technique, demonstrating unequivocally that recording from the brains of conscious animals was both possible and well tolerated by the animals. Evarts then took the technique a step farther, developing and largely perfecting a system almost identical to the one in widespread use today. The development of this technique was critical because it meant that the parietal association areas could finally be studied in action.

The Command Hypothesis
The first laboratory to use this new technology to study parietal cortex in action was Vernon Mountcastle's research group at the Johns Hopkins

University in Baltimore. Mountcastle had made a name for himself by using microelectrodes to study the somatosensory cortices of anesthetized animals, the sensory cortex responsive to touch stimuli. He and his students had performed landmark studies that laid the foundation both for our modern theory of how the cerebral cortex in general works and for our modern theory of how the somatosensory system in particular works. Mountcastle was at the center of the neuroscience establishment, and his decision to use single-neuron recording in conscious animals to study an association area was a critical step. It gave the stamp of approval from the scientific establishment for physiologists to use what was coming to be called the *awake-behaving preparation* to do what is now called *cognitive neuroscience.*

Mountcastle and his team of young physiologists (Mountcastle et al., 1975) proceeded by training monkeys to sit quietly while visual and tactile stimuli were presented to them. They also trained the monkeys to use specific visual stimuli as cues to produce behavioral responses that, if performed correctly, would yield rewards. For example, a monkey might be trained to reach toward a light whenever the light was illuminated, regardless of where the light was positioned in the space around the monkey. If the animal did reach for the light, she would receive a drink of fruit juice. Or the monkey might be trained to reach out and touch a button as it moved past along a track. In 1975 Mountcastle's group published a landmark paper that reported the results of these experiments. (See figure 10.4.)

The major conclusion we draw from the observations described above is that there exist within the posterior parietal association cortex sets of neurons which function as a command apparatus for the behavioral acts of manual and visual exploration of the immediately surrounding extrapersonal space.

. . .

The projection and hand-manipulation neurons of the parietal cortex appear to be neither sensory nor motor in nature, but stand in a selective *command* [my italics] relation to movements of a particular sort.

. . .

We wish to emphasize the following: that our concept of command centers explicitly assumes that there exist within the central nervous system many sources of commands to the motor apparatus. The source of the command and its nature will differ remarkably in different behavioral reactions, even though the peripheral musculature engaged in the different acts may be virtually identical.

. . .

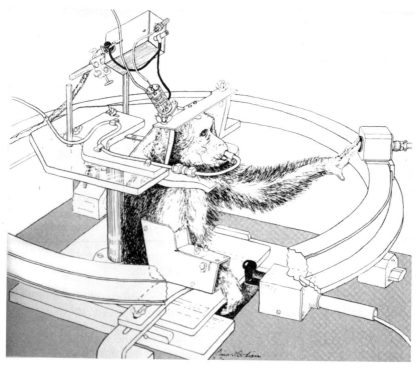

Figure 10.4
Mountcastle's experimental setup. (From Mountcastle, Lynch, Georgopoulos, Sakata, and Acuna, 1975, Posterior parietal association cortex of the monkey: Command functions for operations within extrapersonal space. *J. Neurophys.* 38: 871–908.)

We propose that several of the abnormalities of function that occur in humans and in monkeys after lesions of the parietal lobe can be understood as deficits of *volition*, of the will to explore with hand and eye the contralateral half-field of space, a deficit caused by the loss of the command operations for those explorations which exist in the parietal association cortex. (Mountcastle et al., 1975)

These single-neuron studies led Mountcastle and his colleagues to suggest that a nonsensory and nonmotor process was taking place in parietal cortex, something they named a command process. While they argued that this process should be considered neither sensory nor motor in nature, it seems clear that they viewed it as more closely related to the generation of a movement than to the processing of sensory signals. The name "command center" alone makes this clear.

Shortly after the Mountcastle lab published this manifesto arguing for the existence of a parietal command process, evidence began to accumulate that would challenge their proposal. Initially, this challenge came from Michael Goldberg (then at the U.S. National Institutes of Health), a scientist who had been developing an alternative conceptual approach to understanding how sensory signals could act to precipitate movements.

Attentional Enhancement

In the years immediately before Mountcastle published the command hypothesis, Goldberg had worked with his colleague and mentor, Bob Wurtz, to perform the first characterization of eye movement-related activity in the superior colliculus, using the awake-behaving monkey technique. It was a technique that Wurtz had learned from Edward Evarts while Wurtz was himself a postdoctoral fellow at the U.S. National Institutes of Health. (See figure 10.5.)

In Goldberg and Wurtz's first experiments on neurons in the superior colliculus, monkeys had been trained to perform two behavioral tasks. In the first, which they called a fixation trial, monkeys were trained to stare at a visual stimulus located straight ahead while a secondary stimulus was illuminated at some other location. The secondary stimulus would be abruptly extinguished and the monkey would be rewarded for entirely ignoring the existence of this secondary visual stimulus. In a second task, which they called a saccade trial, while the monkeys were staring straight ahead at the central stimulus, a secondary stimulus would be illuminated and the central stimulus would then be extinguished. During these trials the monkey was rewarded if she looked to the secondary target after the central target was extinguished.

Each day, as soon as Goldberg and Wurtz had placed their electrode near a single collicular neuron, they would begin by identifying the location of that neuron in the collicular topographic map. This would allow them to place the secondary stimulus at the precise location in visual or motor space for which that neuron was specialized. Once the secondary stimulus had been fixed at that location, they had the monkey execute a set of fixation trials followed by a set of saccadic trials. On fixation trials they found that the collicular neurons became weakly active when the secondary stimulus was illuminated, and that this weak activity petered out after the secondary stimulus was extinguished. When

Fixation Task

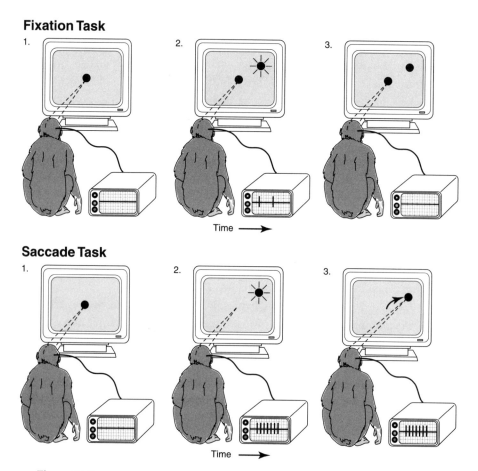

Saccade Task

Figure 10.5
Goldberg and Wurtz's fixation task and saccade task. The oscilloscope beside the monkey displays activity in the superior colliculus during each phase of the task.

they then switched the monkey to saccade trials, they observed that the weak initial response of the neuron grew vigorous late in the trial, just before the monkey made her eye movement. But what surprised them was that as the animal executed saccade trial after saccade trial, the initial response to the onset of the secondary target grew stronger and stronger. It was as if the more certain the monkey grew that the secondary stimulus would be the target of a saccade, the more vigorous was the initial neuronal response.

Because the size and timing of this enhanced initial response had no obvious effect on the movement, Goldberg and Wurtz reasoned that this initial activity must not be a movement control signal. Their observation that the strength of the initial response grew from trial to trial even though the stimulus stayed identical from trial to trial led them to conclude that the enhanced early response must not be purely sensory in nature either.

So what was this signal that was neither sensory nor motor and that they had described several years before Mountcastle's lab had published the command hypothesis? Goldberg and Wurtz had seen no need to postulate anything like Mountcastle's command function to explain their results. Instead, they argued that this enhancement could be viewed as sensory signal that had been modified by attentional factors.

Their basic idea was that whenever the monkey was planning to look at a particular secondary target, she must be paying greater attention to the onset of that target than when she was ignoring it during the fixation task. They reasoned that as the monkey performed saccade trial after saccade trial, her certainty about the importance of that particular secondary target would grow, and she would therefore pay better and better attention to it. Goldberg and Wurtz hypothesized that this attention might somehow increase the strength of the initial neuronal response in the superior colliculus, and this increase in initial response strength was exactly what they had observed. Attention, in their analysis, was a mechanism that could produce changes in sensory responses that rendered these neural signals not really sensory and not really motor, making them enhanced representations of the sensory world.

Mountcastle and his colleagues had proposed the existence of a command process in posterior parietal cortex to explain the existence of signals that were neither truly sensory nor truly motor, and Goldberg saw a close relationship between these parietal signals and the enhanced collicular signals that he had examined. As a result, Goldberg and two new colleagues, David Lee Robinson and Gregory Stanton, immediately began a search for enhancement-like effects in posterior parietal cortex, using the experimental approach that Goldberg had pioneered in the colliculus. These experiments were completed by 1978 (Robinson, Goldberg, and Stanton, 1978) and replicated many of Mountcastle's findings, but because of Goldberg's earlier work they led to very different conclusions.

Since in their [Mountcastle's] experiments neurons associated with movement did not seem to be excitable by passive visual or somatosensory stimulation, these authors postulated that parietal cortex performs a command function for hand movements and eye movements exploring the visual and somatosensory environment. They stressed that neurons in posterior parietal cortex did not have sensory responses, and hypothesized that this area of the brain provided holistic command signals for the motor system. They proposed that this holistic command view should supplant the more traditional associative view of posterior parietal cortex.

In previous studies of visually responsive neurons in the superior colliculus and frontal eye fields, we showed that their visual response was enhanced when a stimulus in the receptive field was going to be the target for an eye movement. We decided to examine neurons in posterior parietal cortex to see whether cells which are associated with visually guided eye movements could be better understood as behaviorally modifiable visual neurons rather than "command neurons." In this study we recorded from 289 cells in area 7 [the saccade-related portion of posterior parietal cortex]. Every neuron which was associated with movement had a sensory response that could be demonstrated in the absence of the movement. In many cases the sensory response was *enhanced* [my italics] when the animal was going to use the stimulus in the receptive field as a target for an eye or hand movement.

. . .

These experiments show that posterior parietal cortex should be viewed as a *sensory association area.* Cells here integrate visual and somatosensory information from the environment with behavioral data which are presumably generated internally. The behavioral information serves to modify the sensory input. If a stimulus is important, such as a target for a movement, that stimulus will have a greater effect on the nervous system than an equivalent stimulus that is unimportant.

Mountcastle and his co-workers have postulated that neurons in posterior parietal cortex perform a command function for eye movements and hand movements. They described neurons that discharged in association with movement but which they could not drive with passive stimuli. We found that every neuron that we encountered in posterior parietal cortex that could be associated with movement could also be excited by some sensory stimulus independent of movement.

. . .

We propose that parietal neurons are best described according to their sensory properties, not according to epiphenomenological movement relationships. (Robinson, Goldberg, and Stanton, 1978)

At some level, Goldberg and Mountcastle were vying to define the neurophysiological model that would serve as a template for understanding the connection between sensory and motor signals. Mountcastle was arguing that a new process would be required at a conceptual level to understand this connection, a process that was neither motor nor sensory, a command process. Goldberg was arguing that the connection between sensation and movement in parietal cortex could be analyzed using existing ideas about associating sensory and motor signals. The linkage between sensory and motor signals could be accomplished by a modulation of sensory signal strength. When the sensory signal was boosted above some critical level by an attentional process, the final common path was activated.

At heart, Goldberg's proposal embodied Pavlov's dictum of necessity. Under some task conditions, sensory activity elicited by a stimulus gives rise to a movement. Under other conditions it does not. Linking elements produce this effect by responding more strongly on trials in which a movement should be produced. The more likely a stimulus is to produce a movement, the stronger will be the enhanced sensory response, thus increasing the likelihood that the final common path will be engaged. These linking elements reflect the fact that "If a stimulus is important, such as a target for a movement, that stimulus will have a greater effect on the nervous system than an equivalent stimulus that is unimportant." The virtues of this approach were its simplicity and the fact that it so clearly embodied Pavlov's notion of necessity. Goldberg's model was an extrapolation of the Cartesian approach to the parietal cortex and to the cortical sensorimotor problem in general.

Mountcastle's approach was fundamentally different. He was arguing for an abandonment of the reflexological approach when thinking about posterior parietal cortex. He was arguing instead for the existence of an entirely new kind of sensorimotor component. But Mountcastle's model was incomplete at best. What, exactly, were these command functions? How did they work? What computational problem were they trying to solve?

At the time that Mountcastle and Goldberg were having this debate, the publication of Marr's book was still several years away. So the need for a rigorous model of exactly what it was that parietal cortex *should* be doing may not have been as clear as it is today. And in terms of the actual features of such a model, probability theory and economic approaches were just beginning to enter biological studies through ecology departments; in the years between Mountcastle's and Goldberg's papers, Eric

Charnov published the first of his formal models. So perhaps for all of these reasons, the debate quickly began to circle away from a direct analysis of the general models being debated and instead focused on experimental challenges to specific claims Goldberg and Mountcastle were making.

Attention Versus Intention
There is absolutely no doubt that Goldberg and his colleagues demonstrated that the notion of a command function added little to our immediate understanding of parietal cortex. A monkey is presented with an eccentric visual stimulus; sometimes he looks toward that stimulus and sometimes he does not. At least on the surface this seems an indeterminate process, a process that should be hard to explain using classical Cartesian models. One might suspect that an additional indeterminate process would be required to explain such a phenomenon, but Goldberg's idea brilliantly resolves the paradox of this apparent indeterminacy without resorting to an explicitly indeterminate event. The direct connection of sensory signals to motor control circuits is modulated by a gating system, sensory attention. Sensory attention, through the physiological mechanism of enhancement, serves to allow some sensory signals access to the motor plant and to deny that access to others. The process appears indeterminate only because we do not understand how the attentional process operates.

The Goldberg model really could account for what physiologists had observed. By the late 1970s even Mountcastle's laboratory began to encounter evidence that there were signals in parietal cortex which seemed more closely associated with sensory events, as Goldberg had proposed, than with motor events. For this reason, and doubtless for others, Mountcastle's group began to turn their electrodes away from posterior parietal cortex, returning to somatosensory cortex. But before they returned entirely to somatosensory cortex, Richard Andersen would have to complete his postdoctoral studies. (See figure 10.6.)

When he joined the Mountcastle lab, Andersen was interested in understanding how circuits that interface between the sensory and motor nervous systems encode the locations of objects and the trajectories of movements. Imagine, as Andersen did, a monkey looking straight ahead while a visual stimulus is presented 5° degrees to the right of where he is

Figure 10.6
Andersen's coordinate transform experiments.

looking. The sensory stimulus activates neurons at a position 5° to the right of straight ahead on the topographic maps of the retina, the lateral geniculate, and the visual cortices. In order to make a movement that aligns his line of sight with that stimulus, the monkey rotates his eye until it is oriented 5° to the right of straight ahead; he activates the 5° rightward locations on the topographically organized motor control maps.

Next consider the case when the same visual stimulus is illuminated at the same place in the world, but now the stimulus is presented while the monkey is looking 10° to the right of straight ahead. Under these conditions the same light, at the same location in the world, now activates a point on the retina 5° to the *left* of straight ahead. Positions in all of the subsequent sensory maps representing 5° left must therefore be active. But if the monkey wants to look at that light, he must still reorient his eyeball so that it comes to rest at a position 5° to the right of straight ahead.

The problem that Andersen became interested in was this: Many sensing surfaces, like the retina, the skin, or the ears of a cat, move around in the world. This means that the alignment between the topographic maps of the sensory systems and the topographic maps of the motor systems that they must control can shift. Andersen realized that one critical function of any system connecting sensory and motor signals, regardless of how it accomplished that linkage, would be to deal with this problem.

Andersen's work in Mountcastle's lab was largely focused on understanding how sensory and motor maps were aligned, and this interest led him into area 7, a subregion of the posterior parietal cortex specialized for sensorimotor interactions and associated with saccadic eye movements. That work reached a watershed several years later when Andersen, by then a professor at the Salk Institute, published an influential paper with Greg Essick and Ralph Siegel titled "Neurons of Area 7 Activated by Both Visual Stimuli and Oculomotor Behavior" (Andersen, Essick, and Siegel, 1987).

Several laboratories have made recordings of the activity of single neurons in area 7a [a subregion within area 7] of the posterior parietal cortex in behaving monkeys and, by correlating the activity of these cells with sensory and motor events, they have made important advances in understanding its functional role. In the earliest experiments Mountcastle and his colleagues found that many of the cells were activated by certain behaviors of the animal, including saccadic eye movements, fixations, smooth pursuit eye movements, and reaching movements of the arms. It was stated that these cells did not respond to visual or somatosensory stimuli. On these grounds it was proposed that area 7 was involved in issuing general motor-commands for eye and limb movements.

In later experiments Robinson, Goldberg and colleagues found that many of the cells in area 7 responded to visual or somatic stimuli. They argued that the behaviorally related responses reported by Mountcastle and his colleagues could be accounted for either by visual stimulation from the target for movement or from visual/somatosensory stimulation resulting from the movement. It was proposed that area 7a was involved in sensory processes and did not play a role in motor behavior as proposed by Mountcastle and colleagues. In a later report Motter and Mountcastle noted some cells which appeared to be oculomotor and light sensitive and proposed that a gradient existed between cells with strictly eye movement related responses and cells with solely visual responses.

In the present study we have designed experiments to distinguish between visual and motor components of the responses of the fixation and saccade neurons and have found that the activity of the cells in these two classes is related both to sensory stimuli and to oculomotor behavior. The nature of the eye movement and fixation (eye position) signals suggests that they play a role in establishing spatial constancy rather than in the initiation of oculomotor behavior. (Andersen, Essick, and Siegel, 1987)

Andersen and his colleagues went on to argue that the most fundamental role of posterior parietal cortex was to solve a problem that was much more clearly defined than how sensory and motor systems are interconnected. As the eyes, limbs, and head move, the relationship between topographic maps of the sensory world and the topographic maps of the motor systems is constantly shifting. Regardless of how we decide which stimuli should trigger a response, we must somehow decide which response that stimulus should trigger. It was this issue—how to link the shifting sensory and motor topographies of the brain—that Andersen identified in 1987 as a central function of posterior parietal cortex.

But in the next year Andersen and his colleagues discovered an unexpected property in parietal cortex that forced them to revisit the command hypothesis. Working as a postdoctoral fellow in Andersen's laboratory, Jim Gnadt trained monkeys to perform a remembered saccade task (Gnadt and Andersen, 1988; see figure 10.7). In that task, while the monkey stared at a central stimulus, a secondary visual stimulus was briefly flashed on and off. The monkey's job was to look at that secondary stimulus, but only after Gnadt turned off the central stimulus. And Gnadt would often leave the central stimulus on for quite a while *after* the secondary target was extinguished. The monkeys had, in effect, to remember what movement they were supposed to make during this enforced delay, which could be up to 1.5 sec. When Gnadt and Andersen used this task to study the activity of neurons in the saccade region of area 7, a region that had by now acquired the name *area LIP*, they made an amazing discovery. They found that neurons activated by the brief flash of the secondary stimulus remained active after the visual stimulus went out, and that this activity persisted until the monkey made the saccade which aligned gaze with the *remembered* location of the stimulus.

We have shown that there is memory-linked activity in the lateral bank of the intraparietal sulcus which is associated with saccadic eye movements of specific direction and amplitude. The activity can be disassociated from the visual stimuli which guide the eye movements.... Therefore, these cells' activity appeared to be related to the pre-movement planning of saccades in a manner which we have chosen to describe as *motor intention* [my italics]. The term motor intention, as we use it here, is meant to convey an association between the behavioral event (i.e., saccade) and the neural activity. It is not meant to suggest that this neural signal is necessary and sufficient to produce the eye movement.

The posterior parietal cortex of primates contains neural signals appropriate for the building of spatial maps of visual target space, memory-linked motor-planning activity and possible corollary feedback activity of saccades. These findings strongly argue that the parietal cortex is intimately involved in the guiding and motor planning of saccadic eye movements. (Gnadt and Andersen, 1988)

Memory Saccade

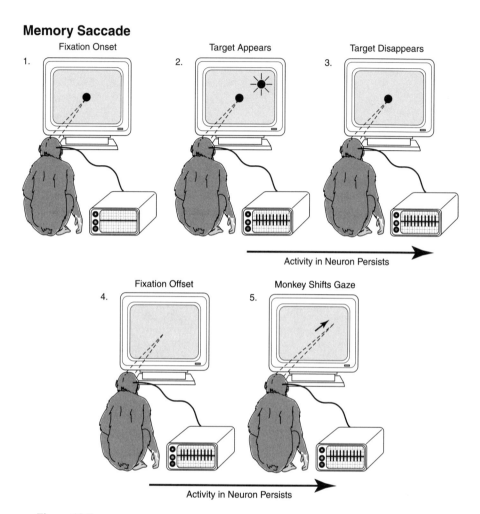

Figure 10.7
Gnadt and Andersen's memory saccade experiment.

Andersen had, in a single salvo, revived a version of the command hypothesis in a new and improved form. He had demonstrated that Goldberg's *enhanced* activity could persist in the absence of a sensory stimulus. This, Andersen proposed, was incompatible with Goldberg's assertion that "parietal neurons are best described according to their sensory properties."

Goldberg and two new colleagues, Carol Colby and Jean-René Duhamel, responded to this new finding by revisiting area LIP. They wanted to know if the results reported by Gnadt and Andersen could be reconciled with their view that posterior parietal cortex was fundamentally a sensory structure. If it could not be reconciled with this view, they wanted to understand exactly what role area LIP played in the sensory-to-motor process.

To begin their new round of investigations, Colby, Duhamel, and Goldberg (1996) taught a new group of monkeys to perform yet another set of tasks. (See figure 10.8.) Of course they taught their monkeys to perform the memory saccade task that Gnadt and Andersen had used, but they also taught them an important pair of tasks that were highly influential and that led to a reinterpretation of Gnadt and Andersen's findings. These two tasks were the fixation task Goldberg had used before, and a new task they called the peripheral attention task. You will recall that in the fixation task the monkey was taught to stare straight ahead at a continuously illuminated central light while a secondary stimulus was turned on. The monkey's job was to ignore the secondary stimulus.

The peripheral attention task was almost identical. Once again the central light illuminated. Once again the monkey was required *not* to make a saccade. But in this task, while the monkey was staring straight ahead and the secondary stimulus was illuminated, the monkey was required to press a lever if she saw the secondary stimulus dim. Goldberg and his colleagues argued that the two tasks were identical from an eye movement control point of view; in neither case was an eye movement produced. The two tasks differed critically, however, in where one might expect the monkey to pay attention. In the fixation task, the eccentric target in the response field was irrelevant, but in the peripheral attention task this same stimulus became highly relevant.

What Goldberg and his colleagues found when they did this experiment was that parietal neurons were much more active in the peripheral

Fixation Task

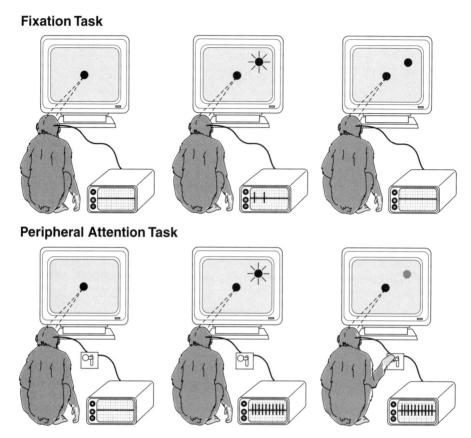

Peripheral Attention Task

Figure 10.8
Colby, Duhamel, and Goldberg's peripheral attention task.

attention task than in the fixation task. Even though neither of the tasks required a movement, they elicited very different responses in LIP neurons. To many scientists this seemed clear evidence that activity in area LIP, and by extension activity in posterior parietal cortex in general, could not simply be a command to make a movement, nor could it reflect the intention to produce a movement. Instead, it seemed that this LIP activity must be correlated with the sensory events to which an animal was paying attention. In communicating these results, however, Colby, Duhamel, and Goldberg took a fairly conciliatory line, perhaps because their relationships with Andersen and his colleagues were growing very strained over this continued dispute.

First, we found that the presaccadic enhancement originally described in area 7 is a *specific enhancement of the visual response* [my italics] to stimulus onset. Second, this enhancement of the visual response in a saccade task is correlated with the degree of enhancement in a purely attentional [movement free] task. [The authors then go on to state two additional findings suggesting that activity immediately before the saccade may well be associated with the movement being produced.]

...

The present results show that LIP neuron activity is multi-faceted and subject to modulation by cognitive factors such as attention and anticipation. LIP neurons have independent sensory responses and saccade-related bursts. Further, attention to a spatial location modulates the sensory response to stimulus onset, and anticipation of a behaviorally significant sensory event affects the level of baseline neural activity.... [These neurons] cannot be regarded exclusively as analyzing visual stimuli because they discharge before saccades even when there has been no recent visual stimulus. They cannot be regarded exclusively as planning saccades because they are strongly responsive in a task in which saccades are expressly forbidden. One way of understanding this varied collection of activations is to consider their point of intersection: the spatial location defined by the preferred stimulus location and the preferred saccade for a given neuron. We suggest that LIP neuron activity encodes events related to a particular spatial location. (Colby, Goldberg, and Duhamel, 1996)

Andersen and his colleagues responded to these new data with a surprising, and quite interesting, hypothesis that was meant to further challenge Goldberg's position. They proposed that during the attentive fixation task Colby had studied, her monkeys were actually *planning* to look at the secondary stimulus even if they did not in the end make that movement. Colby's monkeys, they reasoned, had seen tens of thousand of secondary stimuli that were supposed to precipitate saccades. Perhaps the strength of activity in LIP reflected not attentional enhancement but the animal's certainty about whether or not it *intended* to make to make that saccade.

To validate this hypothesis, Andersen and one of his students, Martyn Bracewell, trained monkeys to perform yet another task. This time, monkeys would begin by staring straight ahead at a central light. Again a secondary stimulus would flash briefly. As in the remembered saccade task, the monkey's job was to wait patiently until the central light was turned off and then to look at the location where the secondary target had appeared. But on some trials, during this waiting interval, Bracewell and Andersen flashed a third light at yet another location. When that happened, the animal had been taught to change her plan. Now when the fixation light went off, she was to look at the location where the tertiary stimulus had appeared.

What Bracewell and Andersen found was that when they told the monkeys to change their plans, the site of activation on the map in area LIP shifted. Neurons associated with a movement to the secondary target became silent and neurons associated with a movement to the tertiary target became active. The very existence of activity associated with the secondary target, they noted, indicated that neurons in area LIP could encode a movement that a monkey was planning to make, even when that movement was never produced.

Andersen and his colleagues saw this as at least a partial refutation of Colby, Duhamel, and Goldberg's conclusions. Perhaps during the peripheral attention task monkeys were planning a movement that they never executed, just as had been observed in the change of plan task. Goldberg, quite reasonably, responded to this by pointing out that the Andersen group's change of plan task data could also be interpreted as evidence that the monkey was shifting where he was paying attention, shifting his attentional enhancement from the secondary to the tertiary target. These data, he argued, proved nothing about the existence of a motor plan or an intention.

Resolving the Attention-Intention Debate?

To many of us on the outside, the Andersen–Goldberg debate over the function of parietal cortex seemed to have sunk almost to a semantic contest. It was clear that Goldberg had been forced to largely abandon his original hypothesis that "posterior parietal cortex should be viewed as a sensory association area." By the same token, Andersen had been forced to abandon the original command hypothesis of Mountcastle in favor of the much weaker intention hypothesis. What, if anything, could all of this tell us about how the nervous system solves the problem of connecting sensory inputs with motor outputs?

At about this time Michael Platt and I, naively, became convinced that we could refocus the parietal debate by designing a single experiment that would directly pit the Goldberg sensory interpretation against the Andersen motor interpretation. What if we could design an experiment in which the movement plan of Andersen's hypothesis and the attentional enhancement of Goldberg's hypothesis were under independent control? Then we could simultaneously test the two competing hypotheses that (1) area LIP carries sensory-attentional signals and that (2) area LIP carries motor intention plans. To do this, we designed yet another set of tasks, tasks that combined the attentive fixation approach Colby, Goldberg, and Duhamel had used with the change of plan task Bracewell and Andersen had used.

I need to pause here to say that this was, to put it simply, a silly idea. Platt and I were doing nothing more than trying to replicate what had already been done. We had stepped right into the middle of this fractious semantic debate with yet another task and without any new theoretical insights. The experiment that we conducted should have earned us no more than a footnote in a history of the Goldberg–Andersen debate. The reason I want to tell you about this last classically styled parietal experiment is that the results it produced convinced us that deciding to do this experiment had been silly. To understand how it convinced us of this, I have to tell you a bit more about the experiment itself.

The Cued Saccade and Distributed Cue Experiment

We reasoned that we would need to design an experiment in which we could attempt to simultaneously falsify each of these two competing hypotheses: the hypothesis that area LIP carries attentional signals and the hypothesis that area LIP carries intentional signals. If our experiment falsified only one of these hypotheses, this would provide support for the other model of parietal cortex and would validate the notion that area LIP could be understood within the framework of that model (Platt and Glimcher, 1997). (See figure 10.9.)

We began by training monkeys to perform, in sequential blocks of trials, two tasks that independently controlled both the location of a secondary stimulus the monkey would be required to look at, and the location and behavioral relevance of a tertiary stimulus at which the monkey would never look. At the start of our experiment each day, and before having the monkey perform the actual experiment, we isolated a single neuron in area LIP for study and had the monkey make a series of eye movements that shifted his gaze into alignment with secondary

Cued Saccade

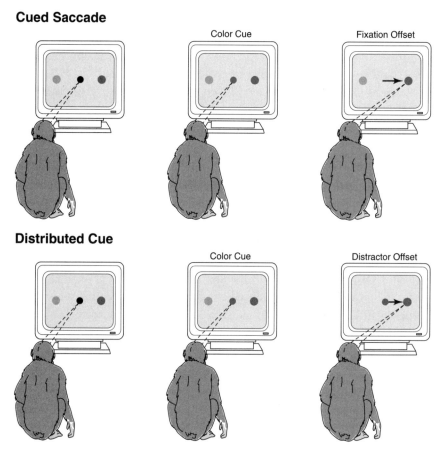

Distributed Cue

Figure 10.9
The cued saccade and distributed cue experiment.

stimuli presented sequentially at a large number of locations. We used these data to identify the location of our neuron in the area LIP topographic map, the *best location* for this neuron. We also used these data to identify a stimulus and movement for which the neuron was inactive, a null location for this neuron.

Once these two locations had been identified, we next had the animal perform a block of cued saccade trials, shown in figure 10.9. Each cued saccade trial began with the illumination of a central yellow light at which the monkey had to look. After a brief delay, the secondary and tertiary targets were illuminated, one at the best location and one at the null location. After a further delay, the central yellow light changed color. On a randomly selected 50 percent of trials it turned green. On the other trials it turned red.

The monkey had been taught in advance that on trials in which the central fixation stimulus turned red, the left light served as the secondary target (the saccadic goal) and the right light served as the tertiary target (a completely irrelevant distractor). On trials in which the fixation stimulus turned green, the converse was true; the right light served as the target and the left light was irrelevant. The monkey was, however, not allowed to look at the secondary target until we turned off the central fixation stimulus. If, after that point, the monkey looked at the correct target, she received a fruit juice reward.

Amazing though it may seem, the monkeys readily learned this task. That made it possible for us to test the motor-intentional hypothesis by comparing two classes of trials that were nearly identical in their visual properties but differed profoundly in their movement properties. In both classes of trials, two eccentric targets were illuminated, one at the best location and one at the null location. The trials differed in the meaning of the eccentric stimulus at the best location. On 50 percent of these trials, the stimulus at the best location had served as the saccadic goal, and in the other 50 percent it served as a totally irrelevant visual distractor. We reasoned that if neurons in area LIP were motor-intentional elements, they should respond strongly when the stimulus within the response field was a target, but *not at all* when it was an irrelevant visual distractor.

The left panel of figure 10.10 shows the average firing rate of forty area LIP neurons during these two classes of trials at three points in time: just after the two eccentric targets turn on, after the fixation stimulus had changed color (identifying the saccadic goal), and just before the saccade began. The solid line shows the activity of the neurons when the fixation stimulus turned red and the monkey looked at the best location. The dashed line in the left panel shows the response of the neurons on trials in which the fixation stimulus turned green and the monkey looked away from the best location.

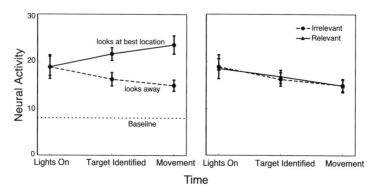

Figure 10.10
Results of the cued saccade experiment.

We clearly found that the population of LIP neurons discriminated between these two conditions. They were very active before and during a movement to the best location. But although they were less active, *they were not silent* when the stimulus at the best location was completely irrelevant. In fact, although neuronal activity was low, it was significantly above the baseline level of activity for these neurons, as shown by the horizontal dotted line. If anything, then, these data suggested to us that our first experiment had falsified the intentional hypothesis because our population of neurons responded to a stimulus at the best location even when the monkey intended to look at the null location.

We next had the animal perform a block of distributed cue trials while we continued to study each neuron. Distributed cue trials, shown in figure 10.9, were almost identical to cued saccade trials. They differed in only one respect: In distributed cue trials it was the offset of the tertiary (or distractor) stimulus, not the offset of the central fixation stimulus, that signaled to the animal that his saccade should be initiated. Because of this difference, gathering data from each neuron during both types of trials (cued saccade and distributed cue) allowed us to compare the behavior of the area LIP population under a second set of nearly matched conditions. Under both of those conditions the animal was instructed to look at the null location. In one case (the cued saccade trials) the stimulus at the best location was completely irrelevant. In the other case (the distributed cue trials) the stimulus at the best location was critically important because it carried the command to initiate a saccade.

We reasoned that if the attentional hypothesis were true, then the neuron should be more active during the distributed cue trials than during the cued saccade trials. In the first case the best location was important and in the second case the best location was irrelevant. Indeed, Carol Colby's experiments with the attentive fixation task *almost* required that this be the case. The right panel of figure 10.10 shows the data that we obtained. The solid line plots the average firing rate on trials in which the stimulus at the best location was relevant, and the dashed line plots average firing rate when the stimulus at the best location was irrelevant. Note that the neuronal responses under these two conditions are virtually indistinguishable, apparently falsifying the attentional hypothesis as well.

Initially, Platt and I found these data tremendously disappointing. Although we tried to put the most definitive spin possible into our paper, the results just confirmed something almost everyone else already knew: The attentional and intentional hypotheses were both wrong at some level.

Ultimately this was a tremendously important thing for us to realize, because it forced us to reconsider our belief that all of the signals in the sensorimotor process had to be characterizable as either sensory or motor. We were forced to ask if nonsensory and nonmotor signals could, in principle, be elements of the sensorimotor process. This was the observation that first led us to consider abandoning the classic Cartesian approach for understanding the connection between sensation and action.

An Alternative Approach: Goals, Probability, and Valuation

What were our animals trying to do when they performed the cued saccade task we had taught them? What was the behavioral goal our animals were trying to achieve? While no classical neurophysiologist had ever asked that question directly, it was the question David Marr had been urging us to ask in the pages of *Vision*. And it was actually a very simple question. What should a rational monkey be doing when he performs the cued saccade task? He should be trying to get as much Berry Berry Fruit Juice as he can, as quickly as possible.

If we begin by assuming that the monkeys do have a goal, and that their goal is to maximize the juice they receive, then we ought to be able to use an economic approach to figure out how they should go about achieving that fairly straightforward goal. An economic approach would suggest that first, the monkeys would need to know the prior probability that looking at the upper target and looking at the lower target would yield rewards. Second, our monkeys would need to know the amount of juice that they could hope to receive for looking at either the upper or the lower target; they would need to know the value of each movement. Finally, our monkeys would have to combine an estimate of the prior probability of reward with an estimate of the value of each movement to determine something like the expected utility of each possible response. Then our monkeys would select and produce the movement with the higher expected utility.

We also realized that for a rational monkey, the expected utility for each movement would change as each trial progressed. Early in each trial, before the fixation light changed color, expected utility would be based on the prior probability that each movement would be rewarded, times the value (or, more precisely, the utility) of each movement. But after the fixation light changed color, the monkey could perform something like a Bayesian probability estimation to determine the posterior probability that looking at the upper or lower target would be rewarded. After the fixation light changed color, which in the cued saccade task indicated with 100 percent certainty which movement would be reinforced, the monkey could combine a posterior probability estimate with an estimate of value to produce a more accurate expected-utility estimate for each movement. Of course, in the experiment we had done, none of these variables, which were the only variables any economist would have considered worth varying, was ever manipulated.

Encoding Probability

Accordingly, we modified our cued saccade task to test a simple hypothesis (Platt and Glimcher, 1999). Since any rational decision-making system must encode the likelihoods of all possible outcomes, we designed an experiment to ask if neurons in area LIP carry information about the probability of obtaining a reward. In all existing physiological studies of LIP, the likelihood that any movement would yield a reward had always been held constant. But if area LIP participated in solving the computational problem of deciding where to look, and if that computational problem could be solved rationally only by a system that kept track of probability, then the activity of neurons in area LIP might well be influenced by the likelihood that a movement would yield a reward.

The goal of our experiment would have to be to present an animal with exactly the same visual stimulus and have her make exactly the same motor response while varying the likelihood that the movement encoded by the neuron we were studying would yield a reward. If we saw evidence that the activity of neurons in area LIP was correlated with either the early prior probability or the later posterior probability, then we would have made an important step. (See figure 10.11.)

We therefore returned our monkeys to the cued saccade task, but this time the probability that the central fixation light would turn red or green on each trial was varied systematically. Animals would be presented with a block of 100 sequential trials in which the probability that a movement toward the right eccentric target would be reinforced might be 80 percent and the probability that a movement to the left eccentric target would be reinforced was 20 percent. That block of 100 trials might be followed by a second block in which these probabilities were reversed. Of course we couldn't tell the monkeys in advance what the relative probabilities were. They would have to work that out for themselves as each block progressed, but after 100 trials we might well expect

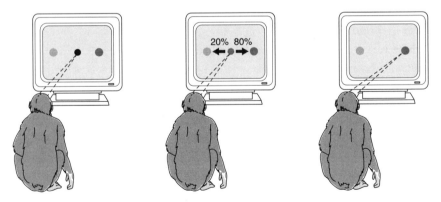

Figure 10.11
Changing probability that a movement will produce a reward in blocks.

them to know something about the likelihood that the central fixation light would turn green. After all, theories of rational decision making require that choosers track this kind of data. Surely evolution would have figured that out and built it into our monkeys' brains.

Now recall that our goal was to test the hypothesis that the prior or posterior probability an upward movement would be reinforced was encoded by upward-preferring neurons in area LIP. Classical studies had focused on whether signals in area LIP should be considered sensory or motor, attention or intention. To steer clear of that debate, we decided to find a way to hold all sensory and all motor properties of the task constant while varying only the probability of reward.

In the standard cued saccade task, on some trials the fixation light turns red and on others it turns green. These different colors represent a disparity in the sensory input provided to the monkey on these two trials. On some trials the monkey looks left, and on others she looks right, a disparity in the motor output. In order to eliminate these sensory and motor properties from our analysis, we made the following adjustment. After the monkey had completed a set of seven blocks of trials (each under a different probability condition), we examined only trials on which the fixation target had turned one color and on which the monkey had correctly looked in the same direction. This subset of trials would be identical in both sensory and motor properties. They would differ only in the likelihood that each of the two movements would yield a reward. What we were trying to do, in essence, was to reverse our old approach. When we had first used the cued saccade task, we had held probability and value constant so that we could determine whether LIP activity was related to sensation or movement. The answer had been Neither. Now we wanted to hold sensation and movement constant while we varied probability.

When we actually did this experiment, the cells produced an unequivocal result. Once we had selected from our data set only those trials on which the same stimulus was presented and the same movement was produced, what we found was very clear. When there was a high prior probability that an upward movement would be rewarded, LIP neurons associated with the upward movement responded very strongly as soon as the upper target was turned on. When there was a low prior probability that an upward movement would yield a reward, the same LIP neurons responded weakly to target onset. This variation in firing rate was observed even though the stimulus and the movement, the only variables employed in the classical models, were identical on all of these trials. To us, this strongly suggested that prior probabilities were being encoded by LIP neurons.

What about posterior probabilities? If one analyzes the pattern of neuronal activity over the course of a trial, one sees that this second measure of probability is also encoded by these neurons. At the beginning of each trial, when the prior probability that the upper target will be identified as the goal is either 80 percent or 20 percent, LIP neurons fire at a higher or a lower rate, depending on the prior probability. But after the fixation light turns red, allowing the animal to compute that the posterior probability is now 100 percent, the firing rate rises. And because we selected out trials from the 80 percent and 20 percent blocks that required the same movement (and thus have the same posterior probability even though they have different prior probabilities), these two blocks of trials should show an identical neuronal firing rate after the color change. Again, this is exactly what we observed. Early in the trial the prior probability seems to be encoded by LIP neurons. Late in the trial the posterior probability seems to be encoded.

Perhaps the most critical aspect of this observation is how it seems to fly in the face of Pavlov's "necessity" criteria. In this particular task it is not necessary for the animals to keep track of the prior probabilities. After all, at the end of each trial the fixation light turns red or green. The posterior probabilities are always clear and unambiguous. Nonetheless, these neurons seem to track probabilities closely throughout the trials.

Figure 10.12 shows an example of how a typical neuron in area LIP responded during this experiment. Both the thick black line and the thick gray line plot the average firing rate of the neuron on groups of trials in which the fixation stimulus turned red and the monkey looked upward. Both the stimuli and the responses are identical in all cases, and thus by definition the behavior was deterministic. The trials plotted in black were drawn from a block in which the central stimulus was 80 percent likely to turn red, and the gray line plots data from a block of trials in which the central stimulus was only 20 percent likely to turn red. Note that

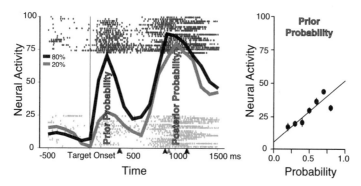

Figure 10.12
Activity of an LIP neuron during the probability experiment. Rows of tick marks in the left panel indicate precise times of neural action potentials during each of twenty trials used to compute the averages shown as thick lines.

even though the sensory and motor properties of the trials were identical, the neuron responded quite differently when the underlying prior probabilities were different.

Early in the trials, when the eccentric stimuli were first illuminated, there was a very large difference between the neuronal firing rates observed under the two conditions. The firing rates then converged just after the fixation stimulus turned red, the point at which the posterior probability becomes 100 percent during both of these blocks. In a sense, then, this LIP neuron appears to carry information related to the *instantaneous* probability that the movement will be reinforced. Early in the trial there is either a 20 percent or an 80 percent probability of reinforcement associated with the movement encoded by this neuron. Later in the trial there is (for both blocks) a 100 percent probability of reinforcement, and at that time the firing rates in both blocks converge. This is exactly the pattern of responding one would expect if neurons in area LIP carried information about the probability that this movement would yield a reward, and it is a pattern of responding that would never have been predicted or required by a reflex-based sensorimotor theory.

In order to determine how efficiently this neuron carried information about the prior probability that this movement would yield a reward, we presented the animal with seven different blocks of trials in which the probability that the fixation stimulus would turn red was systematically varied. We were then able to ask, across seven blocks, how well the average firing rate of this neuron was correlated with the prior probability that the encoded movement would be rewarded. As shown in figure 10.12, firing rate and the prior probability that the fixation stimulus will turn red are strongly correlated. This is exactly the pattern of responding one would expect from a neural element encoding the probability that the upward movement would yield a reward. In order to examine this pattern of responding across several neurons, we performed this experiment on 20 neurons in area LIP. We found that 75 percent of these neurons showed a statistically significant correlation between prior probability and firing rate at some point during the trial.

Encoding Valuation

These data seemed to suggest that there was a nonsensory and nonmotor signal in posterior parietal cortex, just as Mountcastle, Goldberg, and Andersen had suggested. At least in this experiment, it looked like that signal might be related to the probability that a movement would be reinforced. But, as we have seen, essentially all economically based theories of decision making identify two variables as critical in decision making: the likelihood of an outcome and the value of that outcome. This led us to wonder whether neurons in area LIP might also carry information about the value of each movement to the animal.

To examine this possibility, we once again employed the cued saccade task. Animals would again be presented with sequential blocks of 100 cued saccade trials, but for this experiment the likelihood that the fixation stimulus would turn red or green would always be fixed at 50 percent. Across 100-trial blocks we would now vary the amount of reward that the animal would receive for looking up and for looking down. In the first block the animal might receive 0.2 ml of fruit juice as a reward on trials in which he correctly looked left and 0.1 ml of juice on correct rightward trials. In a second block he might receive 0.1 ml on leftward trials and 0.2 ml on rightward trials.

Figure 10.13 plots the behavior of an LIP neuron under these conditions. Again, only trials that were identical in their sensory and motor properties were selected for use in this figure; the trials differ only in the value of the two movements. Note that the neuron fires more strongly

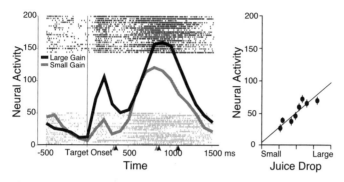

Figure 10.13
Activity of an LIP neuron during the value experiment.

during trials in which the animal could expect to receive a large reward (black line) and more weakly during trials in which the animal could expect to receive a small reward (gray line).

As in the last experiment, we also examined how seven different movement values influenced the firing rates of these neurons early in the trials. Once again we saw that firing rate was well correlated with a classical decision variable, in this case value, even when the sensory and motor properties of the trial were held constant. When we examined 40 neurons in this fashion, we found that 62.5 percent of them showed a significant correlation between the value of the reward and firing rate at some point during the trial.

As a final note about this value experiment, if we examine the relationship between firing rate and value carefully, we see a hint of something that might have been of interest to Daniel Bernoulli. The actual data points rise and then seem to plateau as the amount of juice being obtained nears maximal values. The actual data points seem to curve toward a plateau in a manner reminiscent of classical utility functions. This may be a hint that neurons in area LIP encode the utility of juice rather than the actual value of juice, just as Bernoulli might have suggested.

While these results can hardly be considered conclusive proof of anything, they do raise the possibility that even for a behavior as simple and deterministic as orienting toward a spot of light, economics may form the root of a computational theory that will allow us to understand what the brain is trying to do when it makes a decision. Because we found evidence that neurons in area LIP encode both probability and value (or perhaps utility), it seems possible that neurons in area LIP encode something like classical expected utility.

Variables That Guide Choice Behavior

For Platt and me, these experiments suggested that neurons in area LIP carried information about the expected utility of movements that would be made at the end of each trial. That was interesting, but it did not tell us what these neurons did when the monkey was, quite literally, free to choose his own movement. If neurons in area LIP actually influence the decisions an animal makes about what movement to produce, then we ought to have been able to show that the value of a movement could influence both the behavior of an animal and the activity of area LIP neurons in a similar way.

In order to test this hypothesis, we needed to develop an experiment in which a monkey would choose, on his own, whether to look up or down while we changed the value of the two possible movements. We could then try to show that both the probability that the monkey would choose to look upward *and* the activity of LIP neurons were correlated with the value of the upward movement. To achieve that goal, we turned to a classical experiment in choice originally described by the Harvard psychologist Richard Herrnstein (1961; for an overview of this literature, see Herrnstein, 1997). In a series of experiments conducted over two decades but which Herrnstein originally designed in the 1960s, pigeons were allowed to press either of two levers. One lever rewarded the pigeon with a large food pellet but did so only rarely; the other lever rewarded the pigeon with a small food pellet but did so often. By controlling the distribution of the intervals governing how often each lever would be permitted to deliver a pellet, as well as the size of the pellet, and the distance between the two levers, Herrnstein and his colleagues found that the pigeons could be induced to respond alternately on both levers. The pigeons would pick one lever or the other for each press. At a global level, Herrnstein had found that the rate at which the pigeons pressed each lever was equal to the fraction of the total available reward that they could obtain at that lever per unit time, a relationship he referred to as the matching law.[3]

In an effort to employ this basic approach, we trained our monkeys to perform a modified version of the cued saccade task that we called the free choice task. In that task, while animals stared straight ahead at a central yellow stimulus, two eccentric yellow stimuli were illuminated. After a delay the central stimulus was extinguished and the animal was free to look at either of the two eccentric stimuli. Regardless of which he looked at, he would receive a reward. All that we changed across blocks of trials was the value of each of the two movements to the animal. In one block the animal might receive 0.2 ml of juice as a reward on trials in which he decided to look rightward and 0.1 ml on trials in which he decided to look leftward. On a second block the converse might be true.

It is, however, important to note that our experiment was not identical to Herrnstein's experiment. In Herrnstein's experiment the optimal solution to the task facing his pigeons was to match the probability of looking at each target to the fraction of total reward available for making that response. *Matching behavior* was an optimal strategy. In our experiment, because of some minor features of its exact design, this was not the case. The optimal strategy for our monkeys was to identify the movement that had a higher value and to keep making that movement until the 100-trial block was complete.

We decided to run the experiment that way because it had been shown that when human subjects perform an experiment like ours, they still show matching behavior, although admittedly only for a while. Only after they get a lot of practice do humans switch to the optimal strategy. After that switch, humans begin each block of trials by testing each lever to see which has a higher value, and then they simply stick with the more valuable lever. In the terminology of choice psychology, the humans

3. To be completely accurate, while Herrnstein laid out the general principles that I described, it was Keller and Gollub (1977) who first demostrated that the magnitude of reward and the variable interval reinforcement schedule could be traded off against each other. More recently, Leon and Gallistel (1998) have developed an exceedingly beautiful application of this approach for the measurement of expected utility.

switch from matching behavior to maximizing behavior. As we will see in a moment, deciding to run the experiment in this way was a critical error on our part.

When we examined the behavior of our monkeys under these conditions, we found that the animals were, in fact, showing classical matching behavior even though this was a suboptimal strategy. We found that the probability that an animal would look at the left target was a lawful function of the fraction of total available reward obtained for looking left. In this case, the probability that the animal looked up was equal to total reward obtained for looking up, divided by total reward obtained.

$$P_{\text{looks left}} = R_{\text{looks left}} / (R_{\text{looks left}} + R_{\text{looks right}}) \qquad (10.1)$$

Where $R_{\text{looksleft}}$ is the reward obtained for looking at the left target summed across trials, $R_{\text{looksright}}$ is the reward obtained for looking at the right target summed across trials, and $P_{\text{looksleft}}$ is the probability that the animal will look at the left target.

What do LIP neurons do under these conditions? To answer that question, we recorded the activity of 40 LIP neurons while animals performed the free choice task. As in our previous experiments, we would select for analysis only those trials on which the animal made the best movement for the neuron we were studying. All of these trials would be identical in the sensory and motor domains, and would come from blocks in which the subject had made his own decision. These trials would differ only in the value of the two movements to the monkey, a variable that under these conditions controlled the matching law behavior of the animal. This was the *average* rate at which he chose to look up or down.

Figure 10.14 plots data from a typical neuron for this experiment. On all of these trials the animal chose to look left. The thick black line plots average firing rate on a block of trials in which the animal was very likely to choose to look left, and did. The gray line plots trials on which the animal was unlikely to choose to look left, but did so anyway. Note how differently the neuron responded during these two blocks of trials.

Given that actual choice and LIP firing rates seemed to covary, we felt that it was time to ask how the behavior and the activity of the neurons were related:

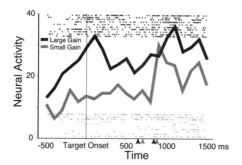

Figure 10.14
Activity of an LIP neuron while a monkey makes his own choice.

The actual choices made by subjects were then used as an estimate of the valuation of each response by the animal on each trial and neuronal data was [*sic*] related directly to this behavioral readout of the animal's decision process....

The goal of this experiment, however, was to directly correlate neuronal activity with the animal's estimate of the value of the two possible movements. Figure 4a presents the choices the subject made across all blocks of trials during this recording session. Consistent with Herrnstein's matching law for choice behavior, there was a linear relationship between the proportion of trials on which the animal chose the target inside the response field and the proportion of total juice available for gaze shifts to that target....

To analyze the relationship between the trial-by-trial activity of this neuron and the valuation of each choice by the subject, on each trial we computed a behavioral estimate of the subjective value of a movement into the response field, based on Herrnstein's melioration theory, by computing the difference in the rate of reinforcement the animal had obtained from each of the two possible choices over the preceding 10 trials (estimated value). Figure 4b [figure 10.15] shows the mean firing rate of the neuron as a function of this estimated value, during each measured interval, for all trials on which the animal shifted gaze into the response field. The firing rate of this neuron increased as the estimated value of a movement into the response field increased.

In our free-choice task, both monkeys and posterior parietal neurons behaved as if they had knowledge of the gains associated with different actions. These findings support the hypothesis that the variables that have been identified by economists, psychologists and ecologists as important in decision-making are represented in the nervous system. (Platt and Glimcher, 1999)

Summary

For me, this experiment served to underline a very important idea. If we want to understand how the brain accomplishes any sensorimotor con-

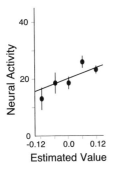

Figure 10.15
Activity of an LIP neuron while a monkey makes his own choice compared to a behaviorally derived estimate of the value of the movement to the monkey.

nection, we need to ask what computational goal the system ought to be trying to achieve. At least since Pavlov, and perhaps since Descartes, the basic technique for understanding how the brain connects sensation and action has been to ask What is the minimally complex stimulus that will elicit this behavior, or this neural response? The focus has, by and large, been on identifying a pattern of motor output and then asking how that pattern could be triggered by events in the outside world. But a definition of the sensorimotor process in those classic reflexological terms can, in principle, include only those neurobiological processes that are either direct products of the sensory world or direct producers of muscular output. Other processes are simply "gates" that control the connection between these two all-important systems.

In contrast, when we ask what problem the sensorimotor process is attempting to solve, we do not begin by excluding nonsensory and non-motor elements from a central position. If we begin by asking what problem, in the largest sense, the nervous system is trying to solve, we derive a very direct answer: The problem that the nervous system is trying to solve is to maximize the inclusive fitness of the organism. In the case of the cued saccade task, monkeys that get more fluid are fitter than monkeys that get less fluid, at least in principle. While in more complicated situations defining the behaviors that maximize fitness may be a very difficult problem, this approach does make clear predictions about how the nervous system should solve the sensorimotor problem. These are predictions that would never have arisen from an effort to identify minimally complex sensory-to-motor linkages.

Falling into the Dualist Trap

The free choice experiment, however, had a critical flaw. Remember that for Descartes, all of behavior could be broken into two principal classes: those behaviors for which stimulus and response were locked together deterministically, and those behaviors for which the relationship between stimulus and response was uncertain or chaotic. The first of these two ideas gave birth to the notion of the reflex, a determinate system of connections that linked sensation and action. The second, he argued, was the product of the soul.

The reflex was, I argued in the first half of this book, the embodiment of determinate mathematics. It was a fully deterministic way of describing sensorimotor linkages. I spent most of these chapters arguing that the reflex was a poor model, that there is no such thing as a reflex, that the kinds of behaviors the reflex was designed to model are better described using a Bayesian statistical approach. But critically, I have not challenged the notion that the world, and the organisms that populate it, are in fact determinate systems. We all agree that we see uncertainty in the world, but it is unclear whether that *apparent* uncertainty just represents an epistemological limitation. Laplace believed that for a superintelligence, who could track all aspects of the universe at once, there would be no uncertainty, no need for a theory of probability. He might have said there is no uncertainty in the universe that is *in principle* irreducible to certainty.

This got us into trouble when our monkeys were allowed to decide whether to look left or right on their own. We designed that experiment because we wanted the monkeys to behave chaotically and unpredictably, in a way that Descartes might have said was the product of volition. And our monkeys did seem to behave somewhat unpredictably sometimes looking up and sometimes looking down. What was absolutely critical, and what we failed to recognize, was that the apparent unpredictability of our monkeys was a suboptimal strategy. The apparent unpredictability simply could not be modeled as optimal within the economic framework which we were advocating.

All through this presentation I have argued that we can define the problems that our animals are trying to solve and then we can derive optimal solutions to those problems. The matching behavior that our monkeys produced, however, was not an optimal solution to the problem posed by the free choice task.

To be honest, the importance of this failure was not clear to me or to Platt at first. It was Michael Shadlen's critiques of our work that finally made the importance of this failure clear. What we came to conclude, which will be described in the next two chapters, was that we were thinking about probability and uncertainty in the wrong way.

Return for a moment to the example of the billiard ball table, in which a single intelligent white cue ball has incomplete knowledge of the locations of the other balls. I argued in chapter 8 that this was a better model of the world our monkeys lived in than a table in which the positions of all other balls were known. But in practice, even this model fails to explain why complex, indeterminate, behavior *should* ever occur.

Even the white billiard ball that has an incomplete knowledge of where the other balls are located lives in a fully determinate, though uncertain, world. Given what little knowledge it has, there is always an optimal strategy that clears the table of balls as quickly as possible. Our monkeys, however, did not seem to behave like that white billiard ball. They did not adopt a single, determined optimal approach. Instead, they adopted what seemed a very *probabilistic* approach. They matched the probability that they would look leftward to the percent of all possible reward available for looking left. They did this even when, in classical economic terms, a determinate behavioral strategy was superior.

Why had our monkeys behaved so suboptimally? So probabalistically? As we were forced to examine this question, we realized that any complete description of the sensorimotor problem would have to be able to account for this probabalistic pattern of behavior our monkeys had shown under conditions that should have elicited a deterministic response pattern. As I hope will become clear in the next two chapters, a recent mathematical addition to the corpus of classical economics was developed to deal with this very problem, the mathematical theory of games.

11
Irreducible Uncertainty and the Theory of Games

Descartes argued that all types of human behavior could be sorted into two categories. His first category was made up of simple, deterministic actions that were reliably triggered by specific stimuli. The second category was made up of behaviors that were fundamentally unpredictable; behaviors that could be attributed to the actions of volition, or the soul.

Descartes proposed that his first category of behaviors could be mechanistically explained by simple sensorimotor linkages, linkages that we now call reflexes. The first half of this book suggested that, in actual fact, reflex-based models often do a poor job of describing both the behaviors and the neural circuits associated with simple, determinate responses.

In chapters 8 through 10, I argued that we could understand simple, determinate behaviors more completely if we thought of them as tools developed by evolution to achieve specific goals, goals that relate, at an ecological level, to the evolutionary fitness of the organism. To begin to think rigorously about the ecological goals of behavior, I argued that we should turn our attention to approaches pioneered in economics and behavioral ecology. The central tools for understanding how the brain produces determinate behaviors should be Bayesian techniques for estimating the likelihood of uncertain events and utility theories for estimating the value of behavioral outcomes in evolutionary terms.

The most fundamental difference between this approach and classical physiological approaches is that it incorporates concepts from probability theory, concepts that are necessary whenever we hope to understand animals that face an environment about which they have incomplete knowledge. Economic tools, unlike reflex theory, were designed to deal efficiently with uncertainty about the true state of the outside world;

they identify a determinate best course of action for the chooser in an uncertain environment. Classical economics, unlike reflex theory, recognizes that choosers are uncertain about the true state of the outside world.

Classical economics, however, retains a deterministic stance with regard to the behavior that the organism actually produces. Given a knowledge of likelihoods and values, classical economics identifies a fixed, optimal behavioral response. The distinction between uncertainty about the state of the external world and the assumption of a determinate behavioral repertoire is important because it engages Descartes's argument that two classes of behavior exist. Not all human behaviors, he argued, are deterministic. Some behaviors are fundamentally, irreducibly, uncertain. If Descartes was correct in this assertion, then classical economics cannot account for all of behavior because it cannot formally account for behavioral unpredictability, a class of responses we often call volitional.

From this belief that both determinate and probabilistic behaviors occur arose the persistent notion of Cartesian dualism, the idea that two independent mechanisms would be required to account for human behavior. At least since 1900 scientists and philosophers have wrestled with the ambiguity that this two-tiered system creates. Pavlov attacked this idea by implicitly denying the validity of Descartes's dualist assertion. His work and his conclusions argued instead that *all* behavior was the deterministic product of a biological clockwork. He argued that fundamentally unpredictable behaviors simply do not exist. More recently, a number of philosophers have extended Pavlov's argument, bolstering his proposal that only a single determinate system may be required for the production of all behavior. Behavior may, these philosophers and scientists suggest, occasionally appear unpredictable, but only because of our own epistemologic limitations as observers.

One interesting example of this approach comes from the matching law studies of Richard Herrnstein. Herrnstein noted that his pigeons, when presented with the opportunity to peck two levers, showed a fixed probability of pecking either lever that could be described by the matching law equation; macroscopically he described this behavior as probabilistic. At a microscopic level, however, even Herrnstein proposed that a simple deterministic process produced the peck-by-peck behavior of his birds (Herrnstein, 1982).

In this chapter and in the next I want to present a fairly unusual critique of both the Cartesian dualist system and the typical monist alternative proposed by scientists like Pavlov. First, I want to suggest that trying to resolve the paradox of dualism by arguing that all behavior is produced by a single class of determinate mechanism is impossible. Classes of behaviors can be shown to exist that are uncertain not because of our own epistemological limitations but because they are, in fact, irreducibly uncertain. They are behaviors that, on a decision-by-decision level, cannot be predicted by an observer. There is no avoiding this fact; empirical data make it clear that we must believe in the existence of this kind of indeterminate behavior. Second, I want to argue that a belief in both determinate and indeterminate behaviors need not require, or imply, dualism of any kind. When properly conceptualized, truly unpredictable behaviors and fully deterministic behaviors both emerge from a single mathematical corpus that can describe optimal solutions to sensorimotor problems. Simple determinate behaviors emerge from processes well described by classical economic theory. Complex indeterminate behaviors emerge when solutions to the sensorimotor problems that animals face begin to require an extension of classical economics into the realm of game theory.

Irreducible Uncertainty in a Populated World

Billiard Balls

To make the concept of irreducibly uncertain behavior clear, we have to return to the billiard table world. This time, consider a billiard table world that more closely parallels the world in which we find ourselves. Once again, imagine a single intelligent white ball placed at random on the table surface. Once again, assume that the ball has a limited field of view. As a result of this limitation, it faces an epistemologic certainty about where the other balls are located. Of course each of the other four balls has a definite location. Our white ball, however, must employ probability theory to overcome this epistemological limitation. Now imagine that the other balls, like our white ball, are intelligent. Imagine that these other balls are not passive environmental components but competitors who also are driven to clear the table of other balls. Under

Figure 11.1
Irreducible and epistemological uncertainty in a billiard ball world.

these conditions the sensorimotor problem faced by the white ball changes precipitously. (See figure 11.1.)

Consider a situation in which a slow black ball is lying in front of a pocket, and within sight of a much faster white ball. The white ball makes a careful mathematical analysis of the situation. She concludes that the best move would be to drive the black ball into the pocket as quickly as possible. The black ball knows this, too. Assume, for argument's sake, that the black ball always adopts a fixed optimal response to the challenge posed by the white ball. It always decides to head off at an angle of 90° to the white ball's expected trajectory. This would move the black ball safely away from the pocket, but only if the white ball does not know that the black ball plans this 90° trajectory. If the white ball knows, or learns, the determinate plan of the black ball, then the white ball can alter its trajectory to compensate. The white ball's new trajectory, which takes into account the determinate evasive action of the black ball, would then *still* succeed at driving the black ball into the pocket.

As long as the black ball employs a deterministic strategy, no matter how complex, the white ball can (at least in principle) infer this strategy and use it against the black ball. So what options does the black ball have? How can he outwit the white ball? To that question there is only one answer. The black ball must become unpredictable. If the black ball can head off unpredictably in any direction, then the white ball will be much less likely to catch him. Only by adding an element of randomness that is irreducibly uncertain to his opponent can the black ball develop a truly optimal response to his intelligent competitor. In this chapter I hope to convince you (1) that the uncertainty a clever opponent introduces by randomizing his or her behavior under circumstances like these is fundamentally different from epistemological uncertainty and (2) that understanding this kind of uncertainty is critical for understanding the relationship between behavior, brain, and mind.

Flipping a Laplacian Coin

Global determinists like Pavlov and Laplace have argued that epistemological uncertainty can be viewed as a property of the animal rather than of his environment. The world itself is a completely structured determinate system, but any individual within that system has incomplete knowledge of that structure. At any given level of knowledge of the outside world, there are still things about which we remain uncertain for epistemological reasons. Probability theory is the tool we use to describe those portions of the environment about which we have incomplete knowledge. By gathering more information we can reduce the uncertainty we face, and thus reduce our reliance on probabilistic models of the world, but we accomplish this at a cost in time and energy.

Consider a clockwork machine designed to flip coins. You can keep the coin it flips if you can predict how that coin will land. If you know nothing about the machine, you can describe the probability that the coin will land either heads up or tails up as a 50 percent likelihood. To make a better guess about whether the coin will land heads up or tails up, you can locate the center of gravity of the coin. You can gather prior probability distributions about whether the coin is more likely to land heads up depending on whether it is placed heads up or tails up on the machine. As you gather data like these, your uncertainty diminishes. You obtain more and more precise estimates until, in the limit, when you have full knowledge of the force that the machine generates and a complete model of the coin spinning in the air, you can predict before the coin is flipped exactly how it will land. This, I would contend, is the essence of epistemological uncertainty of the type that interested Laplace.

An intelligent opponent, however, can introduce a completely different kind of uncertainty that is unavailable to the coin-flipping machine. Consider playing the game of *matching pennies* against an opponent. Two players each have a penny. Both players put a penny heads up or tails up on the table. If both pennies show the same face, player 1 wins. If two different faces show, player 2 wins. Imagine that player 1, in order to maximize his winnings, begins to catalog the prior probability that player 2 will select heads. He even looks for sequential patterns in the behavior of player 2 that will reduce the uncertainty he faces about what player 2 will do. Each time player 1 detects a pattern in player 2's behavior, he has a better than even chance of knowing what player 2 will do, and so will win more than 50 percent of the time. Of course, from player 2's point of view this is exactly what should not be allowed to happen. Under no circumstances does player 2 want the uncertainty associated with his play to be reduced. Player 2's goal is to be completely uncertain in his behavior, to show no patterns, to produce an irreducible uncertainty for player 1.

The Theory of Games

Classical economic theory, of the type described in chapters 8 through 10, was developed to describe rational decision making in an uncertain world. Classical probabilists and economists viewed the world as something that could be described by fixed probability distributions and assessed with a "calculus of probabilities." Classical economic theory was never designed to describe decision making when one faces an intelligent opponent, an opponent who is influenced not only by the static properties of the world but also by the actions of a competitor. This is because in a real two-person competition, your actions and the actions of your opponent form a dynamic system. Understanding such dynamic systems and the irreducible uncertainties that they include is not possible using the approaches contained within classical economics.

In the 1940s, the Princeton mathematician John von Neumann became interested in this limitation of classical economics. Working with the Princeton economist Oskar Morgenstern, Von Neumann began to chart a mathematical theory of how two intelligent competitors should interact when they had contrary, or partially contrary, goals. In a landmark monograph titled *Theory of Games and Economic Behavior*, Von Neumann and Morgenstern (1944) described a mathematical extension of classical economics that was designed to identify an optimal course of action not simply in a stationary and unchanging world but even in a world populated by intelligent competitors who can, by their actions, dynamically change the values of the decision variables that influence many classes of sensorimotor problems.

Consider now a participant in a social exchange economy. His problem has, of course, many elements in common with a maximum problem [a problem in which a single economic actor seeks to maximize his gain]. But it also contains some, very essential, elements of an entirely different nature. He too tries to obtain an optimum result. But in order to achieve this, he must enter into relations of exchange with others. If two or more persons exchange goods with each other, then the results for each one will depend in general not merely upon his own actions but on those of the others as well. Thus each participant attempts to maximize a function (his abovementioned "result") of which he does not control all of the variables. This is certainly no maximization problem, but a peculiar and disconcerting mixture of several conflicting maximum problems. Every participant is guided by another principle and neither determines all of the variables which affect his interest.

This kind of problem is nowhere dealt with in classical mathematics. We emphasize at the risk of being pedantic that this is no conditional maximum problem, no problem of the calculus of variations, of functional analysis, etc. It arises in full clarity, even in the most elementary situations, e.g., when all variables can assume only a finite number of values.

A particularly striking expression of the popular misunderstanding about this pseudo-maximization problem is the famous statement according to which the purpose of social effort is the "greatest possible good for the greatest possible number." A guiding principle cannot be formulated by the requirement of maximizing two (or more) functions at once.

Such a principle, taken literally, is self-contradictory. (In general one function will have no maximum where the other has one.) It is no better than saying, e.g., that a firm should obtain maximum prices at maximum turnover, or a maximum revenue at a minimum outlay. If some order of importance of these principles or some weighted average is meant, this should be stated. However, in the situation of the participants in a social economy nothing of that sort is intended, but all maxima are desired at once—by various participants.

. . .

We hope that the reader will be convinced by the above that they face here and now a really conceptual—and not merely technical—difficulty. And it is this problem which the theory of "games of strategy" is mainly devised to meet. (Von Neumann and Morgenstern, 1944)

Von Neumann and Morgenstern intended nothing less than to completely redefine economic theories of rational decision making. In the real world, decisions often must reflect the existence of intelligent opponents, each of whom seeks to maximize his or her own gain. This is the insight that the theory of games was designed to capture.

An Introduction to Game Theory

Von Neumann and Morgenstern referred to all interactions between intelligent competitors as "games," and they developed a standard set of analytic tools for describing all the patterns of outcomes that a game could produce. Their basic goal was to accomplish something like what Pascal and his colleagues had done for decision making in a passive environment. Pascal had shown how a chooser could obtain the best possible outcome by combining information about likelihoods and values. Von Neumann and Morgenstern wanted to develop a system that would show how a chooser could obtain the best possible outcome, *given that his opponent or opponents were also attempting to obtain the best possible outcomes for themselves.* What Von Neumann and Morgenstern did was to conceive of decision problems involving multiple competitors as interactive dynamic systems in which the gains of one player were counterbalanced by equal and opposite losses to other players. Viewed this way, any economic competition would be seen as a process of trading back and forth the probabilities and values of acceptable losses and desired gains until some stable middle ground was reached. This stable middle ground was, they suggested, a systemwide solution for the optimization problem posed by the competitive game under study.

Of particular interest to Von Neumann and Morgenstern was a class of mathematical games called *zero-sum noncooperative games with mixed strategy solutions.* Although Von Neumann and Morgenstern did study other kinds of games, zero-sum noncooperative games became the foundation on which the theory of games was built, largely because of the simplicity of the zero-sum concept.

In zero-sum games, the gains to one player are always exactly balanced by the losses to another; the summed losses and gains of the

Table 11.1
Von Neumann and Morgenstern's H Matrix

	1: Moriarty goes to Dover to intercept Holmes at ferry	2: Moriarty goes to Canterbury to intercept Holmes on train
1: Holmes gets off train in Dover to escape to the Continent	Holmes: −100 Moriarty: 100	Holmes: 50 Moriarty: −50
2: Holmes gets off train in Canterbury to escape Moriarty	Holmes: 0 Moriarty: 0	Holmes: −100 Moriarty: 100

From Von Neumann and Morgenstern, 1944.

players in any possible outcome must always equal zero. This perfect symmetry between the players simplifies many of the complex mathematical issues that arise in game theory, and for that reason we turn first to an analysis of this class of mathematical competitions.

Consider the matrix in table 11.1, which presents one of the zero-sum noncooperative games Von Neumann and Morgenstern described in what is called *strategic form*. The columns of the strategic form describe two possible actions by Sherlock Holmes's archenemy, Professor Moriarty. The rows describe Holmes's two possible moves. The interior cells describe the relative payoffs to the two gentlemen of each of the four possible outcomes.

Sherlock Holmes desires to proceed from London to Dover and thence to the Continent in order to escape from Professor Moriarty who pursues him. Having boarded the train he observes, as the train pulls out, the appearance of Professor Moriarty on the platform. Sherlock Holmes takes it for granted—and in this he is assumed to be fully justified—that his adversary, who has seen him, might secure a special train and overtake him. Sherlock Holmes is faced with the alternative of going to Dover or of leaving the train at Canterbury, the only intermediate station. His adversary—whose intelligence is assumed to be fully adequate to visualize these possibilities—has the same choice. Both opponents must choose the place of their detrainment in ignorance of the other's corresponding decision. If, as a result of these measures, they should find themselves, *in fine*, on the same platform, Sherlock Holmes may with certainty expect to be killed by Moriarty. If Holmes reaches Dover unharmed he can make good his escape.

What are the good strategies, particularly for Sherlock Holmes? The game obviously has certain similarities to Matching Pennies, Professor Moriarty being the one who desires to match. Let him therefore be player 1, and Sherlock

Holmes be player 2. Denote the choice to proceed to Dover by 1 and the choice to quit at the intermediate station by 2.

Let us now consider the H matrix of Figure 29 [reproduced with additional text as table 11.1]. The fields (1,1) and (2,2) correspond to Professor Moriarty catching Sherlock Holmes, which it is reasonable to describe by a very high value of the corresponding matrix element,—say 100. The field (2,1) signifies that Sherlock Holmes successfully escaped to Dover, while Moriarty stopped at Canterbury. This is Moriarty's defeat as far as the present action is concerned, and should be described by a big negative value of the matrix element [for Moriarty]—in the order of magnitude but smaller than the positive value mentioned above—say, -50. The field (1,2) signifies that Sherlock Holmes escapes Moriarty at the intermediate station, but fails to reach the Continent. This is best viewed as a tie, and assigned the matrix element 0.

[What follows is Von Neumann and Morgenstern's description of their mathematical analysis. I have omitted the formulas that you would need to make much sense of this extract, but I include the text so you can get a feeling for their mathematical style.]

As in [examples] (b), (c) above, the diagonals [of the matrix] are separated (100 is > than 0, -50); hence the good strategies are again unique and mixed. The formulae used before [for modeling the game of matching pennies] give the value (for Moriarty)

$$v' = 40$$

and the good strategies (e for Moriarty, n for Sherlock Holmes):

$$e = \{3/5, 2/5\}, \quad n = \{2/5, 3/5\}$$

Thus Moriarty should go to Dover with a probability of 60% while Sherlock Holmes should stop at the intermediate station with a probability of 60%,—the remaining 40% being left in each case for the other alternative.[1] (Von Neumann and Morgenstern, 1944)

Perhaps the most interesting feature of the Holmes/Moriarty game is that the optimal mathematical solution to the game requires that Holmes leave the train at Canterbury with a 60 percent probability. At one level

---

1. The narrative of *Conan Doyle*—excusably—disregards mixed [or probabilistic] strategies and states instead the actual developments. According to these Sherlock Holmes gets out at the intermediate station and triumphantly watches Moriarty's special train going on to Dover. *Conan Doyle's* solution is the best possible under his limitations (to pure [or non-probabilistic] strategies), in so far as he attributes to each opponent the course which we found to be the more probable one (i.e. he replaces the 60% probability by certainty). It is, however, somewhat misleading that this procedure leads to Sherlock Holmes' complete victory, whereas, as we saw above, the odds (i.e. the value of play) are definitely in favor of Moriarty. (Our result for e, n yields that Sherlock Holmes is as good as 48% dead when his train pulls out from Victoria Station ...) [their footnote].

this seems absurd. Holmes must either stay on the train or get off the train. But like the black billiard ball that cannot adopt a single strategy and still hope to outwit his opponent, Holmes really cannot adopt a determinate strategy or Moriarty will certainly kill him. If Holmes were, as Conan Doyle did in the actual narrative, to replace a 60 percent probability with certainty, then Moriarty would certainly succeed in taking his life. Holmes and Moriarty both know this. In order to maximize their mutual expected utilities, each must produce behaviors that cannot be reduced to certainty by the opponent. Each must effectively roll a set of dice as their trains pull into Canterbury station, and let their actions be guided by this randomizing event. This is, at an absolute level, the best strategy that they can adopt. So Holmes and Moriarty *must* behave probabalistically; they must adopt what is called a mixed strategy.

Opponent Actions and Expected Utility

In the original Holmes/Moriarty game, determining the value of each outcome to both Holmes and Professor Moriarty is a critical first step. As Von Neumann and Morgenstern constructed the game, killing Holmes has a positive value to Moriarty of 100. Losing Holmes on the Continent has a negative value of −50, and keeping Holmes penned in England has a value of 0. These values are critical because they determine the precise probability that Moriarty should adopt each course of action.

Establishing the value, or more precisely the expected utility, of each outcome is therefore as critical for the theory of games as it was for classical economics; each cell in the strategic form of a game must accurately represent the expected utility of an outcome for both players. You will recall that Daniel Bernoulli produced the modern solution to the problem of estimating value when he argued that the expected utility of any outcome could be described as the product of (1) the probability of an event and (2) the monetary value of that event scaled as a concave function reflecting the net worth of the chooser.

Von Neumann and Morgenstern placed within each cell of the strategic form representation the expected utility of that cell to each player. There are, as a result, two kinds of uncertainty embedded in the representation of a game. The first kind is epistemologic, and is embedded in the computation of expected utility that is presented within each cell. In the individual cells of the Holmes/Moriarty game, this epistemological uncertainty does not occur very forcefully: "If, as a result of these measures, they should find themselves, *in fine*, on the same platform, Sherlock Holmes may with certainty expect to be killed by Moriarty." In the Holmes/Moriarty game the expected utility within each cell is computed from a set of outcomes that are certain. But, as we know, this need not be the case. Expected utilities need not be based on certainties; they can easily deal with epistemological uncertainty. The strategic form representation of a game, however, also incorporates the notion of an irreducible uncertainty on the part of each player. That irreducible uncertainty occurs in the form of mixed strategies where players select actions (a particular row or column) with variable probabilities. It is this selection of row and column that embeds the notion of irreducible uncertainty into the strategic form matrix. It is the extension of classical economics to include this secondary class of probabilistic events that was Von Neumann and Morgenstern's masterstroke.

John Nash and Modern Game Theory

In their work, Von Neumann and Morgenstern had focused on identifying optimal solutions to zero-sum games. But by the late 1940s it was becoming clear that this would prove to be a huge limitation. Many classes of games existed in which the gains of one player were not numerically equivalent to the losses of another player.[2] These non-zero-sum games, and particularly those with mixed strategy solutions, were proving very difficult to solve. To understand why these games are important and why they require a very specific, and brilliantly different, approach, consider the classic automotive game of chicken. Smith and Jones sit in cars parked on opposite ends of a bridge. At a signal they drive toward each other as fast as they can. At the instant before the two cars collide,

---

2. In fact, Von Neumann and Morgenstern had devised a zero-sum way to represent non-zero-sum games. This involved including an additional imaginary player whose gains and losses were designed to balance the gains and losses of the other players. This approach, however, provided only limited mathematical power for modeling situations of this sort.

Table 11.2
Game of Chicken

	Smith continues	Smith swerves
Jones continues	−100, −100	50, −10
Jones swerves	−10, 50	1, 1

Smith and Jones each decide whether or not to swerve to the right. Imagine, for the sake of argument, that the strategic form of the chicken game looks like table 11.2.

If neither Smith nor Jones swerves, they are both reduced to pulp—which, following Von Neumann's lead, we will call a loss to both players of 100. If one player swerves, that represents a loss to the swerver of 10 and a gain to the winner of 50. Finally, if both players swerve, we will consider that a draw with a negligible gain to both players. So how would we like to understand this game? Ideally we would like to know the optimal strategy for both Smith and Jones to adopt, but because this is not a zero-sum game, Von Neumann's formulation is of little help. If both players go straight, both players experience a significant loss. If one swerves, the other gains far more than the swerver loses. There is nothing zero-sum here about the losses and gains.

In the late 1940s, John Nash was a graduate student in mathematics at Princeton, then the center of the postwar mathematical world. Einstein and Von Neumann were both there when Nash began to develop into one of the great mathematicians of the twentieth century. As a graduate student looking for a doctoral dissertation subject, Nash saw an interesting level of structure in non-zero-sum games. Let us examine the game of chicken as Nash might have seen it, in an effort to understand how he used the concepts of expected utility and equilibrium to overcome the limitations of Von Neumann's approach.

Nash (Nash 1950a, 1950b, 1951) recognized that if we think of Jones and Smith as playing the game of chicken again and again (neglecting the possibility of their deaths for the purposes of the initial mathematical analysis), the Jones/Smith interaction must come to rest at some sort of equilibrium point. A point at which the losses and gains of the two players are equally balanced, and neither player has an incentive to swerve more or less often than this equilibrium level. But where would that point be? Is there a way to calculate the location of an equilibrium point in a mixed strategy?

Begin by assigning symbols to some important variables. First, we call the probability that Smith will swerve *Psmith, swerves*. Since this is a probability, it will be a number ranging from 0 (he never swerves) to 1 (he always swerves). Since Smith either swerves or goes straight, the sum of the probabilities of swerving and going straight must equal 1:

$$\text{Psmith, straight} + \text{Psmith, swerve} = 1. \tag{11.1}$$

Or, put another way:

$$\text{Psmith, straight} = 1 - \text{Psmith, swerve}. \tag{11.2}$$

By analogy:

$$\text{Pjones, swerve} = 1 - \text{Pjones, straight}. \tag{11.3}$$

We can think of a variable like *Psmith, straight* as the likelihood that Smith will decide to go straight in exactly the same way that we represented the likelihood that a coin would land heads up for the Chevalier du Mere. Starting with this variable, we can figure out the expected utility, for Jones, of the situation in which Jones swerves and Smith goes straight. Since the probability of Smith going straight is *Psmith, straight* and the loss to Jones under these conditions is 10:

If Smith goes straight,

$$\text{Gain to Jones for swerving} = \text{Psmith, straight} * -10. \tag{11.4}$$

In exactly the same way we can use a probabilistic approach to see the gain to Jones if Smith decides to swerve:

If Smith swerves,

$$\text{Gain to Jones for swerving} = \text{Psmith, swerves} * 1. \tag{11.5}$$

So, in total, if Jones makes a decision to swerve:

$$\text{Gain to Jones for swerving} = (\text{Psmith, straight} * -10)$$
$$+ (\text{Psmith, swerves} * 1). \tag{11.6}$$

Or we can say, equivalently:

Gain to Jones for swerving $= ((1 - \text{Psmith}, \text{swerves}) * -10)$

$$+ (\text{Psmith}, \text{swerves} * 1). \qquad (11.7)$$

Nash's critical insight was that a specific course of action for Jones would be an equilibrium point if and only if no other course of action was better for Jones. It could be an equilibrium point only if Jones was indifferent between swerving and going straight because swerving and going straight had equal values to him. Put mathematically, that is equivalent to saying that the equilibrium point is the probability at which the utilities of swerving and of continuing are equal for Jones. So if the gain to Jones for continuing is

Gain to Jones for continuing $= ((1 - \text{Psmith}, \text{swerves}) * -100)$

$$+ (\text{Psmith}, \text{swerves} * 50), \qquad (11.8)$$

and the gain to Jones for swerving is

Gain to Jones for swerving $= (1 - \text{Psmith}, \text{swerves}) * -10)$

$$+ (\text{Psmith}, \text{swerves} * 1), \qquad (11.9)$$

then these two probabilities are equal when

$((1 - \text{Psmith}, \text{swerves}) * -100)) + (\text{Psmith}, \text{swerves} * 50)$

$$= ((1 - \text{Psmith}, \text{swerves}) * -10)) + (\text{Psmith}, \text{swerves} * 1). \quad (11.10)$$

Solving this equation algebraically:

$$90 = 139 * \text{Psmith}, \text{swerves} \qquad (11.11)$$

$$.647 = \text{Psmith}, \text{swerves}. \qquad (11.12)$$

Or, in English, as long as there is a 64.7 percent chance that *Smith* will swerve, swerving and not-swerving are of equal expected utility to Jones. As long as Smith will swerve 64.7 percent of the time, Jones has no incentive to care what he (Jones) does; his two choices are equally good (or bad). This also means that if Smith announces before the race (and for some necessarily suboptimal reason really means it) that there is a greater than 64.7 percent chance he will swerve, then Jones should care very much what he (Jones) decides to do. He should go straight.

The absolutely critical idea here is that Smith's best possible plan is to swerve 64.7 percent of the time, the point at which Jones will be indifferent to his own actions. As soon as either player behaves in a manner that is suboptimal for him (as in Jones's asserting that he will go straight no matter what, and meaning it), then the other player faces a standard economic optimization problem and simply solves that problem using standard tools. But as long as both players are seeking an optimal solution, they have to reach this equilibrium point. The equilibrium point computed in this way defines the only behavioral pattern for which neither the option of swerving nor the option of continuing is a demonstrably better plan. It is at this indifference point, that the players come into equilibrium.

As an aside, this is what is called a symmetric game because the equations describing the equilibrium points for both players are identical and the game yields symmetrical payoffs. The best plan for both Smith and Jones is to swerve 64.7 percent of the time, but this not need be the case. As Nash showed, the equations describing the equilibrium strategies for each player can be different, and the equilibrium point can be nonsymmetrical with regard to the players. Largely because Nash equilibriums can be extended to asymmetrical contests, Nash was able to show that an equilibrium point can be computed for essentially all games of this type.

Nash's insight had an enormous influence, shifting game theory toward the study of equilibrium conditions. Where does a game reach a stable optimal equilibrium? Nash's approach allows us to answer that question, and Nash was awarded the Nobel Prize in economics for this critical formulation.

I think, however, that Nash's notion does much, much more for us. His notion that mixed behavioral strategies can be equilibrium points really goes to the heart of Cartesian dualism. Mixed strategies which are definitionally optimal solutions really require that organisms be able to produce behavioral strategies that are irreducibly uncertain to their opponents. Darwin wrote that the "preservation of favorable variations and the rejection of injurious variations" would be the outcome produced by natural selection. Any organism that possesses the favorable variation of being able to produce probabilistic behavior must, it would seem in principle, be preserved by natural selection. The existence of

Nash mixed equilibriums really means that economic models require both determinate and indeterminate behaviors from animals.[3]

When the sensorimotor problem is framed in this way, all classes of behavior, both deterministic and nondeterministic, can be viewed as solutions to problems that can be rigorously posed by the mathematical tools of economic theory. Some problems, like those posed for the stretch response, require deterministic solutions; others require irreducibly probabilistic solutions.

Limitations of the Equilibrium Approach

Nash's equilibrium approach tells us what strategy to use if we hope to achieve the best possible outcome against an opponent with a similar goal. In this regard, the Nash equilibrium seems to be exactly the extension of classical economic decision theory required for a model of how the sensorimotor problem is solved when an animal confronts an intelligent opponent. It is, however, important to remember that, once one player adopts a nonequilibrium strategy, the optimal response for the other player is also to take a nonequilibrium strategy. In the case of Smith and Jones playing chicken, if Jones announces that he will adopt an 80 percent chance of swerving, then Jones should adopt a pure strategy of going straight; under those conditions Jones always does better by going straight than by swerving. Just how much better he does depends on the precise probability that Jones will swerve, but it is always a better plan.

Of course in practice, Jones and Smith may not know one another's payoff matrices in advance. For them this is a critical problem because

3. Many people respond to this line of reasoning by pointing out that when humans are asked to verbally produce or evaluate random numbers, they often perform quite poorly. And it is certainly true that humans cannot verbally produce truly random patterns of numbers or letters. As we will see in the pages that follow, however, both humans and animals can produce behavioral patterns that are surprisingly random. While it is true that humans do show some small and interesting deviations from perfect randomness behaviorally, they can be shown to behave in a more random fashion than one might expect. While the source of this disparity between what we say and what we do may ultimately have important implications, the critical point for this discussion is that actual human behavior can be surprisingly uncertain.

they may get only one chance to play chicken. For many other games of this general type, repeated plays of the same game are possible and one can imagine that by systematically studying Jones's choices, and constantly adjusting his own choices, Smith could keep improving his winnings until he and Jones reached the equilibrium point. But for single-play games, identifying the Nash equilibrium may be quite difficult in practice.

A second critical limitation of game theory today is that it cannot tell us how Smith and Jones should go about searching for an equilibrium point in the real world. Game theory can describe a system once it reaches a static equilibrium, but it cannot efficiently describe the dynamic process by which an equilibrium is reached. This is a significant limitation because much of the behavior of real animals must be devoted to solving dynamic problems—a problem for which we have no adequate theoretical tools. Fortunately, this is an area of intense research and there is reason to hope that this problem will be solved. For the meantime, however, understanding the dynamics of game play represents a significant limitation with which we must contend. Despite this theoretical limitation, however, the theory of games has already become a critical tool for understanding human and animal behavior. To begin to understand both the limitations and the strengths of game theory as an empirical tool, we therefore turn next to empirical biological applications of the theory of games.

Biology and the Theory of Games

Eric Charnov and his colleagues used ideas from classical economics to model the behavior of animals foraging for food. Like classical economists they successfully treated the environment in which animals forage as a stationary process within which decision makers select an optimal course of action. In the 1940s, Von Neumann and Morgenstern had argued that this approach was sometimes a poor strategy for modeling the real world. The real world includes other organisms that cannot always be described as stationary. Nash had further developed this insight, providing the equilibrium approach as a powerful tool for modeling these nonstationary processes.

At the same time that Charnov was using economic theory, the evolutionary biologist John Maynard Smith began to wonder whether the theory of games could be used as a powerful tool by ecological biologists. As he put it in the introduction to his landmark work *Evolution and the Theory of Games*, published in 1982 (the same year Marr's *Vision* was published):

Paradoxically, it has turned out that game theory is more readily applied to biology than to the field of economic behavior for which it was originally designed. There are two reasons for this. First, the theory requires that the values of different outcomes (for example, financial rewards, the risks of death and the pleasures of a clear conscience) might be measured on a single scale. In human applications this measure is provided by "utility"—a somewhat artificial and uncomfortable concept: In biology, Darwinian fitness provides a natural and genuinely one-dimensional scale. Secondly, and more importantly, in seeking the solution of a game, the concept of human rationality is replaced by that of evolutionary stability. The advantage here is that there are good theoretical reasons to expect populations to evolve to stable states, whereas there are grounds for doubting whether human beings always behave rationally.

He continues, a bit surprisingly, along the same lines as Marr:

To understand wing form [in birds] it would be necessary to know about the atmospheric conditions in which the birds live and the way in which lift and drag forces vary with wing shape. One would also have to take into account the constraints imposed by the fact that birds' wings are made of feathers—the constraints would be different for a bat or a pterosaur.... In the case of wing form, then, we want to understand why selection has favored particular phenotypes. The appropriate mathematical tool is optimization theory [with its roots in traditional decision theoretic mathematics]. We are faced with the problem of deciding what particular features (e.g. a high lift:drag ratio, a small turning circle) contribute to fitness, but not with the special difficulties which arise when success depends on what others are doing, It is in the latter concept that game theory becomes relevant. (Maynard Smith, 1982)

The Hawk-Dove Game

In order to develop this idea, Maynard Smith described what is now probably the most famous of all biological games, the *hawk-dove game*. Imagine, Maynard Smith proposed, a species of animals in which individuals compete for access to territories that increase the number of young they produce. Individuals who hold territories have a measurably greater fitness, but there are more individuals than there are territories.

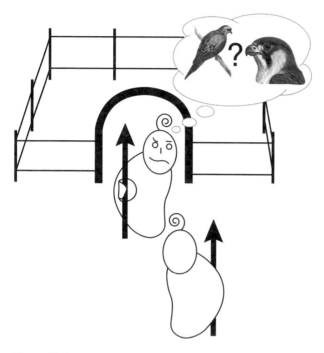

Figure 11.2
Maynard Smith's hawk-dove game.

In this hypothetical species, animals must compete to obtain the valuable territories. (See figure 11.2.)

In the hawk-dove game, competition begins when an animal without a territory displays to an animal with a territory, threatening that individual's territorial control. After the display, each animal must make a decision: whether to escalate the conflict (to fight for the territory) or to retreat (to give up the territory without a fight). If one of the animals elects to escalate, behaving as a hawk, and the other to retreat, behaving as a dove, then the hawk assumes control of the territory. If both animals elect to behave as doves, then one of them at random assumes control of the territory. Finally, if both animals elect to behave as hawks, then they fight. One randomly selected hawk is assumed to sustain injuries that reduce the number of young it can produce, and the other gains the territory. This simple game can be written in strategic form. (See table 11.3.)

Table 11.3
Hawk-Dove Game

	Challenger chooses hawk	Challenger chooses dove
Defender chooses hawk	Challenger: 50% chance of gaining territory–50% chance of injury Defender: 50% chance of retaining territory–50% chance of injury	Challenger: nothing gained Defender: retains territory
Defender chooses dove	Challenger: gains territory Defender: loses territory	Challenger: 50% chance of gaining territory Defender: 50% chance of retaining territory

For Maynard Smith, each of these values can be expressed in evolutionary terms: the gain or loss in reproductive fitness that an individual achieves with each outcome. Gaining a territory confers an increase in fitness. Sustaining an injury results in a decrease in fitness. Using this approach one can conclude that if the value of a territory is high and the magnitude of injury in a hawk versus hawk fight is low, then animals genetically disposed to behave as hawks will be more fit than those genetically disposed to behave as doves. Under these conditions, Maynard Smith reasoned, the population will evolve toward a set of individuals who show a single pure strategy equilibrium. All animals in the population will eventually be hawks.

Similarly, if the value of a territory is low and the magnitude of injury sustained in a hawk versus hawk fight is high, then hawks should eventually die out. All animals that behave as doves will produce more offspring, will be more fit, than animals that act as hawks. Under these conditions the population should evolve toward a pure strategy of behaving as doves.

But if the value of a territory is high, and the cost of an injury is also relatively high, then an interesting result can be predicted. The only evolutionarily stable equilibrium strategy under these conditions is for there to be a fixed probability that any individual will play hawk or dove on a given encounter. To be more specific, a single dominant and unbeatable strategy should emerge in a population playing the hawk–dove game at an evolutionary level. The population will reach an evolutionary equilibrium point when the probability that on any given encounter an individual will choose to behave as a hawk is equal to the value of a territory divided by the magnitude of the injury sustained in a hawk versus hawk conflict. Critically, on each encounter individuals must behave in an unpredictable fashion, never allowing their opponent to know in advance whether they will be a hawk or a dove. But across many such encounters the only evolutionarily stable and unbeatable solution for the population is for the probability of being a hawk to be equal to the value of a territory divided by the cost of injury.

Maynard Smith goes on to point out that there are two ways for the species to accomplish this equilibrium. Either each individual could develop unpredictably as a hawk or a dove for life, or individuals could behave unpredictably from encounter to encounter. Both between-individual and within-individual unpredictability can thus be produced at an evolutionary level. In this specific game, Maynard Smith points out that a population in which each individual behaves unpredictably will be slightly more stable than one that relies on between-individual unpredictablility.[4]

Maynard Smith referred to equilibrium evolutionary strategies that result from games of this type as evolutionary stable strategies, or ESSs. ESSs reflect an extension of the Nash equilibrium concept toward a much more biological and evolutionary solution, the details of which I have not really described. At a more general level, however, there are two critical insights presented by Maynard Smith's analyses. First, these game theoretic studies suggest that there are mathematically defined conditions under which animals *must* evolve the ability to behave in an

---

4. I have presented the hawk-dove game here in a extremely simplified form. First, it is assumed that during the display phase individuals gain no information about whether they will win or lose the conflict. Second, all individuals are presumed to be equally likely to win or lose any conflict in which they participate. Third, I have completely avoided describing the beautiful mathematical proof that Maynard Smith develops. In Maynard Smith's book each of these issues is carefully addressed, and proofs dealing not only with this simplified hawk-dove game but also with more complex versions involving the exchange of information prior to conflict are described. I urge the reader to examine Maynard Smith's book for details.

irreducibly uncertain fashion. Put another way, the behavior of animals must be stochastic, unpredictable at the micro level of individual acts, but lawful and predictable at a probabilistic level. Second, these complex and unpredictable patterns of animal behavior can be lawfully described by the theory of games.

Can Animals Really Produce Unpredictable Behaviors?

One core criticism often raised against this general line of argument, particularly by empirical scientists, is that physical systems as large as actual animals simply cannot behave unpredictably. While we all agree that modern physicists have proved the existence of uncertainty at the subatomic level, many people believe that uncertainty in macroscopic systems like organisms is an impossibility. In essence, the argument gets made that randomly picking whether to be a hawk or a dove on a given encounter is simply impossible for real animals. It is important to note, however, that the theory of games does not actually require that animals be truly, fundamentally, random in their behavior. Game theory requires only that the behavior of each individual be irreducibly uncertain *to his opponents*. It does not require that animals be *fundamentally* unpredictable. I should add, however, that although the theory of games does not require fundamental unpredictability, I see no a priori reason to rule out the existence of such behavior. As Maynard Smith put it in 1982:

I cannot see the force of this objection. If it were selectively advantageous, a randomizing device could surely evolve, either as an entirely neuronal process or by dependence on functionally irrelevant external stimuli. Perhaps the one undoubted example of a mixed ESS is the production of equal numbers of X and Y gametes [male producing and female producing sperm] by the heterogametic sex: if the gonads can do it, why not the brain? Further, in so far as animals can adopt "probability matching" tactics in experiments on learning, they are demonstrating that they possess the equivalent of a roulette wheel. (Maynard Smith, 1982)

Maynard Smith makes two points here. The first is that we should not be too quick to dismiss the idea that devices as complex as our brains could have evolved the ability to produce random processes at the neuronal level. His second point is that in order to produce irreducibly uncertain behavior, organisms do not have to employ a true neuronal randomizer. Organisms could employ "functionally irrelevant external stimuli" as seed values from which unpredictable responses could be generated by some internal and nonrandom process. The critical point is that animals must be able to produce behavior that is irreducibly uncertain from the point of view of their opponents.

Applying Game Theory to Animal Behavior

Mathematicians, economists, and ecological biologists have argued, at a theoretical level, that game theory can predict the stochastic patterns of behavior which animals produce when facing intelligent competitors. Has this theoretical assertion been verified empirically? In the preceding chapters I argued that more classical forms of economic theory could be used to describe foraging behavior at a theoretical level. I then reviewed empirical tests of this claim which suggested that current economic models did a good, although imperfect, job of predicting the behavior of real animals. Can the same be said for game theoretic models of animal behavior?

To be honest, there are very few tests of the validity of game theoretic models of animal behavior in the literature. In chapter 12 I will present experimental evidence from my own laboratory that suggests game theoretic models are effective tools for both behavioral and physiological studies of animals. Before turning to those neurobiological experiments, however, I want to describe one example of game theory as a predictive tool in a more natural setting.

In 1982 D. G. C. Harper performed what is generally considered a landmark study of group foraging among ducks in Cambridge, England. Thirty-three mallard ducks spent the winter of 1979 on a lake in the botanical garden of Cambridge University, and Harper wondered how these ducks might interact as they competed for access to small bread balls thrown sequentially into the lake.

Each day, Harper and an assistant would walk down to the lake, each with a basket of either 2-gram or 4-gram bread balls. The two humans would take up positions along the edge of the lake about 20 meters apart. At a signal, they would begin throwing bread balls. One would throw bread balls once every 5 sec, and the other would throw them either once every 5 sec or once every 10 sec. The question Harper asked was How does each of the thirty-three ducks decide where to stand?

Take a situation in which the human named Swerve is throwing a 2-gram bread ball every 5 sec and a human named Continue is throwing a 2-gram bread ball every 10 sec. What should a duck do? Formally, this is a 33-duck game, and one that we can solve for a Nash equilibrium as a 33-player problem. To keep the solution fairly simple mathematically, we will make two simplifying assumptions. First, we will treat this as a two-player game: a single duck playing against a flock. We could solve this as a 33-player game and it would yield the same result, but at a tremendous increase in complexity. Second, we will assume all of the ducks standing in front of Swerve or Continue have an equal chance of catching any bread ball that is thrown.[5]

Now, to determine the Nash equilibrium point for this game, we have to determine when the particular duck we are studying, say the duck named Smith, is indifferent about the bread ball thrower in front of whom he stands. We have to find Smith's equilibrium point, the point at which Smith sees the two patches (Swerve's and Continue's) as being of equal value. To find this, we begin by defining the value of each patch to Smith.

The value of Swerve's patch per hour must be equal to the total amount of bread thrown into the patch per hour, divided by the average number of ducks in the patch per hour:

$$\text{Value of Swerve's patch} = \text{gain}_{\text{swerve}}/\text{ducks}_{\text{swerve}} \qquad (11.13)$$

If we define the number of ducks in Swerve's patch as the fraction (θ) of the total flock size (Size),

$$\theta^* \text{size.} \qquad (11.14)$$

Then the value of Swerve's patch to the duck named Smith is

$$\text{Value of Swerve's patch} = \text{gain}_{\text{swerve}}/(\theta * \text{size}). \qquad (11.15)$$

---

5. In fact, this is a fairly interesting assumption for several reasons. First, this assumption has played an intriguing role in theoretical analyses of this kind of foraging. For details the reader is referred to Fretwell's classic 1972 book, *Populations in a Seasonal Environment*. Second, Harper found that this assumption was in fact violated in his flock. Dominant ducks got more than their fair share. Third and most important, as long as each individual duck has a probability of getting a bread ball that is influenced only by his dominance rank and the number of other ducks at that feeding site, this assumption has no real effect on the game theoretic model developed here.

In a similar way, the value of Continue's patch is

Value of Continue's patch = $\text{gain}_{\text{continue}}/((1-\theta) * \text{size})$.   (11.16)

At equilibrium, the value of these two patches to Smith must be equal. That is, they are of equal value when the number of ducks in each patch is such that the value of each patch *to Smith* is equal. Thus equilibrium occurs when

$\text{Gain}_{\text{swerve}}/(\theta * \text{size}) = \text{Gain}_{\text{continue}}/((1-\theta) * \text{size})$,   (11.17)

where gain is the total volume of bread thrown per minute at Swerve's and Continue's patches. Performing a little standard algebra:

$\text{Gain}_{\text{swerve}}/\text{Gain}_{\text{continue}} = (\theta * \text{size})/((1-\theta) * \text{size})$.   (11.18)

Then

$\theta = \text{Gain}_{\text{swerve}}/(\text{Gain}_{\text{continue}} + \text{Gain}_{\text{swerve}})$.   (11.19)

Now if, as in the example Harper's experiment presents, Swerve is throwing a 2-gram bread ball every 5 sec and Continue is throwing a 2-gram bread ball every 10 sec, then the total gain per minute is 24 grams from Swerve and 12 grams from Continue:

$\theta = 24/(12+24) = 2/3$.   (11.20)

The two patches are of equal value to Smith when, and only when, two thirds of the ducks are at Swerve's patch and one third are at Continue's patch. Whenever this is not the case, the right choice for Smith is to go to the patch with too few ducks. In this way, the game theoretic decisions of each duck will drive the flock toward equilibrium.

What this all means is that a Nash equilibrium is reached when two thirds of the ducks are standing in front of Swerve and one third of the ducks are standing in front of Continue. Under those conditions, Smith is completely indifferent about the patch in front of which he stands. Since this is a symmetrical game, each of the other ducks is indifferent when Smith and his cohort are spending two thirds of their time in front of Swerve and one third in front of Continue.

Perhaps amazingly, this is exactly what Harper found. Under these conditions the population of ducks had assorted itself precisely at the Nash equilibrium as predicted by theory. And they did this within 60 sec of the start of bread ball throwing, a time when less than half of the ducks had received a single bread ball. Perhaps even more amazingly, each of the ducks maintained a one third/two thirds ratio of its own time in each patch, again exactly as predicted by theory. Whenever Harper and his assistant changed either the size of the bread balls they were throwing or the rate at which one of them threw bread, the ducks immediately reassorted themselves according to the equations shown above.

To a first approximation, then, game theory does seem to do a fairly good job not only of modeling unpredictable behavior at a theoretical level but also of predicting the actual behavior of animals engaged in competition. Game theory really does seem to be an extension of economic decision theory that can account for unpredictability in animal behavior when it reaches a stable equilibrium.

The great limitation of contemporary game theory is that it fails to provide tools for describing the dynamic process by which equilibriums are reached. Being able to model the dynamics of sequential decision making before an equilibrium is reached will, ultimately, be of critical importance. The theory of games in its current form, however, still provides a critical asset. It is a fundamental tool for understanding the unpredictable behavior humans and animals produce.

Summary

When the sensorimotor problem is framed in economic terms, all classes of behavior, both deterministic and nondeterministic, can be viewed as solutions to problems that can be rigorously posed. Some problems, like those posed for the stretch response, require deterministic solutions. Others, like the hawk–dove game, may require irreducibly probabilistic solutions. The theory of games completes the economic approach in the sense that it eliminates the need for a dualist neurobiology. While game theory demonstrates that both determinate and indeterminate behaviors are necessary, it explains how both are the product of a single efficient decision-making system.

Given this theoretical advantage, can game theory be used as an effective tool for neurobiological research? Can we actually identify irreducibly uncertain behaviors that can be modeled at a behavioral *and* neurophysiological level with game theoretic tools? To begin to answer those questions, we turn in chapter 12 to a series of experiments that Michael Dorris and I began in the year 2000.

12

Games and the Brain

Volition, Free Will, and Mathematical Games

Imagine yourself a young woman at a summer party, outside in the park. At the other side of the lawn you see a close friend talking with a fantastically handsome young man. He seems to laugh easily and to listen well. Should you go over and ask him to dance? A hard decision. Will he say yes or no? If he says yes, do you want to risk getting involved with him right now?

Understanding decisions like these seems intuitively beyond the reach of neuroscience. One has such a clear sense of deciding, of exercising free will. It seems so unlikely that a scientific theory of the brain could ever fully describe a process like this in mathematical and physiological terms. Of course that was what Descartes thought as well; exactly the kind of decision that he was referring to when he wrote in *Passions de l'Âme*:

It is easy to understand that there remains nothing in us that we should attribute to our soul but our thoughts, which are principally of two genera—the first, namely, are the actions of the soul; the others are its passions. The ones I call its actions are all of our volitions, because we find by experience that they come directly from our soul *and seem to depend only on it* [my italics]; as, on the other hand, all the sorts of cases of perception or knowledge to be found in us can generally be called its passions, because it always receives them from things that are represented by them. (Descartes, 1649)

Can we ever expect tools like classical economics and the theory of games to bring decisions like these under the umbrella of neuroscience? I would argue that if there is a way, it is to use the scientific method Francis Bacon and his colleagues invented during the Enlightenment.

First, we would need to identify a behavioral decision that everyone agrees reflects an "action of the soul," as Descartes put it. Once we had such a behavior identified, we would need to determine what goal, in David Marr's sense of the word, that "action of the soul" was intended to accomplish. Then we could proceed to develop a computational description of the behavior itself and to begin to analyze the neural hardware that generates the behavior.

What are the defining characteristics of these "actions of the soul," volitional decisions that cannot be called reflexlike or determinate? First and foremost, decisions of this type seem to "depend only on volition," to paraphrase Descartes. They must be unpredictable, irreducibly uncertain with regard to external sensory events. The decision about whether or not to ask the young man to dance does seem to have this property. Any scientific study of this class of decisions must dissect neural processes that have this property of unpredictability. Second, it must be a decision that seems, subjectively, to require free will. Unlike pulling one's hand away from a sharp tack, or simply shifting one's line of sight to a newly illuminated target, it has to *feel*, at a subjective level, like we are making a decision. If we were to find such a decision, and then learn how to model it and study it in the laboratory, we might be able to test the idea that neuroeconomic approaches could be used to model even the most complex processes brains can produce.

Playing the Inspection Game

Imagine playing the following game against me. Pretend that I am your employer and you are my only employee. At the beginning of each day you have to decide whether or not to come to work. As you know, coming to work is hard. It costs you something in time and energy. A cost on which we could probably place a dollar value. You also know that I, as your employer, have other responsibilities that make it difficult for me to check up on you each day. Once in a while I do come to the office to see if you came to work that day, but I try to do this as rarely as possible.

Imagine yourself on a Monday morning. You wake up tired. Lying in bed, you have to decide whether or not to come to work. Will I inspect today? Assume for argument's sake that I always adopted a strategy of inspecting on Mondays and never on any other day. If you knew that this was my strategy, it would doubtless influence the decisions you made on Monday mornings. You could, for example, decide never to shirk on Mondays, but rather to put off your shirking until later in the week. Of course I know that you know that, and so I am inclined to be as unpredictable in my inspections as possible. In practice I have to be sure that you will never know exactly when I will inspect.

Each morning, as you lie in bed, you have to reflect on whether there is some kind of pattern in my behavior which indicates whether or not I will inspect on that day. In a similar way, I try to anticipate exactly when you will shirk. Like the white and black billiard balls in chapter 11, we find ourselves locked in a game of unpredictable strategy.

As you imagine this game, I want you to note that you have a clear sense of having to *decide*; to think about what I might do and then to exercise your free will in making a decision about whether to work or to shirk.

Theory

Let me proceed by formalizing these decisions that we make in strategic conflict as the classic mathematical *inspection game*, also known as the game of *work or shirk*. We begin by formalizing your sense that going to work is costly. Work costs you some unpleasant effort, E. For simplicity we will put a dollar value on your effort, an amount of money for which you would not quite be willing to work.[1] When you do go to work (or when you shirk and I fail to catch you), I pay you a wage, W. Necessarily W will have to be bigger than E, or you would, at best, be a very indifferent employee. In mathematical terms this means that one of your conditions for playing this game with me is that W must be greater than E.

Now what about me? I have to pay your wage, W, but what do I get in return? When you come to work, your effort yields a product, P. Necessarily, the value of P must be greater than what I pay you or my

---

1. To be more precise, it would be the wage that made you indifferent, in the long run, about whether or not it was ever worth going to work at this particular job.

Table 12.1
Work or Shirk

	I inspect	I do not inspect
You work	You: W − E Me: P − W − Insp	You: W − E Me: P − W
You shirk	You: 0 Me: −Insp	You: W Me: −W

hiring you would be irrational. My condition for playing is therefore that P must be greater than W. Finally, we come to inspections. As I said earlier, checking to see if you have actually come to work costs me something. Every time I have to come to the office, I have to pay for that with time I could have used elsewhere. We take this into account with the variable *Insp*. *Insp* is how much it costs me, in dollars, each time I make an inspection. That brings our list of variables to the following:

E—The effort you expend working

W—The wage I pay you

P—The value of your production during a day at work

$Insp$—The cost, to me, of inspecting.

(12.1)

Examine what the costs and benefits of each of our possible actions are in strategic form. I have two possible courses of action each day. I can either inspect or not-inspect. You also have two possible courses of action: You can either work or shirk. (See table 12.1.)

If on Monday I inspect and you work, then you gain your wage but lose your effort. You have a net gain of *W-E*. On the other hand, I gain your product but lose both your wage and the cost of my inspection; *P-W-Insp*. If you work and I fail to inspect, you still gain your wage (less your effort) and I still gain my product (less your wage), but this time I do not lose the cost of my inspection. This outcome is best for me. If you shirk and I do not inspect, then you gain your wage without expending any effort and I lose your wage without gaining any profit. This outcome is best for you but worst for me.

What does this formalization of our game capture? To see that, we begin by turning all of these variables into numbers. Imagine that I pay

Table 12.2

	I inspect	I do not inspect
You work	You: 50 Me: −25	You: 50 Me: 25
You shirk	You: 0 Me: −50	You: 100 Me: −100

Table 12.3

	I inspect	I do not inspect
You work	You: 50 Me: 20	You: 50 Me: 25
You shirk	You: 0 Me: −5	You: 100 Me: −100

you $100 per day as a wage, and that you produce a product worth $125 to me. Imagine that you see a day off (your effort) as worth $50. Finally, assume that an inspection costs me $50 in gas and time because I live 25 miles from the office. The strategic form of the game under these conditions, with payoffs in dollars, is shown in table 12.2.

Taking a look at these conditions shows that inspecting is very expensive. You know this, which means you will probably feel that you can shirk fairly often, a strategy I will tolerate as long as your rate of shirking is not totally out of control. Now compare that with a situation in which I live around the corner from where you work. Under those circumstances, we might think of an inspection as costing me only $5. Under those conditions you might expect that I will tolerate very little shirking. If I think that you are getting away with anything, I will start inspecting often, and you will get caught often. Again, the strategic form seems to capture this intuition. (See table 12.3.)

In some sense, work or shirk resolves to a series of trade-offs between the two of us. You shirk as much as you can and I inspect as little as I have to, in order to keep you at work and to maximize my profits. We both know this each morning when we wake up and decide, respectively, whether to work and whether to inspect, on that day. Of course shirking as much as you can get away with is what John Nash was talking about when he invented the concept of the Nash equilibrium. It is a formal mathematical way to define how often you *ought* to shirk. Now I am not saying, at least not yet, that the free will you exercise lying in bed can be described as the solution to an optimization problem. I am just saying that Nash's model allows us to identify the best strategy you *could* adopt. It tells us how often you *ought* to decide to shirk.

Formally, the probability that you will shirk at Nash equilibrium is the precise probability of shirking that makes me indifferent between inspecting and not inspecting. At that level of shirking I see inspecting and not inspecting as equally attractive. If you shirk more than this equilibrium level, then I should always inspect if I want to maximize my profits. If you shirk less than this equilibrium level, I never have to inspect because inspecting is not worth what it costs. Mathematically, the probability that you will shirk should be equal to the cost of inspection divided by the value (to me) of your wage:

Probability of you shirking $= I/W$. (12.2)

And in a similar way,

Probability of me inspecting $= E/W$. (12.3)

All of this means that, for the strategic game shown above in table 12.2, in which an inspection costs me \$50, you earn \$100, your effort costs you \$50, and your product is worth \$125, the absolute best that we can do *against each other* is for you to shirk 50 percent of the time and me to inspect 50 percent of the time. That is, quite simply, the best that we can each do, given our competing goals. If, however, the cost of inspection were to drop to \$5, as it does in table 12.3, then your shirking should drop to 5 percent.

So far so good. The Nash equilibrium tells us what you ought to do as you lie in bed each morning. As you try to decide whether or not to go to work, the Nash equilibrium calculation identifies a computational goal for your deliberative process. What about the real world? Does any of this actually predict how you behave when free to choose between working and shirking?

Behavior

To begin to answer that question, Michael Dorris and I asked humans to play this game of work or shirk. We arbitrarily assigned one of our human subjects the role of employer and the other the role of worker. We seated the employer and the worker at computer terminals in separate rooms. Then we had them complete several hundred plays of work or shirk over a period of 1–2 hr. At the beginning of each *play*, we had them independently decide what to do on that "day": whether to work or to shirk, whether to inspect or not to inspect. After they had made their independent decisions, our computer examined the strategic form matrix and informed them of what they had earned for that play. (I should mention that we paid our subjects in cents rather than in dollars, but even so our subjects were able to earn as much as $30 in an hour of play.) For reasons that will soon be evident, I need to tell you that at no time did we explicitly reveal the strategic form matrix to our players. Nor did we explicitly tell them what their opponent had done. We simply paid them whatever they had earned and invited them to play again.

In a typical experiment, we had a pair of subjects play this game 150 times, then changed the payoff matrix, so that a new rate of shirking and inspecting became the Nash equilibrium rate. They then played another 150 trials, and this was typically repeated three to five times.

Of course whenever we asked our subjects to decide what to do on a set of plays, we knew the Nash equilibrium points that defined the optimal solution to the problem they faced. This was because we had a full computational description of the game of work or shirk. The question we asked by having them play the game was whether or not this mathematically defined optimal two-player strategy predicted what our human subjects would actually do.

In figure 12.1 we can see what a typical employer/worker pair did over the course of about 150 plays of the game. The black line plots the percentage at which the worker decided to work, represented as a running average over 20 sequential plays. The gray line plots the rate at which the employer decided to inspect. For this particular set of 150 plays, Dorris and I selected values for *W*, *P*, *E*, and *Insp* that yielded an optimal solution if the worker shirked 50 percent of the time and the employer inspected 50 percent of the time. The thick gray line on the graph indicates that optimal rate. The jagged lines that hover around that gray line represents the actual behavior of our human subjects.

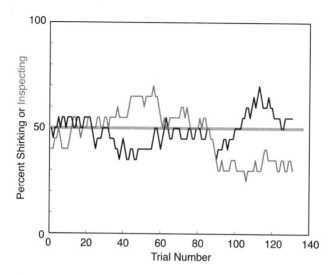

Figure 12.1
Two humans playing work or shirk for money. The behavior of the employer is plotted in gray and that of the worker is plotted in black.

The amazing thing about these graphs, at least to us, was that over the course of the first 100 plays both the employer and the worker seemed to adjust their percentages back and forth until their behavior came into fairly precise accord with the Nash equilibrium. Their behavior then remained at or near this stable equilibrium until we changed the payoff matrix. Acheiving the Nash optimal strategy seemed to be exactly what the employer and the worker were doing when they decided what to do on each play.

Recall that we never explicitly told our players what the payoff matrix looked like, and we certainly never told them anything about the theory of Nash equilibriums. In fact, most of our players were neuroscience graduate students who had never heard of a Nash equilibrium. When we asked them, after the experiment, what they thought they were doing and how they did it, they never made any particularly mathematical replies. If we asked a typical worker, after the hundredth trial, Why did you shirk that time? He might answer, "It seemed like I would probably get away with it that time." Despite their ignorance of game theory and their strong feelings of independence, these players did seem to be accomplishing mathematically defined behavioral goals. They were selecting a rate of working or inspecting that was nearly optimal, a rate fully described by the Nash equations.

As we reflected on these data we realized that they could do something much more; they could begin to tell us something about the irreducible uncertainty which I argued was central to understanding Descartes's complex behaviors. Return to the situation in which the Nash equilibrium rates for shirking and inspecting are 50 percent. The data I have already described indicate that human players do a good job of approximating these equilibrium rates. What about the specific pattern of working and inspecting by which our players achieved those overall rates? Are their specific patterns of working and inspecting irreducibly uncertain, as predicted by game theory? Remember that our worker could have achieved a 50 percent rate of shirking simply by alternating, play after play, between working and shirking, working on every odd-numbered trial and shirking on every even-numbered trial. If, however, our employer had noticed this pattern, then he could have made good use of that knowledge. Knowing in advance when the worker would shirk, the employer could have inspected only when necessary. What follows from this is that the worker has to shirk (and the employer to inspect) in as truly random a fashion as possible. And that seems, at an intuitive level, to be the pattern that we expect to find when studying a truly volitional decision.

So how unpredictable, how irreducibly uncertain, was the behavior of our human subjects? In figure 12.2 we plot, on the left, the total number of times that the worker chose to work or shirk during the 150 plays of a game in which 50 percent shirking was the optimal strategy. Note that he worked 51 percent of the time and shirked 49 percent of the time. As you move to the right on the diagram, we plot the number of sequential plays on which he worked and then shirked. We plot how often a decision to work was followed by a second decision to work. On the line beneath that, we plot the number of times a decision to work was followed by a decision to shirk. On the lines beneath that we plot the fraction of trials on which he decided to work after a decision to shirk and the fraction of trials on which he shirked after shirking. In essence, what we are doing is looking for sequential patterns in the way our human worker decided whether to work or to shirk.

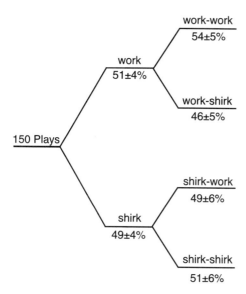

Figure 12.2
Randomness in the behavior of a human "worker" playing work or shirk.

If our worker had been alternating back and forth between working and shirking, we would have seen many more works followed by shirks than works followed by works. On the other hand, if the worker was being irreducibly uncertain in his or her behavior, then there would be an equal distribution among all of these possibilities. What we actually see is a fairly equal distribution, indicating that there is no obvious pattern in the behavior. True to theory, the worker seems to be randomly deciding what to do each time.[2] This randomness also seems to explain yet another feature of our data. You probably noticed that in the plot of shirking across trials (see figure 12.1) the graph was very jagged-looking. While the players seemed to hover around the Nash equilibrium, they only rarely stayed exactly on the equilibrium line. Now we can see that this reflects a fundamental randomness in their behavior, a pattern that we see not just in this worker but in essentially all of our human workers and in all of our employers as well.

2. A more formal mathematical test for randomness in this behavior is known as the Ljung-Box Q-statistic. It also reveals randomness in the behavior of our human subjects.

Summary

When we ask our players what it feels like to play work or shirk, they report a very strong sense that on each play they have to *decide* whether to work or to inspect. They report that they try to be as clever and unpredictable as possible. Our numerical data support this claim. Their behavior really is quite unpredictable at a decision-by-decision level. Based on these data, I want to argue that the game of work or shirk does seem to be played by humans in an unpredictable fashion. The behavior our human subjects produce when they play work or shirk is a behavior of the type that Descartes would have described as a product of the soul, or of volition. It is a complex and unpredictable behavior that no determinate or reflex-based system could ever hope to explain.

When we examine this behavior through the lens of economic theory, however, even this unpredictability seems terribly lawful and easy to understand. The behavior, randomness and all, accurately meets the computational goal set out by a game theoretic description of the problem the players are facing. There seems nothing mystical about these behaviors when they are viewed as the evolutionarily derived solution to problems that require probabilistic solutions. Rather than appearing to be a unique element in a dualist system, this class of behavior seems remarkably similar to the more determinate behaviors we have already examined. How, then, can we use this approach to begin to study the neurobiological underpinnings of a behavior that we might very well label volitional?

Shifting to a Single Player

For Mike Dorris and me, the next step toward the physiological study of a volitional behavior was to reduce the number of players from two to one, while preserving all of the important features of the original work or shirk game. This would allow us to focus our attention on the behavior of the single remaining player and would ultimately allow us to devote all of our resources to examining the physiological processes that were occurring when work or shirk was being played. To do that, we developed a computer program that could replace the human employer, and would play work or shirk unpredictably, according to the laws of game theory.

In order to develop such a program, we turned to a colleague of ours, the computer scientist Dana Ballard, who works at the University of Rochester. Ballard and his graduate student Sheng Huo Zhu had recently become interested in developing computer programs that could compete effectively with humans in strategic games. They had used classical equations from both animal and machine learning theory to develop computer opponents that slowly but surely learned how to earn as much money as possible by evaluating the behavior of their opponents and planning irreducibly uncertain strategies. Like human players, these computer programs almost always adopted Nash equilibrium strategies. This was not because the programs knew anything about equilibriums but because the equilibriums, once found, were optimal strategies.

We began by designing our computer employer around one of Ballard and Zhu's algorithms, after adding an important change. We had noticed that their computer opponents never checked to see whether there were any predictable patterns in the behavior of the human or computer they faced. Ballard's algorithms just assumed that their opponents were behaving unpredictably. That was, however, an assumption that we felt we could not make. Irreducible uncertainty, we had argued, evolves from the existence of opponents who search for patterns. We therefore added a search for patterns in the behavior of one's opponent to their algorithm.

Once the computer program was complete and we had shown that it could detect patterns in an opponent's behavior and use that pattern to advantage, we once again invited human subjects to play work or shirk in our laboratory. The human subjects were again seated at a computer terminal and again invited to play the game for real money. From the point of view of one of our human workers, everything was exactly the same as in the original game. We did not even tell the human subjects that they were now playing a computer.

Remember that the reason we were going to all of this trouble was to replace one of our players with a standardized computer program, and we wanted to do this without changing any feature of the worker's behavior. Our goal was to show that even after the substitution of a computer program for the employer, our human subjects behaved in fundamentally the same way. Figure 12.3 shows the behavior of one of

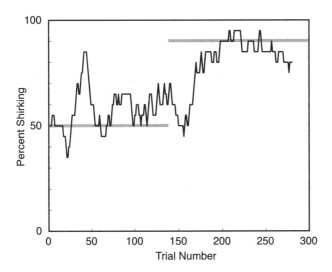

Figure 12.3
Behavior of a human worker playing a computer employer for money.

our typical human workers when playing against our computer opponent under two sequentially presented equilibrium conditions. Note that
our human workers perform in the same way when they face this computer opponent as they did when facing another human. With our earlier
work, this suggested to us that we had captured an irreducibly uncertain
behavior which was ready for a scientific examination at the physiological level.

Game-Playing Monkeys

What we did next may seem a bit unorthodox, but it was absolutely
necessary. We trained rhesus monkeys to play this same game, work or
shirk, against our computer employer. The idea was first to ask whether
or not the patterns of decisions that our monkeys made looked just like
the patterns produced by our human workers. If that were the case, then
asking what the monkeys' brains were doing when they played work or
shirk would tell us something about human volitional decision making.
Of course we could not pay the monkeys in coins, so for this version of
the experiment we paid the monkeys in milliliters of Berry Berry Fruit
Juice delivered after each play.

From the monkey's point of view, the experiment looked as much like a standard neurophysiological experiment as we could make it. The monkey was seated facing a computer display. At an unpredictable time a central fixation stimulus was illuminated, and the monkey had to stare at that light. The computer employer then secretly selected one of two possible trials to present to the monkey, the *Inspect trial* or the *No-Inspect trial*. In both trials, two eccentric visual targets were next illuminated; one to the left and one to the right of the central stimulus. After a brief delay the central target was extinguished and the monkey had to decide whether to look left or look right. Looking to the left counted as working and looking to the right counted as shirking. Based on what kind of trial our computer opponent had selected, and what movement the monkey had selected, our experimental system consulted the payoff matrix and paid the monkey worker in juice and the computer employer in virtual dollars. Then, after a brief interval, the next round of play began.

Our goal was to keep this as close to the human experiment as possible. As in that experiment, if the monkey worker began to shirk too often, the computer employer responded by inspecting more often. If the monkey worker decreased the probability that he would shirk, then the computer employer reduced the rate of inspection. Figure 12.4 plots an example of a typical monkey's behavior during a typical set of plays conducted over a daily 1- to 2-hour session. On the day presented in this figure, we examined two payoff matrices in series. I intentionally selected an experiment in which the Nash equilibriums for these matrices were the same ones shown for the human versus computer games presented in the preceding section.

First we set the juice rewards so that a 50 percent rate of shirking was optimal for our monkey. After about 80 plays we switched the payoff matrices for both the monkey and the computer opponent so that a rate of 90 percent shirking was optimal.

Notice that the monkey tracks the equilibrium point accurately, at least as accurately as our human players, but also stays irreducibly uncertain in his behavior. Just like our human players, the monkeys seem to decide on each trial whether to work or to shirk. On each trial our monkeys are, like the humans, unpredictable. But on average the behav-

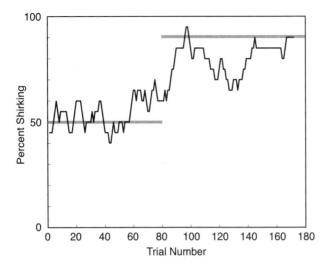

Figure 12.4
Behavior of a monkey worker playing a computer employer for juice.

ior of the monkeys is carefully sculpted to achieve the computational goal of maximizing what the monkey earns when he faces an intelligent opponent.

The very close parallel between these data and our human data suggested to us that we had in fact succeeded in our first goal: We had brought a complex and unpredictable decision into the laboratory and had shown that a computational approach based in game theory could describe that behavior.

The Physiology of a Complex Behavior

In the physiology experiment that Michael Platt and I did, which was described in chapter 10, we looked for evidence that decision variables described by classical economic theory were encoded in parietal area LIP. Traditional sensorimotor theories had predicted that activity in parietal cortex must be either sensory or motor in nature. We found that when we held the sensory inputs and motor outputs constant, but varied either the probability or the value of an outcome, the firing rates of LIP neurons were strongly influenced by those decision variables. As a result of that observation we suggested that area LIP neurons were most likely reflecting the relative expected utility of the movements they encoded.

In chapter 11 I noted that this finding did not, and could not, address the deeper question of whether a neuroeconomic approach could be used to specify all possible sensorimotor problems both the simple and the complex in computational terms. In that chapter, I argued that classical economics could not account for all types of behavior because it could not account for complex, or *unpredictable*, patterns of behavior. When, however, game theory is employed as a part of the overall economic corpus, then it becomes possible to account for predictable as well as complex, or irreducibly uncertain, classes of behavior.

The theoretical work of Von Neumann and Morgenstern argued that all kinds of behavior, both simple and complex, could be viewed as points along a single mathematical continuum, a continuum that ranges from determinate behavior to probabilistic behavior. This theoretical claim raised what Michael Dorris and I considered a crucial question: Did neurons in area LIP also see this is as a single continuum, a single continuum governed by the same rules and computations? Or, alternatively, did neurons in area LIP see simple and complex behaviors as distinct in the way Descartes had originally proposed?

In order to begin to answer that question, we recorded the activity of single neurons in area LIP while our trained monkeys played the work or shirk game. At the beginning of each day's experiment, Dorris and I would isolate a single neuron in parietal area LIP, but now we would have the monkey play work or shirk. On each trial the shirk target would appear at the best location for the neuron we were studying and the work target would appear at a null location. The monkey's job was to indicate whether he had decided to work or to shirk on that trial by looking at one of the two targets.

To understand the results of those experiments, two concepts are critical. First, recall that in the original economics experiments conducted by Michael Platt, each neuron encoded something like the expected utility of its movement *relative* to the other possible movement; movements that were worth 0.4 ml of juice were represented twice as strongly as movements worth 0.2 ml of juice. The second concept that must be borne in mind is the mathematical definition of a Nash equilibrium. A Nash equilibrium occurs when a chooser is indifferent between the options available. More formally, a behavior is a Nash equilibrium only when the relative expected utilities of the possible movements are exactly equivalent.

Taken together, these two concepts lead to a rather surprising prediction. In the Platt and Glimcher (1999) experiment we had shown that as we varied the amount of juice earned for each movement over five or more blocks of trials, LIP firing rates varied enormously from block to block. On a given day in this new experiment, Michael Dorris and I might also study five different blocks with different rewards, but in this experiment the animals were always at or near the Nash equilibriums. Under these conditions, despite the fact that both the movements made by the animals and the amounts of juice earned were changing from block to block, the relative utility of the two options was always by definition equivalent. That is what defines a Nash equilibrium. So if the monkeys were maintaining a Nash equilibrium, they were doing so by keeping the relative expected utilities of their two options equivalent. If the monkeys were computing and maintaining Nash equilibrium behaviors, then across all of the different conditions we studied there should never have been a change in LIP firing rates if LIP firing rates encode relative expected utility.

Surprisingly, this is exactly what we found. In figure 12.5, the left-hand figure plots the behavior of one of our animals on a typical day, a running average of the probability that he will chose to shirk. You can see that this varied significantly, and systematically, over the course of the day as we presented the monkey with five different Nash equilibrium blocks. The critical data are presented in the right-hand figure, which plots the firing rate of the neuron. Just as predicted by theory, the firing rate of this neuron was pretty stable throughout the day, even though the animal's behavior varied significantly from one block of trials to the next. To us, this provided compelling evidence that LIP neurons were encoding relative expected utility, a single decision variable which was required both for the generation of more determinate behavior in the Platt experiment and for the generation of this irreducibly uncertain behavior.

On reflection, we realized that this analysis could even be taken a step farther. The analysis we had completed suggested that, on average, LIP neurons reflected something like relative expected utility during a Nash equilibrium behavior. What would happen if we examined the neuronal responses at a much finer-grained level of analysis?

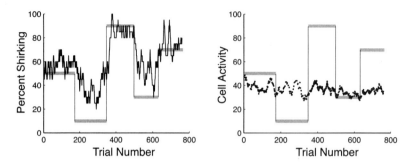

Figure 12.5
(*Left*) Behavior of a monkey worker playing a computer employer for juice under five different Nash equilibrium conditions. (*Right*) Simultaneous measurements of the activity of a neuron in area LIP. The neuron does not track the Nash equilibrium values, as predicted for a system encoding relative expected utility.

Remember that our computer opponent, the employer, actually achieved a Nash equilibrium response through a play-by-play analysis of the behavior of the monkey worker. On each trial, the employer was programmed to search for a best strategy, given the observed behavior of the monkey. Overall this yielded a Nash equilibrium solution. The play-by-play analysis of the monkey's behavior, however, had also revealed small but systematic fluctuations from the equilibrium rate. Indeed, it was the sensitivity of our computer employer to these fluctuations that forced our monkey to stay, on average, at the Nash equilibrium rate. Similarly, it was the sensitivity of the monkey to these same fluctuations on the part of the computer employer that forced it to maintain a Nash equilibrium rate. This is how a Nash equilibrium of any kind works.

If the monkey was performing a calculation similar to that performed by our computer employer, then we reasoned that we could examine the behavior of LIP neurons on a play-by-play basis for evidence of these small fluctuations in relative expected utility.

To look for these fluctuations, we began by developing a computer program that could serve as a simulated worker, a version of our computer employer that played the part of a worker. We then presented the computer worker with exactly the same pattern of gains and losses that our real monkey had encountered during a previous day's work. After each play the monkey had made, we asked the computer worker to assess the relative expected value of the two movements, work or shirk, available on the next play. We then compared the analysis of the computer with the firing rate of the LIP neuron we had studied earlier.

When we did this, we found a positive correlation between the relative expected value estimated by the computer and the firing rate produced by the neuron. The neurons seemed to be reflecting, on a play-by-play basis, a computation close to the one performed by our computer. At both the macroscopic and the microscopic scales, game theory seemed to account for both the behavior of our monkeys and of the activity of area LIP neurons. Game theory thus accounted for the average Nash equilibrium behavior of our monkeys and for the average firing rates of the neurons. At a more microscopic scale, we were able to use game theory to begin to describe the decision-by-decision computations that the neurons in area LIP were performing. And critically, these computations seemed to be the same regardless of whether the monkey was in a deterministic task like the one Platt had used or an irreducibly uncertain task like the one Dorris had used. Neurons in area LIP *did* seem to see all of behavior as a single continuum governed by a single set of goal directed rules and computations.

Summary

Philosophers who refer to themselves as monists, rather than as dualists, have typically argued that all human and animal behavior must be viewed as fully deterministic. They have argued that macroscopic physical systems in the real world must, a priori, be deterministic, and as a result the brain must also be deterministic.

In the first part of this book I argued that Sherrington had proposed reflex theory as a determinate logical calculus for constructing behaviors using simple neurophysiological elements. It was my contention that although brilliant, this was a mistake. Animals operating in the real world do not—in fact, I argued that they cannot—solve all problems in a determinate fashion if they are to survive. Instead organisms must represent at least two kinds of indeterminacy: one based on the epistemological limitations that animals face, and the other an irreducible indeterminacy required for effective competition with other organisms.

At an epistemological level, I argued that animals often have incomplete information about the world around them, and they therefore have to make statistical estimates of the likely state of the world and the likely outcomes of their actions. Recognition of this uncertainty was a breakthrough that allowed the birth of economics. Michael Platt and I hypothesized that economic theories might serve as excellent computational models for how the brain actually solves some kinds of decision-making problems. Our studies of determinate decisions in parietal cortex seemed to support that hypothesis.

At the level of irreducible uncertainty, I argued that whenever an animal must make a strategic decision which can be influenced by an intelligent competitor, game theory must be used to describe the computational problem the organism faces. In fact, I went a step farther and argued that for any game which requires a mixed strategy at equilibrium, as in work or shirk, behavioral indeterminacy is required if the behavior is to efficiently meet the needs of the animal. In the studies Michael Dorris and I have done, when monkeys played work or shirk, we hypothesized that game theory might serve as a computational model for indeterminate decision making. Our studies in parietal cortex seemed to support that hypothesis. Together with Platt's observations, these data suggested that a unitary economic approach might serve as a complete computational model for all components of the sensorimotor process.

Since the 1970s ecological biologists have begun to apply economic approaches like these to the study of behaving animals in the wild and in the laboratory. They have found that these models provide good descriptions of both the computational problems these animals face and the behavioral strategies they adopt. The results I have presented here extend those observations in an almost trivial manner. They suggest that these animal behaviors are the product of calculations performed by the brain.

13

Putting It All Together I. Behavior and Physiology

The Neuroeconomic Program

The ultimate goal of neuroscience is to understand how the brain produces behavior. In the preceding chapters I have reviewed theoretical and empirical evidence suggesting that this goal can be achieved only through a two-step process. First, we have to develop the tools required to determine, formally, what it is that a behavior accomplishes; we have to be able to determine the efficiency with which behavior approximates fully defined goals. Second, we have to learn to use quantitative measurements of these behavioral efficiencies as a mathematical corpus for linking behavior and neurophysiology.

In the second half of this book I have suggested that the process of defining the goal of a behavior for real-world animals must rely, in a fundamental way, on a theory of probability. I drew this conclusion from the work of mathematicians and economists who have argued that one can specify in mathematical terms the goal of any behavior if notions like probability and value are adequately formalized. In the 1960s biologists began to test this hypothesis within the ecological domain, attempting to show that the goal of any biological system can be characterized as an effort to maximize evolutionary fitness. They made this argument first with regard to foraging for food and later with regard to more abstract social phenomena like mate selection. Developing these ideas over four decades, ecological biologists gathered significant evidence supporting their claim that economically based models could describe optimal behavioral solutions to the problems animals face in terms of inclusive fitness.

During this same period, classical economics focused on deriving a theory of optimal response selection for humans while eschewing the empirical strategies that ecological biologists employed. Indeed, by the early 1960s classical economics seemed near to achieving a complete theoretical economic corpus. This *rational choice theory*, it was argued, defined the computations that any agent must perform in order to achieve a specified goal with maximal efficiency. Economics as a discipline, however, stumbled in the period after these mathematical successes were achieved because empirical observations revealed that rational choice theory often did a poor job of describing actual human behavior.

Over the last several decades this failure of classical economics and a growing awareness of ecological biology have led to some revolutions in economic circles. A group of economists have begun to challenge the notion that humans seek to maximize monetary utility and have instead suggested more ecological goals drawn from the biological sciences. Others have attempted to expand the field of economic research by employing behavioral experiments of the type pioneered by behavioral ecologists.

Until the 1970s very few neurobiologists had attempted to conceptualize neural function with regard to the kinds of goals that both behavioral ecologists and experimental economists were beginning to employ in their research. Marr and his colleagues had convinced many neurobiologists that studying the nervous system with regard to goals was important, but his approach provided very little guidance for identifying biologically meaningful computational goals. And even when biologically meaningful computational goals were proposed, among neuroscientists there was a tendency to avoid the study of systems in which probabilistic analyses were required, systems like those engaged by behavioral ecologists and experimental economists.

More recently, however, there has been a growing movement within the neurobiological community to employ goal-based approaches to describe behavioral and neurophysiological phenomena. There has even been a growing sense that statistical and probabilistic approaches may be central to this goal-based strategy. William Newsome and his colleagues, for example, used statistical and probabilistic approaches in the early

1990s to characterize the efficiency with which monkeys made decisions about the direction in which a stimulus was moving. They then used these measured efficiencies to identify neurons whose activity could, in principle, be used to produce the precise behavioral pattern they had observed.

In the second half of this book I have argued that the goal of neuroscience today should be to expand on this approach. We should begin to employ probabilistically based approaches to understand how the brain takes information from the outside world and uses that information in concert with stored representations of the structure of the world to achieve defined computational goals. It has been my central thesis that this goal can be best achieved through the synthesis of economics, biology, and neuroscience.

The central challenge facing neural scientists is to link behavior and brain. It seems clear that to accomplish this goal, a theory of behavior will eventually be required. Economics was designed to be just that, a mathematical corpus which attempts to describe how *any goal* should be achieved in an uncertain world like the one we inhabit. Behavioral ecologists recognize this; their field is focused on the study of how animals approximate economically defined goals with regard to the maximization of inclusive fitness. Experimental economists recognize this; their field is focused on the study of how human behavior approximates economically defined goals with regard to the maximization of utility. Neurobiologists are also beginning to recognize this, and today it seems natural to assume that some form of neuroeconomics will play a critical role in explaining how the brains of humans and other animals actually solve the maximization problems these two other disciplines have identified.

Using Neuroeconomics

Several of the experiments I have described in previous chapters seem to validate this notion that economic models, with roots in both game theory and more classical economic approaches, will be useful tools for linking brain activity with behavior. As an example, many of the experiments from my own laboratory have focused on demonstrating that both the choice behavior of monkeys and the behavior of individual parietal neurons are well described by economic tools. The goal of a neuro-economic approach, however, has to be much larger than an attempt to understand the activity of a few parietal neurons. The ultimate goal of any neuroeconomic approach must be to provide an overarching theory of how the computations that underlie behavior are organized and produced by the brain.

Building a complete neuroeconomic theory of the brain is an enormous, and largely empirical, task. This book serves more as a description of how one might begin to build such a theory rather than an indication of what such a theory would ultimately look like. To begin such an undertaking one would have to use an economically based theory to describe individual behaviors. Then one would have to use physiological tools to search for neural modules that perform some or all of the computations required by the behaviors under study. Finally, one would have to develop a cellular-level explanation of how those computations were performed. Unfortunately, we cannot know in advance how the brain performs or modularizes any computation, so a neuroeconomic approach would necessarily be iterative. Theory would be followed by both behavioral and physiological-cellular experiments that would lead to changes in theory and then to new experiments. And because the neuroeconomic program is in its infancy, early theories at both behavioral and physiological-cellular levels would necessarily be crude, and of course wrong.

Neuroeconomic Examples

Regardless of our certainty that these early models will be wrong, they are an essential first step if the empirical program of a neuroeconomic approach is to ultimately bear fruit. Recognizing the necessity of these crude early models, laboratories like mine are attempting to develop and test neuroeconomics with experiments that describe processes such as decision making, attention, learning, reward, and even emotion. I want to stress, however, that these current models and experiments serve as no more than examples, a demonstration of neuroeconomics in action.

Nonetheless, examples are important because they show how a neuro-economic approach actually works. With that in mind, what follows are four additional examples that present neuroeconomic approaches to traditional problems in neuroscience: (1) How can we hope to separate visual-sensory attention from decision making? (2) How can constantly changing prior probabilities be used by the nervous system to select an optimal behavioral response? (3) How can we measure and study the way visual-motor learning updates knowledge of the likelihood that a response will be reinforced? (4) How can we quantitatively measure the process by which the value of a reward is computed and updated? I present these examples simply to provide a better sense of how neuro-economic strategies can be employed in practice.

Example 1: Visual Attention

The American psychologist William James provided what is probably the most famous definition of attention when he wrote:

Everyone knows what attention is. It is the taking possession by the mind, in clear and vivid form, of one out of what seem several simultaneously possible objects or trains of thought. Focalization, concentration, of consciousness are its essence. It implies withdrawal from some things in order to deal effectively with others.... (James, 1890)

Since William James wrote those words, other definitions of attention have been proposed, but all of them share a common feature: Attention is that process by which the speed or accuracy of normal sensory processing is enhanced, an enhancement that occurs in association with some focus in the sensory world. Working from that starting point, George Sperling and Barbara Dosher (1986) proposed that our ability to pay attention could be viewed as a limited resource which one allocates to an object or a location in the world in order to enhance the speed or accuracy of sensory perception at that location. Thinking about attention as a resource which must be allocated efficiently, Sperling and Dosher proposed that one could use a simplified utility theory to define an optimal allocation of attention in theoretical terms. Sperling and Dosher even recognized that efficiently gathering sensory data, and deciding what behavioral response to make, could be modularizable problems, at

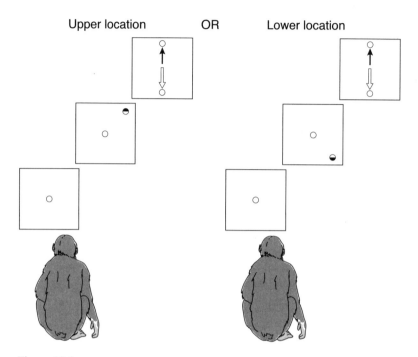

Figure 13.1
Separating attention and decision experimentally.

least in principle. To make that logical modularity clear, we begin with a concrete example. (See figure 13.1.)

Imagine an experimental situation Vivian Ciaramitaro and I have explored (Ciaramitaro, Cameron, and Glimcher, 2001). A monkey is trained to look straight ahead while paying attention to a location 10° above where he is staring. At a predictable time, a spot of light flashes on and then off at that location, either brightly or dimly. The job of the monkey is to make an upward eye movement if the spot appeared in a dim state, and a downward movement if the spot appeared in a bright state. After the monkey makes his movement, he receives a fruit juice reward if he has made the evaluation correctly. The task is difficult for the monkey because the bright and dim lights are very similar—so similar that if the monkey focuses all of his attention on the one spot, he can tell bright trials from dim trials with an accuracy of only 80 percent. Notice that in this experiment we can gain independent control over two classes of variables that Pascal would have recognized. We can control the likelihood that the spot will be bright or dim, and we can control the value of each outcome (bright or dim) to the monkey.

Imagine that across large groups of trials we systematically manipulated the likelihood that any given trial would be a dim trial. We have every reason to believe that with experience the monkey would determine the likelihood, the prior probability, that on a given trial the light would be dim. If, for example, the monkey has observed 100 sequential trials during which the spot of light appeared dim 99 times, he must remember that the spot was almost always dim. Formally, the prior probability of a dim trial would be 0.99, and we have every reason to believe the monkey would learn and remember something like this likelihood.

Of course the monkey can rely on more than memory to determine whether this trial is more likely to be bright or dim. He can use the sensory information that his eye receives to determine whether this particular trial appeared to be bright or dim. Economic theory provides a mathematical description for this process. The way in which sensory information ought to influence his estimate of the probability that this is a dim trial is described by Bayes's theorem.

To make this clear, consider a group of trials on which there is a 50 percent prior probability of a dim trial and the monkey is 60 percent accurate at identifying dim trials. Under these conditions, if it looked dim, it most likely *was* dim. Now consider a group of trials in which there is a 99 percent prior probability that the trial was bright; dim trials are very rare. Under these conditions, even if it looks dim, it probably is really a bright trial. So if he is to perform the task efficiently the monkey's guess must reflect more than just what he saw. It must represent the outcome of a calculation that describes a posterior probability as a combination of prior knowledge and current observation.

As we know from expected utility theory, the Bayesian estimate of the most likely state of the light is not the only factor that the monkey must consider when deciding whether to look up or to look down. The monkey must also know the value of each response in milliliters of juice. If looking down on a bright trial yields 20 ml of juice, looking up on a dim trial yields 0.02 ml of juice, and all other actions yield no juice, then we expect the monkey to look down irrespective of the sensory stimulus.

In contrast, if the rewards for looking down on a bright trial and up on a dim trial are equivalent, then the posterior probability should control whether the monkey chooses to look up or down.

To summarize, the monkey should solve this problem by performing an expected utility calculation. The relative utilities of the two possible conditions must be determined. Each of these utilities must then be multiplied by the posterior probability estimates to derive an expected utility for each course of action: *look up* and *look down*. A rational monkey then chooses to look in the direction that yields the highest expected utility.

The economic approach yields an objective description of the decision-making task that the monkey faces in this experiment. An optimal monkey solves the problem this task presents by executing these Bayesian expected utility calculations. But what about the process of paying attention to the spot of light? How does that figure into a neuroeconomic analysis?

To answer that question we have to make the task slightly more complicated. In a new version of the task, the spot of light that the monkey must observe might now appear, on any given trial, at one of two possible locations: one location 10° above and one location 10° below the monkey's fixation point. Imagine, for a moment, that it appears at the upper location 90 percent of the time and at the lower location 10 percent of the time. If our monkey can monitor two locations simultaneously, and be just as accurate at performing the task at either location, then this modified task is just like the last task but requires twice as many calculations. But what if the monkey's resources for visual processing are limited? What if splitting his attention between the two locations decreases his performance on the bright/dim discrimination? If we think of the monkey's ability to perform the bright/dim discrimination as a limited resource, then this new task requires that the monkey make a second decision. The monkey has to decide in advance where to pay attention (or, more formally, how to allocate his visual processing resources) in order to maximize the amount of juice he receives.

Consider a situation in which the monkey's ability to perform the bright/dim discrimination is a limited resource and works the following way. If the monkey devotes all of his attentional resources to studying the upper location, he gets the bright/dim discrimination right 80 percent of the time at the upper location and only 60 percent of the time at the lower location. If, alternatively, he splits his attention between the upper and lower locations, then he gets the bright/dim discrimination right only 70 percent of the time at either location. At an intuitive level we might say that describes an attentional system which can modulate the accuracy of visual processing. What would a neuroeconomic model of this kind of attentional process look like? Sperling and Dosher provided an answer to this question with their utility-based analysis. Under these conditions an optimal attentional process would allocate attentional resources, would adjust the accuracy of the visual system, so as to maximize the juice the monkey obtains. That would be the *goal* of attention under these conditions.

Consider a situation in which there is a 90 percent chance that the bright or dim spot will appear at the upper location, there is a 50 percent chance that the spot will be bright or dim regardless of where it appears, all correct responses yield 1.0 ml of juice, and all incorrect responses yield 0 ml of juice. From a decision-making point of view, this task is very simple. The prior probability that this is a bright trial is 50 percent. The utility of bright and dim trials is equivalent. Only the location at which the spot will appear is asymmetric. What should the monkey do? At an intuitive level it seems obvious that the monkey should allocate almost all of his attention to studying the upper location. This will make his posterior probability estimates as accurate as possible at that location, the only location that is really important under these conditions. Of course this allocation of attention will decrease the accuracy of his posterior probability estimates at the lower location, but that is a cost he ought to be willing to incur. Viewed this way, the role of spatial attention in economic terms is, speaking generally, to optimize estimates of posterior probability at important locations. That is just a way of saying formally, and with the power of Bayesian mathematics, what we have already said semantically.

Now consider a situation in which there is still a 90 percent chance that the bright or dim spot will appear at the upper location, there is still a 50 percent chance that the spot will be bright or dim regardless of where it appears, but now all correct evaluations of the lower locations yield 1.0 ml of juice, and other responses yield 0 ml of juice. Under these conditions the monkey should devote all of his attention to the lower location even though it is only the pattern of rewards that has changed.

These examples should make it clear that from an economic point of view, the role of attention is not to reduce errors in some general sense, but rather to specifically reduce errors in the posterior probabilities that will be useful for maximizing gain. In economic terms, attention can be described as a process that works to achieve a very specific goal. Paying attention efficiently means allocating sensory processing resources so as to maximize the accuracy of important posterior probabilities. In contrast, making efficient decisions about what course of action to take is a different process. That process must maximize local gains by combining utilities and the posterior probabilities that attention and perception yield. An economic analysis reveals how clearly modular these two processes can be, in principle.

When Vivian Ciaramitaro and I performed an experiment very much like this one, we found that the efficiency with which both human and monkey subjects performed the bright/dim discrimination varied systematically as a function of the probability that the spot would appear at a particular location. Under no conditions were the animals perfectly efficient, but the efficiency with which they performed the bright/dim discrimination at a particular location was inarguably a function of the probability that the spot would appear at that location. Importantly, at the same time that animals were accurately allocating attention to optimize the efficiency of their posterior probability estimates, our data showed that there was no effect on the decision-making process itself.[1] This observation seemed to validate the economically derived hypothesis that attention and decision were separable. The monkeys were able to independently regulate their attentional and decisional processes.

Example 2: Evaluating Visual Motion

In chapter 5 of this book I described William Newsome's experiments on the perceptual judgments made by monkeys when they view a field of moving spots of light. In those experiments, monkeys were trained to

1. As assessed with signal detection theory.

stare at a display of chaotically moving spots and then to report whether, on average, the spots seemed to be moving toward the left or toward the right. Newsome found that when the majority of the spots actually moved to the left or right, monkeys easily identified the average direction of motion. As the percentage of spots moving in a single coherent direction was reduced, however, the task became harder and harder for the monkey subjects to perform. Once the percentage of spots moving in a single coherent direction was as low as 1 or 2 percent, the monkeys behaved as if they were being forced to guess.

In 1998 Josh Gold and Michael Shadlen, then both at the University of Washington, became interested in how monkeys performed this task when it was so hard that the monkeys were almost, but not quite, forced to guess. They had noticed that under those conditions the monkeys would stare intently at the display for up to 2 sec before making their judgment. This led them to suspect that over the course of the 2-sec period the monkeys were gathering more and more evidence upon which to base their left versus right decisions.

Gold and Shadlen (2000) realized that in a formal mathematical-economic sense, this process could be modeled as the use of sensory data to perform something like a continuous Bayesian analysis of the likelihood that this was a trial on which the spots were moving to the right. To test the hypothesis that animals really were performing this maximum likelihood analysis, Gold and Shadlen developed a clever experimental protocol. On a typical trial, monkeys would simply be expected to stare at the display and then to decide whether the spots were moving left or right, indicating this decision with an eye movement at the end of the trial. On an occasional trial, however, Gold and Shadlen would directly stimulate one of the eye movement control maps before the presentation of the spots was complete. They knew that the stimulation would, in the absence of the display, induce an upward eye movement. They reasoned that if the monkey was in the process of deciding whether to look left or right, then the movement elicited by stimulation should be deviated leftward or rightward by an amount proportional to the monkey's certainty that the motion of the spots was leftward or rightward. In fact, this is exactly what they found. When they stimulated immediately after the dot display was turned on, they saw neither leftward nor rightward deviations in the stimulation-induced eye movement. The longer they waited to turn on the stimulator, the larger the leftward or rightward deviation they observed. This is just what you would expect if the continuously presented display was gradually increasing the monkey's certainty about whether this was a leftward or a rightward trial.

This suggested, at a neuroeconomic level, that the monkeys were performing something like a Bayesian maximum likelihood calculation as each frame of the display was presented. The idea was that after each frame, the monkeys computed the formal posterior probability that the spots were moving to the right, and used that to strengthen or weaken their developing plan to look left or right. Gold and Shadlen (2001) even succeeded in developing a mathematical model of this process which provided compelling evidence that the decision about whether to look left or right really could be described in economic terms as a maximum likelihood calculation.

These experiments began with the hypothesis that the process of deciding whether to look left or right, when made in the face of significant epistemological uncertainty, could be described with the formal tools Bayes and Laplace had developed in the eighteenth century. Their behavioral and mathematical analyses suggest that this economically based model can, in fact, account for the observed behavioral phenomena.

Example 3: Learning Prior Probabilities

Up until this point, in this entire book I have treated the external world as a relatively unchanging place, a world in which the prior probabilities that govern both decision and attention are fixed. In the real world, however, these probabilities change constantly. The changing state of our memories, as well as our estimates of the values of any course of action, reflect this dynamic property of our environment.

All economically based theories presume that animals can learn about the prior probabilities that describe the world around them and can store those prior probabilities for future use. Can we also use the neuroeconomic approach to measure the instantaneous values of the prior probabilities that animals store and then watch them change as new experiences update them? Put another way, can we test the hypothesis that prior probabilities, a formal definition of at least some kinds of working memories, are lawfully updated in identifiable brain structures as an animal learns?

To accomplish that goal, one could train monkeys to perform the following task. While the monkey sat in front of a video display, a central visual target would appear, and the monkey would be required to fixate that target. We could then illuminate four more visual targets at four randomly selected eccentric locations. The monkey's job would be to look outward toward one of those targets and then back to the fixation spot. When he had done that, the outer spot he had looked at would disappear. Next the monkey would have to look outward toward one of the remaining eccentric spots and again back to fixation. Once again, the eccentric spot the monkey had just looked at would be extinguished. The monkey would have to repeat this for each of the remaining eccentric spots until he had looked at each one once.

Once the animal had looked at all four eccentric spots, he would receive a reward. But critically, the size of the reward that he received would be determined by the order in which he had looked at the four eccentric spots. Without informing the monkey, we would have randomly selected a *correct* order at the beginning of each day. If the monkey happened to visit the spots in that order, he would receive a large reward, typically about 1.0 ml of fruit juice. If he visited only two of the spots in the correct order, and got two of them out of order, he would receive only 0.5 ml of juice at the end of the trial. Similarly, if he visited only one spot, or none of the spots, in the correct order, he would get 0.25 ml or 0 ml of juice, respectively.

The goal of the monkey each day would be to learn the correct sequence as quickly as possible, so as to maximize the juice he earned. At the beginning of the day, when a brand-new set of four eccentric spots appeared, the monkey would have no choice but to randomly try different sequences. As the monkey gained more experience, and learned more about what movements yielded rewards, he would get closer and closer to producing the correct sequence.

To understand the rationale for this experiment, consider the first movement in the sequence that the monkey produces during the first 50 trials of a given day. Since the monkey does not know at this point which movement is the correct first movement, we might expect him to randomly try each of the four eccentric spots, varying his choice from trial to trial. If we were to make a graph of this, it would show that the probability of his looking at any one of the four spots on his first movement was equal, and thus 25 percent. Put in economic terms, he would be, through his behavior, telling us that in his estimation the prior probability that each of the four eccentric spots was the correct first spot was 25 percent.

If we performed a similar analysis on the last 50 trials, we would presumably find that he almost always made one movement, the correct first movement, and almost never made any of the other three possible movements as the first movement. At the end of a day of learning he would be telling us that he believed the prior probability of that particular spot being the correct first spot was 100 percent.

If we examined his performance on the intermediate trials, we would probably find that he refined his prior probability estimate as he got better and better at that array of targets. His estimate of the prior probability would shift gradually from 25 percent to 100 percent over the course of many trials. By looking at any 50 trials, we could always determine the monkey's current estimate of the prior probability that a particular spot was the correct spot for that movement.

If we hypothesize that neurons in some brain area, say in the basal ganglia of the telencephalon, encode prior probabilities like these, then this is a very easy hypothesis to test. We simply have to ask whether the firing rates of these basal ganglia neurons are tightly correlated with the continuously changing estimate of prior probability that we see our animal subject express. An experiment like this allows us to define a working memory quantitatively and then to test the hypothesis that some brain area encodes that working memory.

Example 4: Learning About Values

Similar approaches could also be applied to understanding how animals might learn to estimate the value of producing a particular response. Wolfram Schultz and his colleagues at the University of Fribourg have begun to explore this problem in their studies of the dopaminergic neurons of the substantia nigra and the ventral tegmental area of the monkey brain. In a now famous set of experiments, Schultz examined the activity of these neurons while monkeys pressed levers for juice rewards (Schultz, Dayan, and Montague, 1997; Schultz, 1998). In a typical experiment, a monkey might begin by pressing a lever and receiving 1.0 ml of juice for each lever press. Schultz found that under these conditions, the dopamine neurons he was studying fired action potentials at a fixed baseline rate after each juice reward was delivered. If, however, he suddenly and without warning doubled the reward produced by a lever press, these same neurons reacted with a burst of action potentials after the juice was delivered. Over the course of many sequential trials during which the larger reward was provided, the neuronal activity gradually returned to the original baseline level. If he then suddenly dropped the size of the juice reward back down to the original level, the neurons responded with a reduction in activity. Once again, he found that over the course of many sequential trials which presented the reward at this lower level, the firing rates of the neurons returned gradually to baseline.

Based upon these experiments, and others I have not described, Schultz hypothesized that these dopamine neurons carry an error signal. He proposed that the firing rates of these neurons indicate whether the reward just obtained is larger or smaller than expected. This seems important from an economic point of view because a signal like this one could be used to update an estimate of the value of a response.

One could test the hypothesis that these neurons carry a signal appropriate for updating an estimate of value by training monkeys in a task very similar to the one described in the last section. Consider a task in which four targets are illuminated, each of which yields a different reward—say 0.25, 0.5, 0.75, and 1.0 ml of fruit juice. In this task, the monkey is free to visit the eccentric spots of light in any order he desires. As in the last experiment, the monkey receives his summed reward only after the trial ends, but in this experiment he does not know in advance which target yields which reward. Now we add one additional feature. Trials can end, unexpectedly, after the first, second, third, or fourth movement. An unpredictable 25 percent of trials end after the first movement is complete, regardless of which movement the monkey produced. Twenty-five percent end after the second movement is complete, and so on. This unpredictability has two effects. First, it allows the monkey to determine the differential value of the four movements because on some occasions he completes only one, two, or three movements. Second, it places a premium, for the monkey, on ranking the movements according to value and making the most valuable movements first.

Formally, in this task the prior probability that he will be permitted to make the first movement is 100 percent, and the prior probability that he will be permitted to make the fourth movement is only 25 percent. The expected value of the fourth movement is thus 25 percent of the expected value of the first movement, assuming you know nothing about the relative values of the four possible movements. For this reason a rational monkey should always produce the most highly valued movement first and the lowest valued movement last.

By analogy to the experiment described in the preceding section, one could use this approach to examine both behavior and neuronal firing rates to determine whether they are correlated with the rate at which animals update their estimates of reward value.

Limits of the Theory: Will It Be Good Enough?

All of these experiments bring up a very important point. The behavioral data produced by animals in these experiments, and in others like them, suggest that subjects never really perform optimally. A number of people have argued that this proves economic models of optimal behavior cannot be useful for studying behavior or the brain. I want to respond to that objection. Economic models describe the task that animals and humans face in any decision-making situation. They define how a problem *should* be solved. Real animals and real people deviate from these solutions; they perform suboptimally. I want to suggest that, perhaps somewhat surprisingly, from a neuroeconomic point of view this deviation from optimality turns out to be a good thing.

The goal of neurophysiology is to understand what computations the organism makes, and how it makes those computations. Whenever the organism deviates from an optimal strategy, this tells us something fundamental about how the organism makes its computations. When we find neural circuits that deviate from optimal economic computations in the same way that the behavior of our animals deviates from optimality, this serves as evidence that we may have identified the neural circuitry that underlies a mathematically described, though imperfect, behavior.

To make this very clear, I want to return to an example developed by Gerd Gigerenzer and presented in chapter 8 (Gigerenzer, Todd, and ABC Research Group, 2000). Imagine a bacterium that lives in a world where food is completely randomly distributed. The prior probability that food will be present at any given location is a constant number, regardless of location. Next assume that this bacterium can only swim in stretches 1 ml long. What is the optimal foraging strategy for such an organism?

If food is equally likely to lie in any direction, then the bacterium behaves most efficiently if it swims off in a random direction for 1 ml, stops, checks for food, and then either eats or swims off in another random direction. Now how might the bacterium perform the computations that guide this behavior? One possibility is that the bacterium builds a cognitive map of food source locations. The bacterium stores data about every food item it ever encounters, and from these it computes a spatial map that encodes the prior probabilities of encountering food at any possible spatial location. Since this map would show a uniform prior probability for all possible locations, the bacterium could compute a random pattern of movements as an optimal foraging strategy. Alternatively, consider a bacterium that has evolved an internal process which automatically sends it off in a random direction. This organism forages randomly because that is the only way it can forage.

Experiments on the physiological processes that guide the foraging strategies of these two bacteria become interesting when we place the two bacteria into an environment in which the food is distributed nonrandomly. Of course the bacterium that computes cognitive maps of prior probability still achieves optimal foraging, but under these conditions the randomly searching bacterium does not. To be more precise, the bacterium which moves at random begins to perform suboptimally in a way that suggests how it generates its foraging behavior. It continues to swim off in random directions regardless of the structure of the environment. To use the expression that Gigerenzer proposes, the random bacterium uses a simple heuristic. A rule that, in the environment in which it evolved, provides an optimal (or near optimal) foraging strategy. The nature of this heuristic becomes obvious when the animal is placed in an environment for which it did not evolve.

In many ways we learn most about the bacterium when we study it in an environment where it performs suboptimally. It is the economic variables which the bacteria cannot track that may actually tell us most about the physiology of this organism. This suggests that neuroeconomic approaches may be, somewhat paradoxically, most useful when animals do not behave in the optimal manner predicted by theory.

Summary

Unlike the traditional determinate models that have served as the foundation for modern reflex-based approaches, neuroeconomic approaches allow for the generation of models which can both analyze and produce uncertainty. These models provide a benchmark against which to correlate both behavioral and neuronal data across the entire spectrum of problems that evolved systems must engage. They provide a linking hypothesis without which it is impossible to convincingly argue that an identified neurobiological circuit underlies the computation and expression of a particular behavior.

These kinds of models and the empirical results that they generate are essential not just for biologists interested in the brain, but also for economists interested in human behavior. As early as 1898 the economist Thorstein Veblen made this point in an essay titled "Why Is Economics Not an Evolutionary Science?" He suggested that in order to understand the economic behavior of humans, one would have to understand the mechanisms by which those behaviors were produced. More recently the biologist E. O. Wilson (1998) has made a similar point. Arguing that a fusion of the social and natural sciences is both inevitable and desirable, Wilson has suggested that this fusion will begin with a widespread recognition that economics and biology are two disciplines addressing a single subject matter.

Ultimately, economics is a biological science. It is the study of how humans choose. That choice is inescapably a biological process. Truly understanding how and why humans make the choices that they do will undoubtedly require a neuroeconomic science.

14

Putting It All Together II. Philosophical Implications

Classical Dualism and Physiological Monism

Our classical view of how the brain gives rise to behavior stems from the work of Descartes three and a half centuries ago. Linking brain and behavior, he argued, was not a single problem but a dual one. For simple deterministic behaviors Descartes postulated a straightforward mechanical linkage between sensation and action. For complex indeterminate behaviors he proposed as the linking agent an extraphysical process: the soul or free will.

Having removed the cause of all nondeterminate action from the physical universe, Descartes went on to describe the minimally complex nervous system that could produce his straightforward mechanical linkage. The reflex, as Descartes described it, was an effort to apply the geometrical technologies of seventeenth-century mathematics to the problem of understanding how brains could produce determinate behavior.

Since that time, physiologists have chafed under the limitations imposed by this dualism, which partitions the causes of behavior into physical and nonphysical categories. In the physical sciences it is assumed that everything we observe is the unitary product of scientifically describable processes. Why, physiologists have wondered, should the study of brain and behavior require a uniquely dualist approach?

In an effort to reconcile a unitary view of the physical world with studies of brain and behavior, a number of physiologists have suggested a monist approach. All action, these physiologists have argued, must be the product of determinate, reflexlike mechanisms. For working neuroscientists this argument has tremendous appeal. It eliminates the need for a dualist explanatory system and reinforces our belief that the modern scientific method, which has been so successful in the physical sciences, will be adequate for explaining all possible linkages between brain and behavior. Essentially, it resolves the paradox of dualism by first accepting the logical limitations of Descartes's determinate mathematical approach to physical systems and then by rejecting his claim that indeterminate behaviors do in fact exist.

It is important to remember, however, that the logical mathematical premises from which this dualist formulation emerged were developed in the middle of the seventeenth century, a time when notions of probability and uncertainty had not yet appeared in Western thought. When Descartes wrote the *Treatise on Man*,[1] Pascal was only a boy and even the most rudimentary Western notions of probability were still decades away. As a result, Descartes was forced to develop these ideas, which serve as the roots of both the monist and the dualist traditions, with exclusively deterministic mathematical tools.

Alternatives to Classical Dualism and Physiological Monism

Throughout this book I have argued that the limitations of classical dualism and physiological monism both stem from the inability of determinate mathematical tools to describe behavior in all its complexity. Even modern dualists recognize this at some level. Their use of a nonphysical process called volition or cognition to link the brain to complex behavior acknowledges this limitation.

In the first half of this book I examined traditional dualist and monist approaches, and argued that any future model of the linkage between brain and behavior must respect three critical conclusions. First, it must acknowledge that biological organisms arose through an evolutionary process that included natural selection. When two animals are equally complex, but one can shape its behavior more efficiently, the organism that can engage the future state of the world more efficiently will enjoy greater reproductive success.

Second, I argued that we must acknowledge the epistemological limits animals face. No organism can ever have complete knowledge of the fu-

---

1. Although it was not published at that time.

ture state of the world. Even if we believed in a fully determinate Laplacian clockwork world, we would have to accept that no real organism with finite resources can aspire to a state of *complete* knowledge. Animals unavoidably operate with a limited horizon of knowledge, and this means that future states of the world cannot be predicted with certainty. Future states of the world can be known only probabilistically. If we believe that animals evolved in an environment that includes epistemological uncertainty, then it would be odd to suppose that 600 million years of evolution have overlooked this constraint.

Once we shift our emphasis from determinate models to probabilistic models, much of the gulf between simple and complex behavior that tormented Descartes disappears. Models of the mind rooted in probability theory allow us to explain, at a mechanistic level, much more complex behavior than can any determinate model.

The third point I developed was that even the much broader scope of epistemologically driven probabilistic models cannot entirely close the gap between the brain and all classes of behavior. This last critical issue is that there are aspects of the world which are irreducibly uncertain. Heisenberg made this clear at the subatomic level, but our everyday experience tells us that this is true in the macroscopic world at a much more personal and intuitive level.

For an organism to compete efficiently with other organisms, there are often times when behavior *must* be unpredictable. One of the central insights of Von Neumann's theory of games was that optimal interactions between competitors often require that each individual adopt a *mixed* strategy. Mixed strategies are those in which, at a play-by-play level, the behavior of each individual is irreducibly uncertain, but across hundreds of plays behavior is lawfully probabilistic. John Maynard Smith extended this idea. He agreed with Von Neumann that single individuals must often be able to produce irreducibly uncertain behavioral responses. He also suggested that evolutionary circumstances could arise in which populations show irreducible uncertainty from individual to individual. Unpredictability, he argued, should be encountered both within and between individuals.

Accurate neurobiological models must be able to account for patterns of behavior that are richer than the determinate patterns to which classical monist models are limited. At one level this seems so clear: The deepest intuitive problem that we all have with a classically monist explanation for human behavior is the uncertainty we experience each day. Not just the uncertainty we see in others, but the uncertainty we see in ourselves. Today, neuroscientists and philosophers are beginning to recognize that there is a mathematical corpus which predicts that just such a level of uncertainty should exist, and it even provides the tools for quantifying and formalizing that uncertainty.

Probability theory is, at some level, a monist approach to linking behavior, brain, and mind, but one very different from the determinate strategy of classical monism. It is a single mathematical corpus that can describe all classes of behavior, a corpus predicting that some behaviors will be simple and deterministic while others will not just *appear* uncertain, but will actually *be* uncertain. Unlike the traditional monist approach of classical physiologists, this theoretical strategy does not argue that behavior is the product of incredibly complex sets of interacting reflexes. Instead, it suggests that there are no such things as reflexes. Determinate reflexes are, in this view, an effort to explain a tiny portion of behavior with an inappropriate theory. I mean this in a very real and concrete sense. Reflexes are a model of how sensory signals give rise to motor responses. We now know that the breadth of behavior which these model systems can explain is tiny. At this point in time, reflexes are simply a bad theory, and one that should be discarded. In place of the determinate reflexes employed by classical physiological monists, and in place of the indeterminate nonphysical process required by classical dualism, neuroeconomics argues for a third alternative: an explicitly indeterminate monism.

Free Will

Philosophers, like the Jansenists and Jesuits of the seventeenth century, have always recognized the complexity and contradictions inherent in a theory of behavior that includes unpredictability. Classical monist theories have engaged this issue by arguing that all behavior is the product of determinate mechanisms, and thus that the experience we have of freely *deciding* what we will choose to do must be false. If, as Laplace might have said, the precise state of the world ten days hence can be predicted, then it must follow that the decisions each of us will make within that world can also be predicted. Free will cannot exist.

Classical dualists, in contrast, avow the importance of both the subjective experience that we *decide* and the irreconcilability of free will with a purely physical view of the world. The dualist approach argues that some nonphysical mechanism, often called volition or free will, plays a causal role in the future state of the world and gives rise to both indeterminacy and our experience of deciding.

From a game theoretic point of view, some economists and philosophers have argued that this debate is misdirected. The efficient solution of game theoretic problems requires that the future state of the world cannot, in principle, be predicted by the organisms which inhabit it. When organisms adopt mixed strategy solutions in competition with other organisms, they make the future state of the world unpredictable to their opponents. Models of the world which seek to exclude free will by insisting that the world is determinate fail because animals make them fail. From the point of view of animals that inhabit it, the world must be considered an indeterminate system.

A game theoretic approach does not, however, argue that this indeterminacy must be the product of a nonphysical process which we might label "free will." If I play the game of matching pennies with you, my behavior on each play is unpredictable. My behavior is, however, lawful and regular at a probabilistic level. It can be fully described as the product of an optimization process that can employ randomization at both the developmental and the neuronal levels. Developmental randomization (whether innate or learned) produces indeterminacy across the population of opponents you may encounter in matching pennies. Neuronal randomization produces indeterminacy within an individual. The theory of games was designed to explain these classes of indeterminate behavior in a lawful fashion.

The great challenge faced by classical monism is that it cannot explain nondeterminate behavior. The dualist postulate of free will solves this problem by attributing indeterminacy to a process that cannot, in principle, be studied. Game theory, however, provides the tools for understanding both determinate and indeterminate behavior without resort to an ill-defined nonphysical process.

It seems to me that the theory of games offers a resolution to one of the great conundrums of determinism and philosophy. Free will may simply be the name we give to the probabilistic behaviors that are mixed strategy solutions. Our subjective experience of deciding may be what we experience when a mixed strategy solution requires the activation of a lawful neuronal randomizer.

Consciousness

What does all this say, or not say, about consciousness and the relationship of consciousness to Cartesian dualism?

First, and most important, let me stress that nothing I have said anywhere in this book bears directly on any argument about the existence or nonexistence of consciousness. I have argued that a single body of mathematical theory can be used to model all classes of human and animal behavior, a mathematical approach rooted in modern economic theory. To me, as a neuroscientist, this is a powerful and important hypothesis. The model itself serves as a bridge, a linking hypothesis, between brain and behavior. From my point of view, the most important aspect of this theory is that it allows us to ask how any given behavior can be produced by the physiological components that make up the brain. Neuroeconomics seeks to link the mosaic of behavior to the mosaic of the brain.

Importantly, it is not a theory that can forge powerful links between behavior and consciousness or between consciousness and the brain. But this in itself does have implications for some ideas about consciousness.

Some philosophers and scientists have argued that consciousness is a causal force linked closely to the concept of free will. The whole neuroeconomic approach argues against this conceptualization because free will, or any nonphysical process held responsible for behavioral indeterminacy, is not required by the neuroeconomic approach.

Other philosophers have argued that subjective mental experience exists, but have remained agnostic about what functional role consciousness plays in the generation of behavior. It is in this regard that neuroeconomics may be of some use. At an evolutionary level, a neuroeconomist assumes that animals use their brains to survive. The brains of animals are assumed to represent and exploit structure in the environment. Neuroeconomics provides a model of the architecture that links brain and behavior. Mind, though it may very much exist, simply does not figure in that equation. The concept of mind, when separated from notions of determinacy and indeterminacy, is not an object level engaged by the neuroeconomic approach.

To make what I am trying to say clearer, let us turn to a staple of modern theories of consciousness, the story of the philosophical zombie. Imagine, this story goes, two identical individuals: one of them is a real, conscious person and the other is a zombie who lacks consciousness. They both show exactly the same probabilistic patterns of behavioral response when presented with the same stimuli, but one is a "robotic zombie" and the other is a conscious entity like ourselves.

Many philosophers have argued that we can even conceive of these two creatures as being identical at the physical level. Being composed of the same neurons and synapses. They should be seen as identical in every regard except with respect to consciousness. What, if anything, would a neuroeconomic theory say about such creatures?

My answer goes like this: By definition these two creatures are presumed to behave identically. For every possible sensory input they generate the same probabilistic pattern of behavioral output; these two organisms are described by exactly the same neuroeconomic model of behavior. If one could, in principle, describe all of the behavior that each of these creatures produced, then the equations describing each organism with regard to its behavioral goals would have to be identical. That is, after all, what is meant by being behaviorally identical.

Critically, each of these creatures is also admitted to be very different at an algorithmic, or functional, level. One employs consciousness and one does not. What does this mean at a neurobiological level? My answer, as a biologist, is that they cannot be identical with regard to how their behavior achieves a set of specifiable goals, different at an algorithmic level, and identical at a neurobiological level. They may achieve the same behavior, but if one achieves this behavior by using consciousness and the other does not, then at the level of their biological hardware it seems inescapable that they cannot be the same.

In making that claim I am presuming that consciousness does something for the organism, that it participates in the process by which behavior is generated. I am presuming that, like all other known biological processes, consciousness is subject to natural selection and follows the physical laws of the universe. And I simply state these as assumptions. If I am wrong in those assumptions, if consciousness truly has no function, cannot influence behavior in any way, is not subject to the laws of natural selection, is not constrained by the physical laws of the universe, then it is probably irrelevant to any neuroeconomic analysis.

If, however, we take these assumptions as a starting point, then we really have to conclude that consciousness is what David Marr would have called an "algorithmic technique." It is a process, produced by the brain, that generates behavior. Evolution acts on the algorithmic techniques by which the brain generates behavior, and it must therefore have acted selectively on the biological substrate for consciousness. Consciousness is a part of the algorithm we, and presumably other closely related species, employ to produce behavior. So my answer is that neuroeconomics does suggest something about consciousness, although not much. If consciousness exists, then it exists at or below Marr's algorithmic level. It is presumably an evolved mechanism with which our neurobiological hardware achieves behavior.

Finis

It seems almost certain that only three and a half centuries after its birth, probability theory is still in its infancy. More than three centuries ago Galileo and his peers could not explain how a thrown die would fall. Today that seems a trivial problem. But our own ability to use and understand probabilistic reasoning is still limited. A hundred years ago quantum physicists demonstrated the fundamentally probabilistic nature of matter, but even today most of us find that indeterminacy troubling rather than illuminating. Truly understanding the world in probabilistic terms remains conceptually difficult.

Still, we have made significant progress. In 1738 when Jacques de Vaucanson exhibited his mechanical duck in the Tuileries, audiences were challenged to decide whether the essence of duckishness included some property that could not be captured by a physical clockwork. Most answered yes, a real duck is much more than a determinate machine. Today we know that Vaucanson's audience was correct. A real duck is much more complex than a determinate clockwork. But that does not mean that a real duck is more than a physical system, just that unlike Vaucanson's duck it must be an indeterminate physical system. Descartes, approaching this problem a century before Vaucanson, did not realize that indeterminate physical systems were possible. Instead, he developed a dualist worldview that included determinate-physical and indeterminate-nonphysical processes, a misconceptualization rooted in his own understanding of uncertainty. Unlike Vaucanson's duck, real animals must be both physical and indeterminate, a possibility Descartes never considered.

References

Andersen, R. A., Essick, G. K., and Siegel, R. M. (1987). Neurons of area 7 activated by both visual stimuli and oculomotor behavior. *Experimental Brain Research* 67: 316–322.

Arnauld, A., and Nicole, P. (1662; 1996). *Logic or the Art of Thinking*, J. V. Buroker (ed.). Cambridge: Cambridge University Press.

Babbage, C. (1830). *Reflections on the Decline of Science in England, and on Some of Its Causes*. London: B. Fellowes.

Bacon, F. (1620; 1994). *Novum Organum*, P. Urbach and J. Gibson (trans.) Chicago: Open Court.

Barlow, G. W. (2000). *The Cichlid Fishes*. Cambridge, MA: Perseus Publishing.

Barlow, H. B. (1961). The coding of sensory images. In *Current Problems in Animal Behavior*, W. H. Thorpe and O. L. Zangwill (eds.). Cambridge: Cambridge University Press.

Bayes, T. (1763; 1958). An essay toward solving a problem in the doctrine of chances. *Philosophical Transactions of the Royal Society* 53: 370–418. Repr. *Biometrika* 45: 293–315.

Baynes, K., Eliassen, J. C., Lutsep, H. L., and Gazzaniga, M. S. (1998). Modular organization of cognitive systems masked by interhemispheric integration. *Science* 280: 902–905.

Bell, C. (1911). *Idea of a New Anatomy of the Brain*. London: Strahan and Preston.

Bernoulli, D. (1738; 1954). Exposition of a new theory on the measurement of risk. *Econometrica* 22: 23–36.

Bernoulli, J. (1713). *Ars Conjectandi*. Basel: Thurnisiorum.

Bernstein, N. (1935). The problem of the interrelation of co-ordination and localization. *Arch. Biol. Sci.* 38. Repr. in *Human Motor Actions: Bernstein Reassessed*, H. T. A. Whiting (ed.). Amsterdam: North-Holland, 1984.

Bernstein, N. (1961). Trends and problems in the study of physiology of activity. *Questions of Philosophy* 6. Repr. in *Human Motor Actions: Bernstein Reassessed*, H. T. A. Whiting (ed.). Amsterdam: North-Holland, 1984.

Beuttell, K., and Losos, J. B. (1999). Ecological morphology of Caribbean anoles. *Herpetological Monographs* 13: 1–28.

Boole, G. (1847; 1998). *The Mathematical Analysis of Logic.* Sterling, Va.: Thoemmes Press.

Boole, G. (1854; 1958). *The Laws of Thought.* New York. Dover.

Charnov, E. L. (1973). Optimal foraging: Some theoretical explorations. Ph.D. dissertation. University of Washington.

Charnov, E. L., and Orians, G. H. (1973). Optimal foraging: Some theoretical explorations. Unpublished manuscript.

Church, A. (1944). *Introduction to Mathematical Logic.* Princeton, NJ: Princeton University Press.

Ciaramitaro, V. M., Cameron, E. L., and Glimcher, P. W. (2001). Stimulus probability redirects spatial attention: An enhancement of sensitivity in humans and monkeys. *Vision Research* 41: 57–75.

Colby, C. L., Duhamel, J. R., and Goldberg, M. E. (1996). Visual, presaccadic, and cognitive activation of single neurons in monkey lateral intraparietal area. *Journal of Neurophysiology* 76: 2841–2852.

Creed, R. S., Denny-Brown, D., Eccles, J. C., Liddell, E. G. T., and Sherrington, C. S. (1932). *Reflex Activity of the Spinal Cord.* Oxford: Oxford University Press.

Darwin, C. (1859; 1964). *On the Origin of Species.* Cambridge, MA: Harvard University Press. (Facsmile of first ed.)

Descartes, R. (1649; 1989). *Passions de l'Ame: The Passions of the Soul,* S. Voss (trans.). Indianapolis, Ind.: Hackett.

Descartes, R. (1664; 1972). *L'Homme* (Treatise on Man), T. S. Hall (trans.). Cambridge, MA: Harvard University Press.

Dunbar, R. I. M. (1984). *Reproductive Decisions: An Economic Analysis of Gelada Baboon Social Strategies.* Princeton, NJ: Princeton University Press.

Emlen, J. M. (1966). The role of time and energy in food preference. *American Naturalist* 100: 611–617.

Fodor, J. A. (1983). *The Modularity of Mind.* Cambridge, MA: MIT Press.

Frege, G. (1893–1903; 1964). *Grundgesetze der Arithmetik (The Basic Laws of Arithmetic),* M. Furth (trans.). Berkeley: University of California Press.

Fretwell, S. D. (1972). *Populations in a Seasonal Environment.* Princeton, NJ: Princeton University Press.

Galen, C. (A; 1963) *On the Passions and Errors of the Soul,* P. W. Harkin (trans.). Columbus: Ohio State University Press.

Galen, C. (B; 1968). *On the Usefulness of Parts,* M. T. May (trans.). Ithaca, NY: Cornell University Press.

Galen, C. (C; 1916). *On the Natural Faculties*, A. J. Brock (trans.). Loeb Classical Library 71. New York: G. P. Putnam. Repr. Cambridge, MA: Harvard University Press, 1963.

Galen, C. (D; 1978). *On the Doctrines of Hippocrates and Plato*, P. De Lacy (ed. and trans.). Berlin: Akademie-Verlag.

Galen, C. (E; 1962). *On Anatomical Procedures*, Towers, B., Lyons, M. C., and Duckworth, W. L. H. (trans.). Cambridge: Cambridge University Press.

Galilei, G. (1630; 2001). *Dialogo Sopra i due Massimi Sistemi del Mondo, Tolemaico e Copernicano* (Dialogue Concerning the Two Chief World Systems), S. Drake (trans.). New York: Modern Library.

Gallistel, C. R. (1980). *The Organization of Action: A New Synthesis*. Hillsdale, NJ: Lawrence Erlbaum Associates.

Galvani, L. (1791; 1953). *De Viribus Electricitatis in Motu Musculari Commentarius* (Commentary on the Effect of Electricity on Muscular Motion), R. M. Green (trans.). Cambridge, MA: Elizabeth Licht.

Gigerenzer, G., Todd, P. M., and ABC Research Group. (2000). *Simple Heuristics That Make Us Smart*. New York: Oxford University Press.

Glimcher, P. W. (1999). Eye movements. In M. J. Zigmond et al. (eds.). *Fundamental Neuroscience*. New York: Academic Press.

Gnadt, J. W., and Andersen, R. A. (1988). Memory related motor planning activity in posterior parietal cortex of macaque. *Experimental Brain Research* 70: 216–220.

Gödel, K. (1931). Über formal unentscheidbare Sätze der *Principia Mathematica* und verwandter Systeme, I. *Monatshefte für Mathematik und Physik* 38: 173–198. Repr. and trans. in *The Undecidable: Basic Papers on Undecidable Propositions, Unsolvable Problems and Computable Functions*, M. Davis (ed.). New York: Raven Press, 1965.

Gold, J. I., and Shadlen, M. N. (2000). Representation of a perceptual decision in developing oculomotor commands. *Nature* 404: 390–394.

Gold, J. I., and Shadlen, M. N. (2001). Neural computations that underlie decisions about sensory stimuli. *Trends in Cognitive Science* 5: 10–16.

Goldschmidt, T. (1996). *Darwin's Dreampond*. Cambridge, MA: MIT Press.

Gould, S. J., and Lewontin, R. C. (1979). The spandrels of San Marco and the panglossian paradigm: A critique of the adaptationist programme. *Proceedings of the Royal Society* B205: 581–598.

Graham Brown, T. (1911). Intrinsic factors in the act of progression in the mammal *Proceedings of the Royal Society* B84: 308–319.

Graham Brown, T. (1914). On the nature of the fundamental activity of the nervous centres; together with an analysis of rhythmic activity in progression, and a theory of the evolution of function in the nervous system. *Journal of Physiology* (London) 48: 18–46.

Green, D. M., and Swets, J. A. (1966). *Signal Detection Theory and Psychophysics*. New York: Wiley.

Hall, M. (1833). On the reflex function of the medulla oblongata and medulla spinalis. *Philosophical Transactions of the Royal Society* 123: 635–665.

Hamilton, W. D. (1964a, 1964b). The genetical evolution of social behavior. I, II. *Journal of Theoretical Biology* 7: 1–52.

Harper, D. G. C. (1982). Competitive foraging in mallards: "Ideal free" ducks. *Animal Behavior* 30: 575–584.

Harvey, W. C. (1628; 1843). *Exercitatio Anatomica de Motu Cordis et Sanguinis in Animalibus* (An Anatomical Disquisition on the Motion of the Heart and Blood in Animals). In *The Works of William Harvey*, Robert Willis (trans.). London: The Sydenham Society.

Hebb, D. O. (1949). *The Organization of Behavior*. New York: John Wiley & Sons.

Herrnstein, R. J. (1961). Relative and absolute strength of response as a function of frequency of reinforcement. *Journal of the Experimental Analysis of Behavior* 4: 267–272.

Herrnstein, R. J. (1982). Melioration as behavioral dynamism. In M. L. Commons, R. J. Herrnstein, and H. Rachlin, *Quantitative Analyses of Behavior*, Vol. 2. *Matching and Maximizing Accounts*. Cambridge MA: Ballinger.

Herrnstein, R. J. (1997). *The Matching Law*, H. Rachlin and D. I. Laibson (eds.). Cambridge, MA: Harvard University Press.

Holling, C. S. (1959). Some characteristics of simple types of predation and parasitism. *Canadian Entomology* 91: 385–398.

Hume, D. (1748; 1975). *Enquiry Concerning Human Understanding*. Oxford: Clarendon Press.

James, William. (1890). *The Principles of Psychology*. New York: Henry Holt.

Jasper, H. H. (1958). Recent advances in our understanding of the reticular system. In Jasper. H. H. (ed.) *Reticular Formation of the Brain*. Boston: Little, Brown.

Kandel, E. R., Schwartz, J. H., and Jessel, T. M. (1991). *Principles of Neural Science*, 3rd ed. Norwalk, CT: Appleton Lange.

Keller, J. V., and Gollub, L. R. (1977). Duration and rate of reinforcement as determinants of concurrent responding. *Journal of the Experimental Analysis of Behavior* 28: 145–153.

Kornmuller, A. E. (1932). Eine experimentelle Anasthesie der aussen Augenmuskeln am Menschen und ihre Auswirkungen. *Journal für Psychologie und Neurologie* 41: 354–366.

Krebs, J. R., and Davies, N. B., eds. (1991). *Behavioural Ecology*, 3rd ed. Cambridge: Blackwell Scientific Publications.

Krebs, J. R., Erikhsen, J. T., Webber, M. I., and Charnov, E. L. (1977). Optimal prey selection in the great tit. *Animal Behavior* 25: 30–38.

Kuhn, T. S. (1962). *The Structure of Scientific Revolutions*. Chicago: University of Chicago Press.

Lagrange, J. L. (1788; 2001). *Mécanique Analytique* (Analytical Mechanics), A. C. Boissonnade and V. N. Vagliente (trans.). Norwell, MA: Kluwer Academic Publishers.

LapLace, P. S. (1789–1827; 1969). *Mécanique Céleste* (Celestial Mechanics), N. Bowditch (trans.). Boston: Chelsea.

Laplace, P. S. (1796; 1984). *Exposition du Système du Monde*. Paris: Fayard.

Leibniz, G. W. (1666; 1920). *De Arte Combinatoria: On the Art of Combination*. Trans. in J. M. Child, *The Early Mathematical Manuscripts of Leibniz*. Chicago: Open Court.

Leon, M. I., and Gallistel, C. R. (1998). Self-stimulating rats combine subjective reward magnitude and subjective reward rate multiplicatively. *Journal of Experimental Psychology: Animal Behavior Proceedings* 24: 265–277.

Losos, J. B. (2001). Evolution: A lizard's tale. *Scientific American* 284: 64–69.

MacArthur, R. H., and Pianka, E. R. (1966). On optimal use of a patchy environment. *American Naturalist* 100: 603–610.

Magendie, F. (1822a). Expériences sur les fonctions des racines des nerfs rachidiens. *Journal de Physiologie Experimentale et de Pathologie* 2: 276–279.

Magendie, F. (1822b). Expériences sur les fonctions des racines des nerfs qui naissent de la moelle épiniere. *Journal de Physiologie Experimentale et de Pathologie* 2: 366–371.

Marr, D. (1982). *Vision*. San Francisco: W. H. Freeman.

Marr, D., and Poggio, T. (1976). Cooperative computation of stereo disparity. *Science* 194: 283–287.

Maynard Smith, J. (1982). *Evolution and the Theory of Games*. Cambridge: Cambridge University Press.

McCullough, W. S., and Pitts, W. (1943). A logical calculus of the ideas immanent in nervous activity. *Bulletin of Mathematical Biophysics* 5: 115–133.

Meyer, A. (1993). Phylogenetic relationships and evolutionary processes in East African cichlid fishes. *Trends in Ecology and Evolution* 8: 279–284.

Minsky, M., and Papert, S. (1969). *Perceptrons. An Introduction to Computational Geometry*. Cambridge, MA: MIT Press.

Mountcastle, V. B., Lynch, J. C., Georrgopoulos, A., Sakata, H., and Acuna, C. (1975). Posterior parietal association cortex of the monkey: Command functions for operations within extrapersonal space. *Journal of Neurophysiology* 38: 871–908.

Nash, J. F. (1950a). The bargaining problem. *Econometrica* 18: 155–162.

Nash, J. F. (1950b). Equilibrium points in n-person games. *Proceedings of the National Academy of Sciences* 36: 48–49.

Nash, J. F. (1951). Non-cooperative games. *Annals of Mathematics* 54: 286–295.

Newsome, W. T., Britten, K. H., and Movshon, J. A. (1989). Neuronal correlates of a perceptual decision. *Nature* 341: 52–54.

Newsome, W. T., Britten, K. H., Salzman, C. D., and Movshon, J. A. (1990). Neuronal mechanisms of motion perception. *Cold Spring Harbor Symposia on Quantitative Biology* 55: 697–705.

O'Malley, C. D. (1964). *Andreas Vesalius of Brussels*. Berkeley: University of California Press.

Pascal, B. (1623–1662; 1948). *Great Shorter Works of Pascal*, E. Cailliet and J. C. Blankenagel (trans.). Philadelphia: Westminster Press.

Pascal, B. (1670; 1966). *Pensées*, A. J. Krailsheimer (trans.). New York: Penguin Books.

Pavlov, I. P. (1927). *Conditioned Reflexes: An Investigation of the Physiological Activity of the Cerebral Cortex*, G. V. Anrep (trans.). London: Oxford University Press.

Platt, M. L., and Glimcher, P. W. (1997). Responses of intra-parietal neurons to saccadic targets and visual distractors. *Journal of Neurophysiology* 78: 1574–1589.

Platt, M. L., and Glimcher, P. W. (1999). Neural correlates of decision variables in parietal cortex. *Nature* 400: 233–238.

Pyke, G. H. (1984). Optimal foraging theory: A critical review. *Annual Review of Ecology and Systematics* 15: 523–575.

Reid, R. C. (1999). Vision. In M. J. Zigmond et al. (eds.), *Fundamental Neuroscience*, New York: Academic Press.

Rieke, F., and Baylor, D. (1998). Origin of reproducibility in the responses of retinal rods to single photons. *Biophysical Journal* 75: 1836–1857.

Robinson, D. L., Goldberg, M. E., and Stanton, G. B. (1978). Parietal association cortex in the primate: Sensory mechanisms and behavioral modulations. *Journal of Neurophysiology* 41: 910–932.

Rosenblatt, F. (1962). *Principles of Neurodynamics*. Washington, D.C.: Spartan Books.

Salzman, C. D., Britten, K. H., and Newsome, W. T. (1990). Cortical microstimulation influences perceptual judgements of motion direction. *Nature* 346: 174–177.

Schultz, W. (1998). Predictive reward signal of dopamine neurons. *Journal of Neurophysiology* 80: 1–27.

Schultz, W., Dayan, P., and Montague, P. R. (1997). A neural substrate of prediction and reward. *Science* 275: 1593–1599.

Sechenov, I. M. (1863; 1965). *Reflexes of the Brain*, R. Belsky (trans.). Cambridge, MA: MIT Press.

Sejnowski, T. J., and Rosenberg, C. R. (1987). Parallel networks that learn to pronounce English text. *Complex Systems* 1: 145–168.

Shadlen, M. N., Britten, K. H., Newsome, W. T., and Movshon, J. A. (1996). A computational analysis of the relationship between neuronal and behavioral responses to visual motion. *Journal of Neuroscience* 16: 1486–1510.

Sherrington, C. S. (1906). *The Integrative Action of the Nervous System*. New York: Charles Scribner's Sons.

Sherrington, C. S. (1948). *The Integrative Action of the Nervous System*, 2nd ed. New Haven, CT: Yale University Press.

Simon, H. A. (1997). *Models of Bounded Rationality: Empirically Grounded Economic Reason*. Cambridge, MA: MIT Press.

Sperling, G., and Dosher, B. A. (1986). Strategy optimization in human information processing. In *Handbook of Perception and Human Performance*, Vol. 1, *Sensory Processes and Perception*, K. R. Boff, L. Kaufman, and J. P. Thomas (eds.). New York: Wiley.

Stephens, D. W., and Krebs, J. R. (1986). *Foraging Theory*. Princeton, NJ: Princeton University Press.

Stiassny, M., and Meyer, A. (1999). Cichlids of the Rift lakes. *Scientific American* 283: 64–69.

Stigler, S. M. (1989). *The History of Statistics*. Cambridge, MA: Harvard University Press.

Trivers, R. L. (1985). *Social Evolution*. Menlo Park, CA: Benjamin-Cummings.

Turing, A. M. (1936). On computable numbers, with an application to the entscheidungsproblem. *Proceedings of the London Mathematical Society* ser. 2, 42: 230–265.

Veblen, T. (1898). Why is economics not an evolutionary science? *Quarterly Journal of Economics* 12: 373–397.

Vesalius, A. (1543; 1998–1999). *De Humani Corpus Fabrica* (On the Fabric of the Human Body), W. F. Richardson and J. B. Carman (trans.). 2+ vols. Norman Publishing.

Von Holtz, E. (1937). Vom Wesen der Ordnung in Zentralnervensystem. *Naturwissenschaften* 25: 625–647. Repr. as On the nature of order in the nervous system. In *The Behavioral Physiology of Animals and Man: Selected Papers of E. von Holtz*, R. D. Martin (trans.). Miami, FL: University of Miami Press, 1973.

Von Holtz, E., and Middelstaedt, H. (1950). Das Reafferenzprinzip. Wechselwirkung zwischen Zentralnervensystem und Peripherie. *Naturwissenschaften* 37: 464–476. Repr. as The reafference principle. Interaction between the central nervous system and the periphery. In *The Behavioral Physiology of Animals and*

Man: Selected Papers of E. von Holtz, R. D. Martin (trans.). Miami, FL: University of Miami Press.

Von Neumann, J. V., and Morgenstern, O. (1944). *Theory of Games and Economic Behavior*. Princeton, NJ: Princeton University Press.

Weiss, P. (1941). Self-differentiation of the basic pattern of coordination. *Comparative Psychology Monographs* 17 (no. 4).

Whitehead, A. N., and Russell, B. (1910–1913). *Principia Mathematica*, 3 vols. Cambridge: Cambridge University Press.

Wilson, E. O. (1975). *Sociobiology*. Cambridge, MA: Harvard University Press.

Wilson, E. O. (1998). *Consilience*. New York: Knopf.

Index

Pages containing figures and photos are in italic type. Tables are designated with "t" and notes with "n."